THIS BOOK BELONGS
TO THE

Family

THE Family COOKS

100+ RECIPES TO GET YOUR FAMILY CRAVING FOOD THAT'S SIMPLE, TASTY, *AND* INCREDIBLY GOOD FOR YOU

LAURIE DAVID

RECIPES BY KIRSTIN UHRENHOLDT

FOREWORD BY
KATIE COURIC

PHOTOGRAPHS BY QUENTIN BACON

RODALE.

© 2014 by Hybrid Nation Inc.

Rodale books may be purchased for business or
promotional use or for special sales.
For information, please write to:
Special Markets Department, Rodale Inc.,
733 Third Avenue, New York, NY 10017.

Printed in the United States of America

Rodale Inc. makes every effort to use acid-free ∞,
recycled paper ♻.

Book design by Kara Plikaitis

Photographs by Quentin Bacon

Library of Congress Cataloging-in-Publication
Data is on file with the publisher.

ISBN-13: 978–1–62336–250–8 hardcover

Distributed to the trade by Macmillan

2 4 6 8 10 9 7 5 3 1 hardcover

🌱 RODALE

We inspire and enable people to improve their lives
and the world around them.
rodalebooks.com

To you (yes, you)!
For a life
as healthy,
vibrant, and delicious
as the food
you cook

contents

Recipes

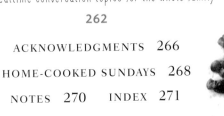

Foreword

Katie Couric

My favorite childhood memories revolve around our dinner table in the house where I grew up in Arlington, Virginia. This is where my two older sisters and older brother would plot future school elections, we all would chat about our lives, and each would bring a new word to the table. My favorite was *ubiquitous.* Those dinners gave me a lifelong appreciation of quality family time, good food, and a great vocabulary.

Once I had children of my own, I did everything in my power to preserve what seemed to be an almost antiquated tradition: family dinners. People weren't eating together anymore because their lives were so hectic and overscheduled and so-called convenience foods were making it easy for each member of the family to grab something, nuke it, and call it a meal. At the same time, it seemed that every year I spent in TV news, the more time I spent reporting on stories about childhood obesity. Type 2 diabetes rates were skyrocketing. Military recruitment was more challenging because people were getting too heavy to enlist. As a nation, we were getting fatter and unhealthier by the minute. At the same time, the exercise craze was in full force, and store shelves were full of low-fat and "healthier" alternatives. What was going on?

This wasn't just a topic I covered on the news. I remember taking some students my daughter Carrie and I mentored from the Harlem Village Academies to the Union Square Farmers' Market several years ago. It was the Saturday before Mother's Day and after we bought lilacs to take home to the moms, we walked around and looked at the bounty of fresh produce spilling over the wooden tables. "Hey kids," I asked, "Do you know what these are?" as I held up a bunch of asparagus. They stared at me blankly. The same thing happened when I picked up mushrooms. One girl said she had never tasted a raw carrot. How could this be? These children were 10 years old! We went to my apartment and prepared some of the vegetables for lunch, where they got mixed reviews. But clearly these kids just didn't know much, if anything, about the foods they were eating on a regular basis . . . .and the foods they weren't.

Slowly but surely, people started becoming more aware of the issue. After all, it was hard to avoid all the news stories and new studies about the obesity epidemic. But it was awareness of the *problem* . . . not the solution. And like many long-term issues, the national will to actually do something was nowhere to be found.

I decided we needed to lay it out in no uncertain terms. We needed to do for this issue what *An Inconvenient Truth* did for global warming. We needed Laurie David. Although I had only met Laurie once, I emailed and asked if she would join forces with me and director and producer Stephanie Soechtig to put together a documentary on childhood obesity. I believe it took her about three seconds to get back to me . . . .and we were off.

We have learned so much since that email exchange almost three years ago, and as we began to understand the causes of this global epidemic, we were shocked and infuriated. Then we felt triumphant. Because once we uncovered the causes, the solution became crystal clear. **The single most powerful thing anyone can do to protect their health, to live a healthy life, and to have a healthy future is to go into their own kitchen and cook food themselves.** It's really that simple.

The Family Cooks is going to help all of us do just that. I love to cook and I love making healthy dishes. But I need help! I'm still learning about fresh ingredients and new ways to prepare real, unprocessed foods. Cooking together as a family is almost as important as eating together. It's educational and fun! So roll up your sleeves, throw on an apron (or not!), and let's get cooking!

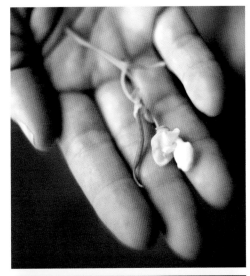

Ready!

–introduction–

I'm so glad you're here! Because there's something I'm bursting with excitement to share with you: Home-cooked, healthy food is the solution to our physical, emotional—and I'd even wager *spiritual*—problems. As if that wasn't enough, it's also a key to bringing pure goodness, vitality, and fun into our lives. It's as simple as that. With our easy and quick recipes and a basket of healthy ingredients, you will discover how truly life-changing, loving, easy, and delicious home-cooked food can be.

It all started for me about five years ago, when I woke up with an irrepressible longing to channel my inner homesteader. To this day, I am not sure where this came from, having grown up on Long Island and lived most of my adult life in Los Angeles. Trust me, farming was not even on my radar as a hobby, let alone as a vocation. As a longtime advocate for environmental causes, I kept my protest sign, but moved aside my pumps to make room for a pair of green muck boots (much to the horror of my fashion-conscious daughters). I tossed my Teflon (which I learned was fuming cancer-causing chemicals into my kitchen!) and bought a now-beloved and well-seasoned cast-iron skillet.

I stuck my hands deep into the earth, planted seeds, pulled up carrots, then stuffed them back down when they looked too small (turns out that is upsetting to a carrot). I figured out how to weed sitting down (much easier on the back) and gave up on man-

icures, my nails requiring such vigorous scrubbing it was a lost cause. My hair went from blow-dry to something crazy only a rubber band and a hat could control. Then, to really seal the deal, I married a blue-eyed farmer down in the field. He taught me how to herd cows (oy, they are so much bigger up close!), to squish bugs (little freeloaders munching on our green beans), and to leave the baby vegetables alone. He is still trying to teach me how to plant a straight row (won't happen). Together, our garden grew, our homegrown dinners got better, and we started organizing Sunday potlucks for friends and family.

I had decided to make some healthy changes in my life, which inevitably led me to improving the food my family and I ate. The more I learned about how real food is grown, the more clearly I saw how messed up our industrialized food system has become. Already deeply concerned about the environmental challenges plaguing us, I found myself pushed to the edge by daily reports of salmonella and *E. coli* poisoning, antibiotic overuse in livestock, rampant food allergies, and links between food dyes and behavioral problems. All these food scares hit way too close to home—you're talking about what I feed my kids! I also started to notice an increase in media coverage about the rapid rise of childhood obesity and diabetes. Today, a shocking one in three American children is overweight or obese. As is one in two adults.

At home, we stopped eating hamburgers and made our first kale salad. We stopped buying packaged foods containing high-fructose corn syrup and soybean oil. We swapped "natural flavors" for truly natural, whole food ingredients. We tossed (into the recycler!) the BPA-lined plastic bottles and cans. We've been growing and eating a lot of our own food ever since, and now we crave kale the way some people crave sweets.

The Family Cooks is a clear, uncomplicated cookbook written to get you and your family craving and cooking the right stuff, too: food that is prepared with love and care and infused with good intentions. You absolutely cannot buy this food ready-made in your supermarket or favorite takeout place. This is food you can only make in your very own home, in the room

trol of your family's health and retrain their palates. Cooking and eating your meals together and making what you eat a priority is the antidote to so many of the issues families are struggling with today.

This book will help you and your kids cook from scratch (by the way, the butter has been churned, the eggs already laid and collected, so you're way ahead of your great-great-grandmother) and bust the myth that cooking is too hard and takes too much time. Nonsense. That is what prepared food marketers want you to believe, but it really isn't true. For the same amount of time required to call in a takeout order, get in your car to pick it up, and bring it home, you can have a more delicious and much healthier home-cooked meal. Study after study has shown that if kids understand where their food comes from (if they can shell peas from an actual pod, rather than just encountering squishy green lumps on their plate) and are regularly exposed to real food, they will eat healthier. Who doesn't have time for that?!

Teaching your kids and yourself how to cook a few simple "recipes by heart," whether it be a tossed salad, a quick tomato sauce, or a pot of soup, will set them up for a lifetime of confident cooking and good eating no matter where in the world they end up. My own recent experience proves this to be true. Both of

"You don't have to cook fancy or complicated masterpieces— just good food from fresh ingredients."

—JULIA CHILD

where everyone already loves to hang out: your kitchen.

Whether you are a new cook, a young cook, or an "I can't cook" cook, everyone can—and really must—give it a try. The more you learn about what your loved ones are eating, what artificial colors are pumped into their favorite yogurt, how much sugar is lurking in their drinks and snacks, and what chemicals are used to preserve their cereals, the more upset you will get. It's exactly what happened to me. But you have the power in your hands to retake con-

my grown-up daughters cook, eat, and prefer home-cooked dinners over anything else. My college freshman, who for years never voluntarily participated in the making of dinner (she always helped eat it though), was so horrified by the low quality of dorm food, she begged to move to an apartment. "Mom, I can't eat this stuff—it's not food!" she said. "I need a stove." I nearly fell off my chair! This year she and a roommate are sharing a kitchen and regularly texting photos of the great dishes they are cooking. She has

tested many of the recipes in this book, and if she can do it, you can, too! The baton (wooden spoon) successfully passed. Amen.

Between you and me, I really need this book, too, because every time I go to cook, I end up having to Google a recipe. Here's my confession: My brain has trouble retaining information. I need easy-to-follow recipes right in front of me so I can refer to the instructions over and over. I can't tell you how many times I look at a recipe while cooking. It's embarrassing.

What I want are simple, delicious dishes with a few accessible, healthy ingredients and clear instructions. **I want family food, not restaurant food. I want to serve one meal for everyone, with plenty of leftovers for another meal tomorrow.** And, of course, like everyone else, I need quick recipes for busy days.

Enter my Danish friend Kirstin, who grew up on a fruit farm, was taught how to cook by her mom and grammy, and spends her days happily whipping up irresistibly delicious and healthy family food. This is our second cookbook together. If you've read *The Family Dinner*, you know that Kirstin and I make a good team. She drafts the recipe, then we test it on our friends and family. If it's a hit, she writes it down. I cook it on my own, and remove all the cilantro. She puts it back. I cut sweet potatoes into "matchsticks." She calls them "wedges." I forget to add the baking powder (fail!); she shows me once again how to line up all the ingredients on the counter before I start to cook. I secretly inspect the garbage to make sure she hasn't "accidentally" tossed away anything compostable. (Busted!)

Well, you get the picture. It's actually a great collaboration, because between Kirstin's professionalism and my amateurism, we end up creating recipes that are delicious, easy, and foolproof, too. Perfect for me, you, our college students, singles, newlyweds, new moms and dads, our budding teen chefs . . . everyone!

It's our sincere hope that these recipes will help you channel your own inner homesteader, because self-reliance is one of the most precious tools you can give yourself in the daily battle against unhealthy, fattening, and downright sickening food. It's bad enough that prefab pseudo-foods don't nourish our bodies, but even worse, they're actually killing us, driving an unprecedented rise in diet-related diseases.

I believe that the case for making home-cooked food is one of the clarion calls of our time. You could even call it a civic duty: If we all embraced healthy home cooking, we could save hundreds of billions of dollars in health-care costs, lost productivity, and all the other unfortunate side effects of our industrialized food chain. This simple fact has so captivated me that my friend Katie Couric and I recently made a documentary about how our children are bearing the brunt of our unhealthy food system. We decided to call it *Fed Up*. We are *fed up* with obesity, diabetes, and allergies. We are *fed up* with depression, hyperactivity, sleeplessness, stomachaches, and headaches (all side effects of the packaged food we are eating). We are *fed up* with industrial food lobbyists who keep the price of unhealthy processed food so low, and fight fairness in labeling, regulation of sugar, and marketing to kids at every turn.

Why entrust one of the most intimate daily acts in our lives—the food we put into our bodies to nourish our brains, our organs, our hearts, and our souls—to a handful of multinational conglomerates? No matter your skills, *you* are a much better cook than they are, even if you just stick some sweet potatoes in the oven (see page 206) and toss a green salad (add some chickpeas and sunflower seeds for a healthy crunch!). That is a better meal than anything you can buy containing dozens of unpronounceable ingredients. You *do* have the time, because it really doesn't take that long. If your kitchen is stocked with some basics, and you are just a little organized, you can have a healthy meal on the table in no time.

Kirstin and I invite you to join us in taking back the responsibility of feeding our loved ones and ourselves in a way that is easy, emotionally fulfilling, and nutritionally satisfying. Now is the time to restake the claim to your home on the (kitchen) range!

something is fishy about these crackers

Why all the increased attention to home cooking? Food guru Michael Pollan and influential *New York Times* columnist Mark Bittman are singing its praises and filling up new books with the topic. Best-selling author Dr. Mark Hyman prescribes home cooking first and foremost to all of his patients. National health-care provider Kaiser Permanente has added more than 50 farmers' markets at its hospitals and facilities across the country. Homemade meals are making a comeback because they are the only way to guarantee healthy nutrition for you and your family.

If I could take back all the chicken fingers and French fries I ordered for my kids when they were little, I would. While I am at it, I would also return the bags of Goldfish, the Go-Gurts and the Capri Suns. I didn't know then what I know now—that most commercial food is booby-trapped. Products you buy in the store are not manufactured with an eye toward your child's good health (despite what the label proclaims). The food industry is interested in one thing only: profits. To accomplish that, they use every trick in the book to hook you and your kids on their products, many of which are unhealthy and even addictive. Unless you are a vigilant advocate for your family's health, they will most likely succeed.

Looking back, although I converted to organic produce when I became pregnant (like so many expectant moms), I was still too trusting and didn't fully comprehend how much food had changed since I was a kid. A typical example was the containers of yogurt I regularly bought. It never occurred to me to look at the ingredients—yogurt is healthy, right?

A close look at the sugar content of an average "fruit" yogurt label, using a calculator to translate (clever how they use the enigmatic gram instead of the more commonly understood teaspoon), revealed a whopping 7 teaspoons of sugar. That's more than twice as much sugar as in a serving of Lucky Charms cereal, which most parents know is not a healthy choice and will likely avoid.

All those chicken fingers and turkey burgers we ordered in restaurants weren't very wholesome, either. They're usually a horrible hodgepodge of animal by-products (gross!), ground up from who knows how many different birds (double gross!). Throw in the ubiquitous French fries, and your meal's nutritional value sinks even lower. The French fry has become the quintessential poster child—along with its sister, the potato chip—for restaurant and processed foods' un-whole-y trinity: salt, fat, and sugar. That trio, cleverly engineered by lab-coat-wearing processed food "scientists" (not chefs!), is literally hijacking our brains and our bodies.

The food companies know that the perfect combination of these three amigos creates a "bliss" point—that heavenly moment when your mouth says, "I love this," and urges your brain to eat more. That's

why this trio is in nearly everything that is packaged, canned, or wrapped. The proof is right there in your fridge, freezer, and pantry. Take a look at the labels and marvel at how many of the words you don't understand, or the odd ingredients you've never heard of. Would it shock you to know that "powdered cellulose" is actually "wood pulp," and used as a thickener for store-bought salad dressing and ice cream? I know that ingredient is not sitting in *your* spice cabinet. Or how about carmine, a common food dye used to color drinks, yogurts, and desserts? It's an additive made from crushed cochineal insects. Okay, I promise I'll stop, but you see the point.

Back to that tricky gram measurement. Dust off that middle school math and use this conversion formula for sugar:

> **4 grams sugar = 1 teaspoon**

Now do the conversion for sugar content listed on the labels of various processed foods in your pantry. I guarantee you won't be happy.

There are also the many milligrams of salt to calculate too. In fact, most of the salt in our diet comes from food industry products, not the innocent little shaker with the teeny tiny holes sitting on your table that you shake once or twice onto your eggs. Corporate food scientists have figured out that salt makes sugar taste sweeter, and bitter less so. It prolongs shelf life, too. So the food industry pours it on.

modern-day snacks

Not only has food become more processed since I was a tot (circa 1958, more math work for you!), entire industries have emerged and exploded. The snack food industry and the beverage industry are two examples. The snack food industry's foundation rests on the seductive charms of the three amigos (salt, fat, sugar). Americans are now buying snacks to the tune of $40 billion dollars a year, and

that is growing. Goodbye carrots and apples, hello Cheez-Its and Doritos! As a new parent, I was sucked in by the products and advertisements, too. Summer meant chips and salsa; fall brought candy corn and pumpkin-flavored coffee creamer. Winter was hot chocolate mix, candy canes, and eggnog pancake mix. Talk about eating seasonally!

Play dates in the park required Goldfish crackers and juice boxes. Rarely did I go anywhere in those toddler years without a ready supply in the diaper bag or car. I remember special trips to Costco to buy mega-bulk cartons of fishy crackers. We filled up punch bowls with them for birthday parties and soccer practice. Ugh! I had no idea those goldfish had enough salt in them to cure a pickle, and that until 2010 their bright orange color came from food dyes that could be linked to allergies and ADHD.

Snack food manufacturers created a whole new market with products like these, items that didn't exist just two generations ago. In the process, they also managed to completely change our culture! The boom in eating between meals, snacking instead of meals, bringing snacks to school and sports practice, snacking in the car, in the stroller, anywhere, anytime, has totally altered what, where, and how we eat.

Ever wonder how that bag of potato chips became the obligatory sidekick to your sandwich? Marketing. A potato chip exec came up with that idea. Who uncovered our desperate "need" for electrolytes after a walk around the park or a kids' soccer game? Thank you, marketing guys at Gatorade. How did protein bars and shakes become so popular? Why does food need to be brought to sports practice at all? Um, that would be marketing, too.

How many fries have we eaten off of our kids' plates? How many Goldfish? We are all going down together, folks! **Our brains are hard-wired from birth for reward—and that salt, sugar, and fat combo is oh-so-rewarding. The problems come later.** We are eating a ton of the bad stuff, less of the good stuff, and our bodies just can't handle it. Our bodies are not equipped to eat chemicals, food additives, hormones, dyes, or excessive amounts of salt, sugar, and fat.

The consequences of living this way have caught up with us. Diet-related diseases are among the top killers in America, second only to tobacco. Diabetes is rampant, expected to affect one in three children by midcentury, right in sync with those obesity rates. Toss in all the stomachaches, jitters, cranky moods, sleeplessness, attention deficit, constipation, diarrhea, sluggishness, and—well, Houston, we have a food problem.

sweet tooth

Sugar in small doses is fine. In the form of fructose, it occurs naturally in foods like fruit and carrots. We are born with the taste for it. Dr. Robert Lustig, a prominent pediatrician whose research points to sugar consumption as the main culprit causing diabetes, puts it this way: "How many times did you have to introduce a savory food to a baby before they would accept it? On average 13 times, that's what science says. But if the food is sweet, how many times? Just once. We are programmed to like the stuff."

But when sugar has been stripped of its fiber (the ingredient that makes our bodies digest it slowly) and added to our foods in large amounts, it becomes toxic. Just how toxic? **Well, eating too much sugar is linked, among other things, to diabetes, obesity, heart disease, cancer, dementia, lipid problems, headaches, depression, acne, high blood pressure, and strokes.** The American Heart Association recommends no more than 6 teaspoons per day for women and 9 teaspoons per day for men. Preschoolers shouldn't consume more than 4 teaspoons (time to recheck that cereal box), children ages 4 to 8 about 3 teaspoons a day, and preteens and teens should cap their sugar intake at 5 to 8 teaspoons.

How much sugar on average are we all actually consuming?
22 teaspoons per day.

It's scary how much sugar we're actually eating without even realizing it. You know it's in the cupcakes you buy, but do you know it's also in the jarred spaghetti sauce and in your regular brand of ketchup, salad dressings, and breads? Sugar is regularly hidden in foods you wouldn't even think of as sweet. Just consider that of the 600,000 food items in a supermarket, 80 percent are laced with added sugar (yikes!).

Astonishingly, sugar is also added to many baby foods and formulas. Added sugar in a baby's diet sets them on a path to a lifetime of overeating, because the earlier your palate acquires the taste for sugar, the more it's going to want. As Dr. Benjamin Caballero, from the Johns Hopkins Bloomberg School of Public Health, says, "The issue is that sweet tastes tend to encourage consumption of excessive amounts, and evidence shows that babies and children will always show a preference for the sweetest food available and they will eat more of it than they would of less-sweet food." Excess sugar consumption suppresses the natural hormones that tell our bodies when we've eaten enough. No wonder we all overeat.

Also lurking in disguise are the names used to identify sugar. There are an astonishing 56 names that are regularly used on ingredient labels to hide the fact that it's just sugar! (See page 13 for all of the code words.) That's just another trick in the bag of the food/beverage/snack industry to keep you from knowing how much sugar they are actually putting in their products and how much you are really eating. Remember, it's just about increasing profits. They know the body craves it, and more and more it's being shown to be addictive. In fact, the industry and our government have known since the early 1970s that sugar is a serious health problem.

Which brings us to the biggest sugar culprit: drinks. Once upon a time, we drank tap water. It was widely available; it was free; it was healthy. Today,

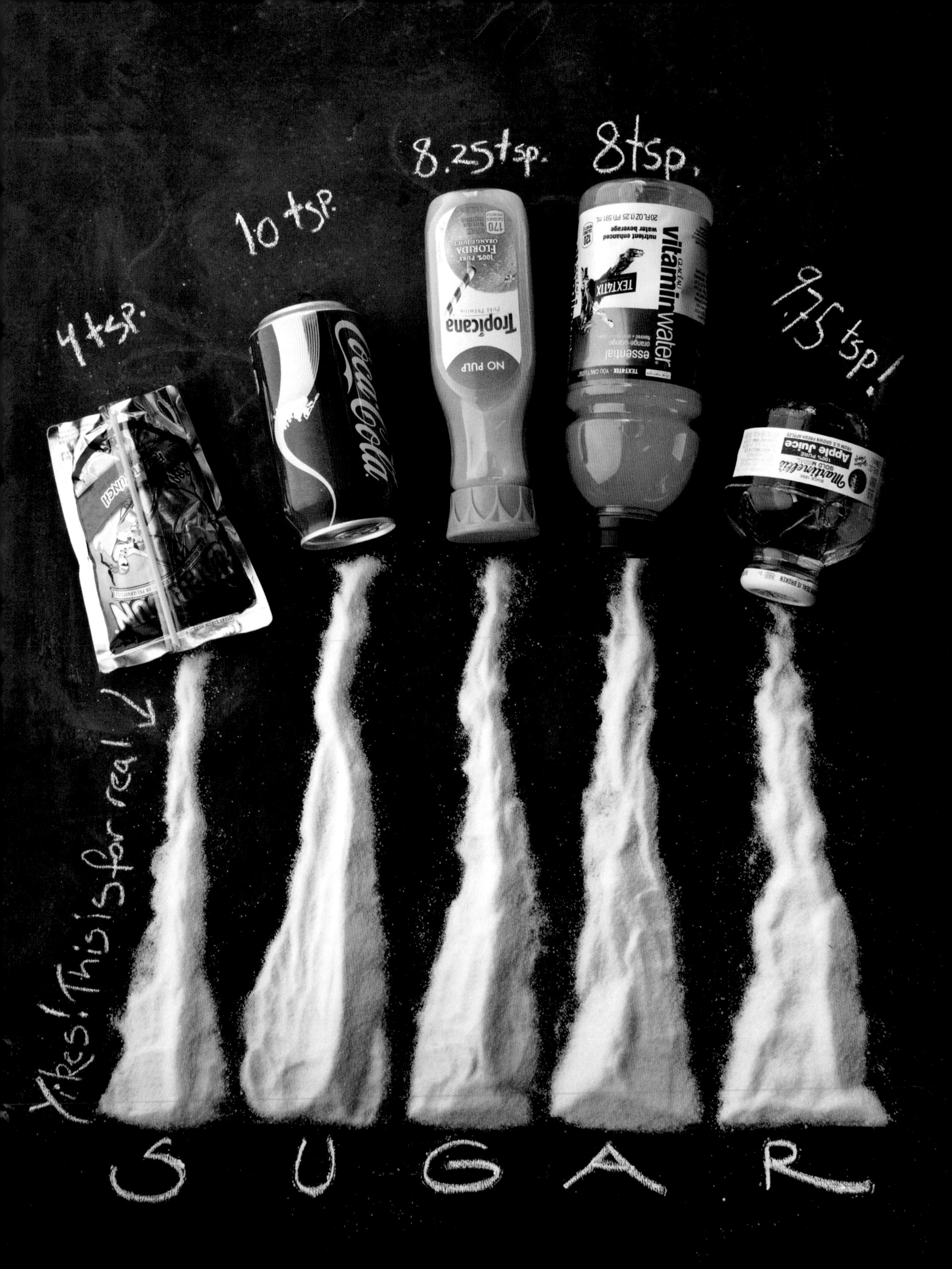
4 tsp.
10 tsp.
8.25 tsp.
8 tsp.
9.75 tsp!
Yikes! This is for real
SUGAR

we have an explosion of moneymaking alternatives, more liquid choices than anyone could ever have imagined. Just like the cleverly created snack food market, a few corporations have created a beverage market so successful that it has actually become a ubiquitous part of our lifestyle. **The drink is as common an accessory in the hand as car keys or a purse!** New products are introduced regularly: energy drinks, specialty soda drinks, coffee concoctions, juice smoothies, flavored waters, protein shakes, sweetened ice teas, lemonades, powdered flavor packets. . . . I'm going into sugar shock just writing this! Wherever you go, make sure you're carrying your water, your coffee, your smoothie. Got to stay hydrated! Funny how we never had hydration problems in the old days, when we were actually far more active!

Even with all of these drink options, soda is still the widely popular choice, especially among teens.[1] Not coincidentally, it is also one of the products most marketed to them. Have to hook them early! Imagine the influence almost $400 million marketing dollars a year can have on a teenager.[2] That's what the soda industry spends to turn your kids into lifelong addicts—I mean customers.

A 20-ounce bottle of regular soda can contain about 16 teaspoons of sugar. I still find that shocking. You probably have a good idea that soda is bad, but did you know that fruit juice drinks are just as loaded with the sweet stuff? Unwitting parents offer their kids endless amounts of juice thinking it's good for them, but even if the label says "100% fruit juice" or "no added sugar," **once the fiber is removed, fruit juice becomes sugar water,** just like soda. A 12-ounce glass of Tropicana orange juice has 8.25 teaspoons of sugar. A 10-ounce Martinelli's apple juice has almost 9.75 teaspoons of sugar, and Welch's grape juice has 10.5. Imagine adding that by hand to a glass you are about to give your child.

And what about Vitamin Water? Some evil marketing genius came up with that one. A 20-ounce bottle of this misnamed beverage contains 32 grams of sugar equaling 8 teaspoons. Snapple lemon iced tea? A 16-ounce bottle has 9 teaspoons of sugar. A 6-ounce Capri Sun fruit punch contains 4 teaspoons; a 14-ounce Nesquick Double Chocolate Low Fat Milk has 14.5 teaspoons of sugar. Let's call this stuff what it really is—liquid candy.

It's sickening when you add up all those teaspoons and imagine drinking that much sugar. And you can bet it's making our kids sick. Just one fruit juice or energy drink contains more added sugar than most kids should consume in a day. That is just the one drink. That doesn't include any other food, desserts, or drinks they will be having during the day, at school, after school, and before bedtime calls.

Oh, and by the way, that serving size listed on the labels to measure your sugar and fat intake is a joke. Most people eat and drink way more than any suggested individual serving size. Take a look at how many servings are in your bag of chips, and then laugh (or cry). The food industry loves them, because they trick you into thinking you're consuming fewer calories (and sugar, fat, and salt) than you actually do. When was the last time you drank just half a bottle of Gatorade, ate only nine chips, or eight dried cranberries? The cranberry recently intrigued me because I saw our 10-year-old voraciously eating them from a bag like she had hit the jackpot. I took a look and measured. One serving size is ¼ cup, about 20 cranberries (yes I counted). Each serving size has 7.75 teaspoons of added sugar. I recalculated

"It may be put down as a rule from which it is safe never to depart that every substitute used for pure cold water as a drink is an injury to health."

—JOURNAL OF HEALTH, PUBLISHED 1853

> *"Each can of soda consumed by children per day increases their risk of being overweight by 60 percent."*
>
> —DR. MARK HYMAN

this five times because I couldn't believe it. I would say those small bags of cranberries can easily be polished off in one or two rounds! That would be 23.25 teaspoons of sugar. You would never visualize that just looking at the serving size and grams as you rushed through the store. Serving sizes purposely deceive you. Research shows that when given a portion, you consume it. If you have a 20-ounce bottle, you will drink 20 ounces. If you are given a smaller size, you will drink less. That was the reasoning behind former NYC Mayor Bloomberg's soda portion campaign, and he was right on the money.

Take a closer look at the misconceptions we've been fed. The conventional wisdom—that all calories are equal, and we just need to show more will power and exercise more—rings hollow. This is the food industry's standard explanation for our obesity epidemic because it conveniently absolves them of any responsibility. But all calories are not equal. The way your body digests an almond is different from the way it digests soda (go see our movie *Fed Up* for a great illustration of this). Also, some calories (like soda) are empty calories, devoid of nutrition, so how could they be equal to calories that provide vitamins and other nutrients? As for exercise, which is crucial to overall health, it would take playing pool volleyball for over 2 hours 45 minutes to work off Subway's Spicy Italian Salad[3] with Chipotle Southwest Dressing, and 4½ hours of walking to burn off a 23-ounce sweetened iced tea. As you can see, we are not going to exercise our way out of this problem. **The obesity and diabetes epidemic is being driven by how processed, industrial food is made, sold, and marketed everywhere you go, 24/7.** It's being driven by our substitution of these products for meals once cooked from scratch and served with water from the tap.

We have lost control, but the blame does not rest with personal responsibility alone, as the food industry would have you believe. And it certainly doesn't explain the explosion of obese infants and toddlers. How much of this is corporate responsibility? When commercially processed food is formulated to deliberately addict us, and advertised in a way that messes with our minds, whose fault is that? Equating sugary drinks and fast food with happiness and love is an especially popular approach because it works. Billions of dollars are at stake, and the conglomerates that stand to profit aren't giving a moment's thought to your family's health. The sooner they hook us, the higher their bottom line. Values, morals, and fairness *do not* have a seat at the table.

If you think that is too strong of a statement, consider children. No child is born wanting to be overweight, eat junk food, or crave Skittles. Children are innocent and they are unfairly targeted, relentlessly bombarded with ads for the lowest quality food imaginable, everywhere they go: at school, on TV, via Web sites and social media. I say "unfairly," because until children reach the age of eight or so,[4] they can't even distinguish between the content of a show they are watching and an ad. Kids think ads are telling them things they should know. The food industry knows this, which makes it all the more cynical and outrageous that they are allowed to use cartoon characters to target children and even embed ads in some of our kids' favorite shows, such as *American Idol* and *X Factor*. We finally got rid of Joe Camel; we need to do the same for junk food mascots. Why should cereal manufacturers selling products filled with unhealthy amounts of sugar and chemical dyes be allowed to use cuddly rabbits, or pirates, or any other kid-seducing creature and advertise on morning cartoon shows?

sugar: not so sweet after all

Below is a list of 56 names, all with one meaning: sugar, sugar, sugar. Check the labels and you will see sugar in its various guises often listed up to six to seven times. Pretty sneaky, huh?

Barley malt Caramel Date sugar **Ethyl maltol** Glucose **Golden sugar**

Barbados sugar **Castor sugar** **Agave nectar** **Glucose solids**

Beet sugar Carob syrup

Brown sugar Dextran Fructose **Fruit juice** HFCS (High Frustose Corn Syrup)

Buttered syrup **Cane sugar** Grape sugar

Corn syrup Cane juice Dextrose Fruit juice concentrate Honey Muscovado

Corn syrup solids

Confectioners' sugar Dehydrated cane juice Galactose Icing sugar **Panocha**

Demerara sugar Golden syrup Lactose Raw sugar

Maltodextrin **Diastatic malt** Diatase **Maltose** Maple syrup

Malt sugar Mannitol **Florida crystals** Molasses Refiner's Syrup **Rice syrup**

Sorbitol

Sucrose Sorghum syrup Treacle **Yellow sugar** **Turbinado sugar** Sugar (granulated)

There are some serious moral issues we need to confront. Is it ethical to enlist popular celebrities and athletes (LeBron James, Peyton Manning, Serena Williams, Michael Jackson, Britney Spears, Michael Jordan, Beyoncé, Katy Perry) to promote unhealthy products to our kids? **Celebrity endorsements work, which is why millions are spent signing them up.** Why don't we demand a stop to this practice? Why don't we make it so politically incorrect to push soda that no smart celebrity would even consider it? Would Justin Timberlake promote cigarettes? Never!

In my opinion, the lowest of the low was Coca-Cola's hiring of Taylor Swift, a singer whose fan base is tweens and younger, to promote artificially sweetened diet soda. Apparently, no one in her camp got the memo that diet soda has been linked to depression[5] and ADHD.[6] Not only do diet drinks hook kids on the taste of sweet (artificial or not, your brain thinks it's sugar), new research shows these beverages actually make you hungrier.[7] Not to mention the whole concept of "diet" being marketed to children in the first place.

It's not a level playing field. It's your ability to ignore your child's persistent urging/nagging/whining versus million-dollar marketing campaigns conceived by the best researchers and advertising wunderkinds (mission accomplished, food execs!). It's you having to repeatedly say "NO!" to clever product placement (did you know that companies pay stores to stock their products at perfect eye level to you and to your kids?),[8] bright packaging colors they know will catch your children's eye, appealing cartoon characters, games, toy giveaways, catchy music, decades of psychological research to help manipulate children's food preferences, and of course as if all that wasn't enough . . . Beyoncé . . . Sigh.

With vending machines around every corner, (over 5 million in America! more than $19 billion in profits!),[9] candy at every cash register (including at toy, drug, office supply, and other nonfood stores!), sugar-coated treats sold in virtually every kind of establishment or given away in the workplace, there is no place left that is safe. Even my local YMCA, whose whole mission is health and well-being, is selling French fries, chicken fingers, and Fruit Loops in the lobby cafe. Our heightened, advertised, food-carnival environment is everywhere, sending off constant cues to eat, drink, and buy. Hardly a level playing field for tired, stressed parents.

Wait, there's more. Culturally we overuse sweets as a common reward, upping the ante on desirability. The standard threat of "no dessert if you don't eat your dinner" sets up a dynamic that what you're eating isn't good, but the sweet thing afterwards is. How many times have we taken our kids for ice cream as a reward for any achievement or comfort? We've got a lot of work to do to change our dysfunctional relationship with sugar.

get cooking!

Outsourcing the feeding of our families to large industrial food manufacturers, fast-food chains, and beverage companies is a recipe for disaster. The proof is in the pudding (so to speak); we are smack dab in the middle of the worst epidemic of food-related diseases the world has ever seen. Here at home or abroad—wherever our processed/fast food is sold—obesity and diabetes are on the rise.

But don't despair. You do have a choice. You can opt out by choosing water as your family's go-to drink, returning sweets to their rightful place as an occasional treat, and cooking most of your food your-self. Yup, you can even make your own salad dressing! It's easier than you think. Talk to your parents, your grandmother, aunts, and uncles—get them to share family recipes with you. Use our recipes, or check out some healthy cookbooks from the library. Get inspired: Hit up friends for their best healthy recipes too, or instigate a school cookbook containing your community's greatest hits.

Or, you can skip the recipes altogether, scramble a few organic eggs with a handful of broccoli and a shaving of cheese. Plant some lettuce in a pot and grow herbs on your windowsill. Put on a straw hat, grab a canvas bag, unplug your kids from their digital devices, and go foraging at the farmers' market. Buy what looks good and ask the farmer for tips on how to prepare it. Or, just go to your local grocery store and pick up some fresh vegetables, fruit, and whole grains. That's all you need to start cooking. Nothing fancy, nothing fake.

You can—and should—be the one who decides how much sugar or salt to add (if any!), whether you want to consume chemicals (I doubt it), and what constitutes an appropriate portion size (hint: Don't look to the Cheesecake Factory for guidance).

By cooking at home, you're saying no to misleading labels, no to long lists of weird ingredients, no to processed foods, no to preservatives, no to chemicals, no to artificial anything. And you are saying yes to real food, cooked with the intention of truly nourishing us. Yes to health. Yes to taking control of your family's well-being, and teaching your kids to love crunchy veggies and a simple, well-made salad.

Show your kids how a carrot grows, and how to scrub it, cook it, and eat it, and you'll give them the critical skills they need to navigate the giant industrial booby-trapped buffet of food that is shoved in our faces everyday. You'll be showing them that yes, they do have a choice, and you're giving them the knowledge and the power to make that choice. We spend a lot of time on a few things that are important to us. We need to make this one of them.

"We want people feeding our kids who really care about them."

—ALICE WATERS

"picky eaters"

Perhaps the quotation marks around this phrase tipped you off to my politically incorrect point of view on this thorny topic. I really do believe that for the most part, picky eating is a modern American expression used to label a behavior that in your grandmother's day would have been widely ignored. I am not talking about allergic reactions or legitimate food sensitivities. I am talking about the overused catch phrase that too quickly labels and excuses what is really a normal reaction of a child tasting something new for the first or second time.

Like so many things a child has to learn—how to share, or ride a bike—developing a palate that accepts a wide range of tastes and textures takes time. In fact, it can take ten or more exposures to a certain food before the palate "accepts" the flavor and starts liking it. (Okay, I admit I am still trying to like raw tomatoes, but that's about it—I'm certain I had some crazy trauma with them in early childhood.) Over the years, I've witnessed many times the happy moment when a young taste bud finally wakes up and says, "Yes!" The scene goes something like this: A child at the table refuses to touch a certain food. I keep serving it, insist that they take a few bites. . . . Then time lapse and cut to, "Please sir, can I have some more?"

Kids today have far too much power over what they eat and, after a rejection or two, parents too quickly give up. There, I said it: Parents give up. This is often for understandable reasons: Guilt, exhaustion, and frustration all play a part. Many working parents want to avoid the food battle, especially when time with their kids is already limited. But a little persistence, patience, and humor when they're small will pay big dividends when they are grown.

My advice: Keep the job of deciding what everyone eats; keep presenting new foods; and make it a family rule that everybody tastes everything. Be careful not to call your kids "picky eaters"—particularly within earshot. One more thing: Remember to enjoy the food yourself. That's a big one, as our kids are always watching what we say and do. A common complaint I hear from moms is that the picky eater in their family is just as likely to be the dad as it is the six-year-old. The next time you all sit down together, be aware of how you—the grown-ups—are eating, what you're saying, and how you're enjoying the food. Your little ones are watching closely and learning.

"When you're pregnant, the foods you eat add taste to the fluid that your baby floats in—and swallows! Amazingly, herbs and spices in the bites you eat give your little baby a delicious preview of future home-cooked yummies . . . and has a huge impact on your child's future food favorites."

—DR. HARVEY KARP, PEDIATRICIAN,
AUTHOR OF *THE HAPPIEST BABY ON THE BLOCK*

include your kids

A great way to encourage "picky eaters" to try new foods is to include them in the process of preparing the meal. Nothing inspires tasting more than ownership. Depending on age, your child's contribution can be as simple as stirring premeasured ingredients in a bowl, or mashing an avocado with a fork. Put younger kids in charge of something small like tearing herbs or being the meal's official taste-tester (that's a surefire self-esteem builder!). Let the older ones take on a dish, and eventually assign them whole dinners. (Don't laugh, it could happen! See my nephews' testimonial, below.) Watch as your child excitedly announces, "I made dinner!" as compliments fly around the table. Kids' confidence soars in the kitchen, while benefits abound.

Check out the **k** icon in many of our recipes for how kids can help.

manage the snack bar

One of the best ways to curb the "picky eater" phenomenon is to ensure that your kids are actually hungry when they come to the table. That means maintaining some control over what snacks—and when—your kids are pillaging in the pantry. If you don't want them to have it, don't buy it.

But snacks aren't available just at home anymore. Our nonstop food environment is constantly providing cues and opportunities to eat junk food. School days offer a parade of treats for birthdays, or TGIF, or any of the countless excuses for which parents are encouraged to send snacks. The access to junk-filled vending machines, often right on school property, isn't helping the situation either. (Come on schools, ban the vending machines once and for all!)

Often, kids leave school hungry because school lunch stinks. Although some meager improvements

a true story, by Alex and Ben Schiff

When we were little, we were very picky (we prefer "selective") eaters. Our pediatrician made us write up a list of five vegetables we agreed we would eat (not including ketchup). At the time, that wasn't easy. Then our mom got us involved in making dinner. We enjoyed learning how to cook—it was like a puzzle at first. The more we cooked, the more we gained control over what we ate, and the more open we became to a wider and wider variety of foods.

Soon, we were growing vegetables in our own garden and cooking Sunday night family dinner by ourselves. Now, at the age of 13, it would be hard for us to pick five vegetables we don't like! We cook all the time (Aunt Laurie even included our Brussels sprouts recipe in this book), and have started our own granola business, A&B Granola. We encourage all parents to let their kids in on the process and cook with them. That's the best way we know of to get kids to try something new!

"Create a snacking rule that suits your family. In our house, children never have to ask for a piece of fruit, but they do have to ask permission for something else."

—KAREN LE BILLON, AUTHOR OF *FRENCH KIDS EAT EVERYTHING*

have been made in the last few years, greater gains have been blocked by industry lobbyists, and so school lunches still tend to be overprocessed and laden with unhealthy preservatives, salt, sugar, and fats. Many fast food joints like Pizza Hut, Chick Fil-A, and McDonalds are shockingly still regular school lunch suppliers.

All the more reason to keep the addictive snacks out of your cupboard and provide yummy healthy snacks instead. After school and before homework begins, put out almonds, carrots, or cucumbers with our hummus recipe. Put out a small bowl of nut butter with apples, or our yogurt parfaits. If it's there, kids will eat it and fill up on the good stuff.

As with adults, the ever-present drink in hand is contributing to the oversnacking problem too. Some of these drinks are meals in themselves, chock full of calories and sugar. Children's ready access to sippy cups, juice boxes, chocolate milk in school, soda, and other sugary drinks has been cited as a major cause of tooth decay and obesity. It really does set bad habits for the rest of their lives.

"Years ago, our mothers never walked around holding drinks of any kind, but today everyone is constantly carrying 'liquid accessories'—coffee, bottled water, and soda," says Dr. Wendy Sue Swanson, a pediatrician at Seattle Children's Hospital. "Kids start to mimic adults at several months old and with parents modeling this constant drinking they are passing this behavior onto their kids."

Despite what the beverage companies tell us, we don't need constant "hydration." We don't need juice, or energy drinks, or electrolytes. We do need water. Serve water with all your meals and water is what your kids will crave for the rest of their lives.

why we hate kids' menus

Restaurants and fast food joints have done their part to encourage "picky eater" syndrome and set kids' nutrition standards as low as they can go. In 1973, a fast food place called Burger Chef had an idea: to offer a "kids' menu" as a way to lure parents. The novelty included a hamburger, French fries, and a soda. Bingo! The kids' menu increased traffic and profits rose. Naturally, the idea was quickly adopted by competitors. Toss in a cheap plastic toy depicting a favorite cartoon or action figure and watch sales zoom!

It didn't take long for kids' menus to catch on as part of our wider restaurant culture, typically offering a limited range of burgers, mac 'n' cheese, grilled cheese, pasta with butter, chicken fingers, and other bland foods, plus a drink and dessert included in the price. **A 2013 study found that the nutritional quality of most "kids' meals" at large chain restaurants do not even meet the standards set by their own National Restaurant Association.**

The money Americans spend on foods made by someone outside the home nearly doubled from 1970 to 2010.[10] The main goal of restaurants is to provide a sensory experience that gets you to come back. Which almost always means more salt, fat, and sugar.

There shouldn't be a category for "kids' food" at all, not in restaurants, not in our homes. Just the term itself sends a negative message empowering kids to reject food not deemed "kid friendly." **Kids should be eating what we eat, just less of it.** It is time for this new normal of white, bland, and processed to go away. It's time to return brightly colored, flavorful, crunchy, fresh food to the table.

Ask Chef Asata: common excuses and no-nonsense responses

Chef Asata Reid is a chef, culinary educator, food advocate, and mother of two strong-willed boys. She works with many organizations to support farm-to-school efforts and promote health and wellness with cooking classes and demonstrations. The founder of Life Chef (www.lifechef.net), Chef Asata focuses on real-world solutions to daily meal dilemmas.

....

Chef Asata:

Often "picky eater" problems are rooted in parents' behaviors. We don't want to own up to that, but it's true. I've had pediatricians at my healthy-cooking demonstrations who stood up and applauded when I said, "An emotionally healthy kid won't starve him or herself. When they get hungry, they'll eat." One doctor elaborated: "I wish parents would let go of their guilt and stop snacking their kids to death. Let them build up an appetite. Let them get hungry and they'll eat." Small kids have small stomachs, and in the land of Supersize Meals, many of us adults have lost all perspective on portion size, which further fuels the dreaded dinnertime drama. Here are some of the most frequently asked questions I get, with my very real, but sincere, responses.

Q: My kid is so picky he will only eat three foods—all of them white or beige.

A: Banish the boring beige plates and invite your kids to eat the rainbow of fruits and vegetables! Insert one colorful food at each meal. Make it fun—the kids can pick the color—then activate the One Bite Rule, and enforce it with loving kindness. Take one bite of everything, and you're dismissed. Simple, right? The trick is to not lose your cool. This is not a platform to fight—it's dinner. Once everyone knows what's expected, hopefully they'll fall in line.

Q: Take-out is cheaper and faster, so it's my go-to on weeknights—there's no way I have time to shop and cook after work.

A: You just nailed the problem—you *don't* have time to shop and cook after work, so do it on the weekends when you *do* have time. Your new favorite quick-cooking techniques are stir-fries and sautés. And your favorite new kitchen appliances are a slow-cooker and a big salad bowl.

Q: I hate chopping vegetables and prepping ingredients—I don't have time for it so I avoid making salads and recipes that require a lot of prep.

A: If you're willing to pay more, you can always buy presliced veggies. However, I have a two-word solution to the problem: food processor. I've picked up a food a processor for as little as $18. It was loud as hell (and I always suspected it had NASA-like aspirations as it was prone to launching off the countertop), but it sliced veggies just fine in the blink of an eye.

Q: I end up having to make three different meals so everyone in my family will find something to eat. How can I avoid that?

A: What are you, a short order cook? Instead of catering to everyone's wants, involve the kids in planning meals throughout the week. Each family member gets a night to create a meal featuring a protein, two veggies (or a fruit and a veggie), and a complex carbohydrate or whole grain. Bonus points for adding a calcium source! So instead of three separate meals every night, each member of the family gets a night to shine, and every one else *respects* that because, after all, their night is coming up next.

Q: My kids always expect dessert at the end of a meal. It seems to be the only reason they eat. How can I make it stop?

A: This is easy. Stop buying or making desserts. Period. Dinner is not the prequel to dessert; it's a necessary part of life and family time. However, for many of us, dinner and dessert have become inextricably linked. Break the habit. Then, if you want, bring back dessert as either a weekend thing, a special-occasion thing, or a family-night-out thing. As the parent, initiate it. You have the power!

Q: When I shop with my kids, they throw junk foods into the cart when I'm not paying attention, and I get so tired of fighting back, I end up buying some of it.

A: Do your kids have a job? If not, why are they putting *anything* in the cart without your permission? And if you get up to the register and find "surprise" items, just tell the cashier to put it back. Simply say, "Sorry, but I didn't approve of that. Will you please restock it?" Done.

Q: I have started going to farmers' markets and come home with beautiful kale and beets and radishes . . . but then I can never figure out how to use them before they go bad.

A: Google. For real. There are a bazillion recipes on the internet just a few clicks away.

Q: My kids snack before dinner (and they are too old for me to "hide" things) so when it's time to eat they're not even hungry.

A: Put your foot down and enforce the "no snacking" rule *and* don't buy any more non-nutritious snacks (they can't eat it if it's not in the house, right?). However, if their snacks are nutritious, maybe it just means smaller portions at dinner time. You may also want to look at what time dinner is served. You may need to make dinner earlier, followed by a nutritious postdinner snack, or make dinner later after the kids have had a chance to build up their appetite.

Q: My husband brings home sweet teas and other drinks that we try not to let our kids drink but doesn't see that he's setting a bad example. How can we get on the same page?

A: Convert the garage to his man-cave and let him "junk out" in there, versus in the house. I kid, I kid. Seriously: It's a grown-folks conversation and you're both grown folks. Come to the table knowing you both want the best for each other and your children, then go from there.

Remind him that in his kids' eyes, he's on par with Superman, so whatever he does, they will mimic and perceive as okay. He's presenting the old adage "Do as I say, not as I do." And we all know that's highly ineffective because actions speak louder than words.

Q: When I ask my kids to help me cook they tell me they don't want to. So I make them do it, they do a lousy job, and I get mad at them and send them away.

A: Your kids are totally "playing" you! They've figured out if they do a half-baked job, you'll banish them, which is what they wanted in the first place. Hmm. I wonder what would happen if *you* decided *you* didn't want to cook. Let's imagine, shall we? This could be a great conversation to have with the kids so they get some insight into your experience and develop some empathy and compassion.

live the life you want your children to live

Dr. Yoni Freedhoff is a passionate doctor of family medicine and a great tweeter (@YoniFreedhoff), which is how we met: online. Affiliated with the University of Ottawa, he is the founder of the Bariatric Medical Institute and author most recently of *Diet Fix*. Here are his wise tips on how best to feed children.

* Encourage a wide and varied healthy diet, introducing new foods frequently and early.

* Don't pressure your children to eat (one-bite rules are fine) or withhold dessert unless they eat their veggies.

* Don't reward them with food.

* Disband the "clean your plate" club.

* Keep plenty of fruits and vegetables handy, accessible, visible, washed and prepared, and literally smile at your kids when they eat them.

* Sit at the table and eat with your kids.

* Don't skip meals.

* Dramatically minimize meals out and takeout.

* Ensure that as many meals as possible a week involve the transformation of raw ingredients.

* Involve your kids in cooking.

* Put even more simply? Live the lives you want your children to live.

Set!

step one to health:
the shopping list

Grocery shopping is where it all begins. Your choices make a difference in how you and your children eat, feel, and live. It's the time when you get to control what temptations are in the house. And if there are no sweet doodleOs, there's nothing to fight about—bonus!

This is when you get to decide where and how the food you eat was grown or raised, and what it contains. Shopping conscientiously will not only feed your family well, it will also send a message to supermarkets, factories, and farms that if they want your business, they need to start taking your family's health very seriously. But how do you do that?

shop like a pro

Before you shop, write a list that you won't lose. Why?

Because you can either shop this way:

You're pushing your cart, with one kid in the seat who somehow is already as sticky as a jujube. Your other child is running at warp speed straight for whatever those evil genius food execs have paid extra to be positioned at your child's eye level (3 feet 1 inch).

You are frantically searching your purse for the envelope on which you wrote your shopping list. But with your own stomach grumbling and younger child acting up, you'll just have to try to remember what you wrote down. The next 20 minutes will be a mad dash from the bananas, to the cheese, back to the potatoes, down the coffee aisle, and shoot . . . back to the cheese for Parmesan. You'll forget milk and beans, you'll get a bag of cheesy poofs to hush your little one (which you'll end up eating half of in the car), and you'll go home with a bunch of stuff your kids put in the cart.

Or you can shop this way:

You arrive at the store with the special book you carry just for shopping lists—small enough to slip into your purse, but big enough so you don't lose it. You add only things that are on the list to the cart, crossing them off as you go and deviating only if the pears are in better condition than the apples, or if the spinach is fresh and local. Your kids will still be sticky and misbehaved . . . but you will have shopped like a pro.

Here are a few more tips on how to run the supermarket gauntlet.

Plan out your meals before you shop. Sit down with tea and a cookbook or two, and think about the days when your schedule will permit you time to prepare food, and the days on which prep for dinner and other meals will be rushed. Make sure that at least two of your planned meals will yield enough leftovers to be repurposed into dinner the next day, or to be frozen for another time.

Write out your list according to where the foods are in the store. Group produce together (trying to keep the herbs with herbs, fruit with fruit, etc.), then make a list of dairy, then dry goods, and so on, so you just hit the parts of the store you need items in. So much the better if you can avoid the aisles laden with temptation—snack foods, cereal, ice cream.

Once at the store, divide and conquer. Laurie likes to give everyone the task of finding a few items, which feels more like a scavenger hunt than a household chore. Have kids compare prices, examine labels for ingredients to avoid, and practice the art of bagging.

Stick to your list. Grocery stores manipulate location and placement to get you to buy things you really (really) don't need. They tend to stock expensive brand names at eye level and less expensive brands on the top or bottom shelves (one exception is the sugary cereal aisle, where the most expensive products are placed at kids' eye level). Abide by your shopping list so you can avoid temptation, stay within budget, and not end up with so much food that much of it goes to waste.

Be aware of labels. Learn how to read nutrition labels and identify which words are important (see page 26). Just because the packaging bears a photo of a bucolic cow, or fresh fruit, or the words "all natural," does not mean the product is healthy or farm-fresh. It's just as likely to come from a factory. Always bring along your reading glasses, if you need them, so you can see these labels, which seem to be shrinking every day (maybe it's our age, but we're pretty sure it's on purpose!).

Manage snacks. Before you put a snack or dessert into your cart, give it a second thought. The only way it can get into your home and your family's tummies is if you buy it. This is your chance to take control of the snack monsters. Also, beware of the yogurt container. Many kids' yogurts contain so much sugar, they really should be regarded as dessert.

Stay strong at checkout. Grocery stores know you are trapped waiting at the checkout stands, so this is where they stock impulse items like candy, soda, and chips. Stay resolute! Stick to your list! Distract your children! In fact, prepare for this inevitability in advance. A good family discussion about checkout behavior can go a long way toward dealing with this supermarket trap.

On days when your shopping list is short, grab a hand basket. The smaller basket curbs impulse buys, and gives your arms a good workout.

"The most important thing you can do is cook for your family. You don't have to worry about nutrients, you don't have to worry about fats, you don't have to worry about sugars. If you cook real food, your family will be eating much better."

—MICHAEL POLLAN, *FED UP*

labels and words: what they mean and why they matter

If labels actually meant what they said, shopping would be fairly simple. But they often don't, and that puts pressure on you to decipher what the heck it all means. To help you avoid falling prey to marketing tricks, we consulted a pro, our friend Urvashi Rangan, who directs the Consumer Safety and Sustainability Group for *Consumer Reports*, an independent organization that has been rigorously testing products and investigating marketing claims since 1936 (wow!).

Below, Rangan guides us in understanding which labeling terms mean what they say—and which are just misleading. For more information, visit Consumer Reports' Greener Choices (greenerchoices.org).

meaningful labels

Organic: The USDA has strict guidelines and a rigorous certification process for use of this term. The USDA Certified Organic seal is put on food products that are either 100% organic or just organic, meaning that at least 95 percent of the ingredients must be organically grown. But what does it mean? Meat, poultry, eggs, and dairy products that carry the USDA Certified Organic label are free of hormones or antibiotics and were fed non-GMO diets. Organic produce is grown without using most conventional pesticides or fertilizers made with manufactured ingredients or sewage, are GMO free, and are not irradiated. Farmers really go the extra mile and cost for this certification.

Grass-Fed: A term for meat that is similar to "pasture-raised," grass-fed is actually defined by the USDA as animals having access to a pasture for most of the growing season and fed a lifetime diet of 99.9 percent grass and forage. The American Grass-fed Certified seal goes even further than the USDA standard and is the best meat raised on a grass and forage diet. The USDA label is only for beef and does not apply to dairy, pork, or poultry and allows the use of antibiotics in feed. By contrast, American Grass-fed Certified does not allow antibiotics and can also be found on lamb, goat, and dairy products.

Non-GMO Verified: GMOs refer to genetically modified organisms and are also known as GE (genetically engineered) or bioengineered foods. It is estimated that GMO ingredients, such as corn and soybeans, are present in as much as 80 percent of processed food. GMO varieties of these crops have never been properly tested for long-term health impacts. As of now, there is no government requirement to label GMOs, and so the Non-GMO Verified label is the most reliable, as it has an independent verification process for GMO-free products.

somewhat meaningful labels

Free-Range: With the horrors of factory farming growing increasingly public, many want to make sure the animals they eat lived decent lives before making their way to their plates. Free-range is one of those terms that sounds great, but doesn't mean much. For meat and eggs there is no standard definition or verification process. When referring to poultry, the USDA requires that chickens have access to an outdoor space, which could be for as little as 5 minutes a day. Hardly the idyllic image of chickens roaming the hills and returning to their coops at night!

Cage-Free: Although chicken broilers are not kept in cages, they are probably kept in a warehouse and are not guaranteed access to the outdoors. So while the USDA can provide optional verification for this claim (look for the additional USDA Process Verified seal), cage-free does not necessarily mean that chickens were living in good conditions.

Gluten-Free: Gluten is a particular protein contained in many grains, such as wheat, barley, and rye. This is an important label for those suffering from celiac disease and gluten sensitivity. However, many gluten-free products are processed with ingredients that are not necessarily healthier than gluten, like corn.

BPA-Free: Recently the synthetic chemical bisphenol-A, commonly known as BPA, has gotten a lot of attention from consumers—which is good, because in addition to being linked to cancer, obesity, and interference with brain development, it's pretty much everywhere: in the lining of canned foods, beer and soda cans, some reusable plastic water bottles, polycarbonate plastic and . . . ATM and cash register receipts. Still, don't get too excited when you see a BPA-Free product, because generally that just means BPA could have been replaced with bisphenol S (aka BPS), a kissing-chemical cousin of BPA that hasn't been thoroughly tested for safety.

Sustainable: This label commonly refers to a philosophy of growing agriculture and sourcing seafood. Sustainable agriculture is an approach that considers long-term profit, impact on the land, energy, and water use, and the lives of both the animals and the farmers. Sustainable seafood is a general term that refers to seafood that is either caught or farmed and that is good for you, good for the oceans, and good for the environment. This is one of those terms that is sure to be overused and misrepresented because it isn't certifiable.

Wild Fish: Wild fish is sourced straight from the sea, so it is naturally "organic"—however, many wild fish are being overfished or caught in a manner that is detrimental to the sea life around them. Check for the best choices at Seafood Watch on the Monterey Bay Aquarium website (seafoodwatch.org).

Farmed Fish: Many types of farmed fish are fed antibiotics, synthetic colors to turn their flesh pink, and fish meal (which essentially means they are being fed huge amounts of ground-up fish that could be used to feed human populations). The farms themselves are often environmental hazards. There are, however, sustainable fisheries that are recommended by the Marine Stewardship Council, so check with them or the Monterey Bay Aquarium Seafood Watch for which fish should land on your plate tonight.

not meaningful labels

Natural: This label is widely used by food companies to create the perception that an item is healthy. The FDA has essentially no regulation of its use and several customers have sued—and won—because some products that claim to be natural are filled with chemicals and additives.

"Natural" Meat: Consumers expect that meat bearing this label comes from an animal that was raised in a natural way: that it spent time outdoors, ate a natural diet, and was not physically altered. But none of those things have to be considered. The animals could have been fed drugs every day and the meat could be enhanced with salt water and called "natural" too.

No Nitrates: Consumers may think this label means that no nitrates (a chemical preservative linked to cancer in animals) were used on a food product like the beloved hotdog. However, it often means that a naturally based nitrate was used, which chemically cures the meat in the same way that a synthetic nitrate would do.

Microwave Safe: Consumers may think that this claim means that an item is safe to microwave and will not leach any chemicals or contaminants into the food. However, this is not the case and chemicals such as phthalates and BPA can leach from plastics and even linings of cardboard cartons. Microwave in glass or microwavable ceramic whenever possible.

Trans Fat–Free: Consumers may think these products are void of heart-unhealthy trans fat, but that is not necessarily the case. The standard for the label is less than half a gram of trans fat per serving. Check the ingredient panel for partially hydrogenated oil, the culprit ingredient. In late 2013 the FDA removed trans fat from the generally recognized as safe status so we should expect to see less of it soon. Bravo FDA!

Made with Real Fruit: We all know we have to eat more fruits and vegetables, and so few things sound more appealing than food that says it's made with real fruit. Except when it's not. Blueberries? Try blueberry bits. Fruit in the bottom of yogurt? Try sugar, high fructose corn syrup, and food dyes. Food companies can feature fruit on the labels as long as they use the word "flavoring." There have been several lawsuits over deceptive advertising. So don't be fooled. Skip the "made with real fruit" label and go straight for the real thing!

No Antibiotics Used: Not too long ago, an infected cut could have resulted in death. Such a thing is

a fresh look at the expiration date

Edible honey has been found in Egyptian tombs, so why does the one in my cupboard expire in March? And what about salt? Didn't it just hang out in mines for a gazillion years, but now that it's in my pantry it's supposed to go bad after a year? Who decides when my food needs to be thrown out?

Not the FDA. With the exception of a few things like baby food, most expiration dates (or sell by, best by, use by dates) are set by the manufacturers. Although they want to keep our food safe and fresh, don't they also have an interest in our buying more of their product as quickly as possible?

There is an easy solution: Whenever you are in doubt . . . *before* you throw it out, use your nose, and go to a "food shelf life" Web site like stilltasty.com or eatbydate.com, which details how long different foods last. Questioning the dates and informing yourself will keep you safe and help you save food and money.

So next time you see a "best by" label, wonder who that's best for!

hard for us to imagine in the age of antibiotics, but the overuse of these drugs is now leading to the rise of drug-resistant bacteria and superbugs, such as MRSA, an antibiotic-resistant staph infection,[11] which is putting public health at risk. According to the Natural Resources Defense Council (NRDC) 80 percent of antibiotics in the US are sold for use in livestock, most for animals that are not sick, but to prevent infection that might result from the unsanitary living conditions. Why we are putting the antibiotics we need for our children's ear infections at risk by using them on healthy animals so they can live in filth? The good news is you can opt out of this insane system. Like "hormone-free," the term "antibiotic-free" is prohibited. Choose meat that is certified USDA Organic, American Grassfed Approved, Animal Welfare Approved, or certified humane—these labels have thorough certification. Your meat may cost a little more, but it will help protect your family's and our nation's health.

No Hormones Added: Hormones are given to make beef cattle grow bigger, faster and to dairy cows to produce more milk. They are a key ingredient of the factory farm system and its horrors. There are growing concerns that these added hormones pose health risks to humans, animals, and the environment as they contaminate the soil, surface, and groundwater. Added hormones are actually prohibited in poultry and pigs, so be aware of those claims. The use of the claim "Hormone Free" is prohibited by the USDA and "No Hormones Administered" is unverified. Instead look for USDA's Organic, American Grassfed Approved, and Certified Humane Raised & Handled, as all are labels that require certification.

For more information please consult

* NRDC.org

* seafoodwatch.org

* Consumer Reports' Eco-labels.org and greenerchoices.org

* EWG.org

set the table

A set table is the signal that something special is about to happen. Knowing how to set the table is a basic skill that parents should teach their children as soon as they are capable—it's right up there with the other skills we pass on to our kids, like brushing their teeth and tying their shoes.

Once you know how to do it the right way, setting the table can be an opportunity for creativity—no need to always be Emily Post correct. Let the table setter decide the centerpiece (this could be flowers picked from the yard, a show and tell object, or a vase of fresh herbs to be used at dinner), fold the napkins, and have the honor of blowing out the candles after dinner.

Go!

Laurie's do's and don'ts for happy family meals

— Do —

* Cook! With love, confidence, and curiosity.

* Embrace the family dinner and make it a ritual! The more meals you eat together as a family—whoever makes up that family—the more benefits you will accrue. Eating together, talking, and sharing are some of the most important activities a family can do together. (Check out our first book, *The Family Dinner*.)

* Cook with the seasons. Get your fruit when it is sweet and your vegetables when they are fresh and crunchy.

* Make extras. When cooking a favorite recipe, double or triple it, wrap up a few portions, and toss them in the freezer (don't forget to label them). Nothing is better than a home-cooked meal after a long day, especially if it's already made.

* Buy organic when you can. It's better for you and it's better for the planet.

* Eat less meat. When you do eat meat, make sure it's organic, humanely treated, antibiotic-free, and grass-fed.

* Try to buy local and support the farmers that surround you, either at farmers' markets, from farm stands, or by subscribing to a Community Supported Agriculture (CSA) service. Take your kids to a pick-your-own farm so they can see how their fruits and vegetables grow and taste them straight from the land. Check localharvest.org to find a farm near you.

* Use sturdy pots and pans that will last forever, like cast-iron skillets, heavy-duty enamelware, stainless steel, and glass. (Teflon-coated cookware releases toxic fumes and can leach these chemicals when chipped during cooking.)

* Use unprocessed heart-healthy fats, such as olive oil, nut oils, and seed oils.

* Stay away from margarine, corn oil, hydrogenated oils or partially hydrogenated oils.

* Use unrefined sweeteners (in moderation), like raw local honey or maple syrup.

* Keep your shopping cart full of fruit, vegetables, and grains, while keeping out the boxes, frozen trays, and crinkly bags.

* Eat your meals in good company, gathered around a table or picnic basket. Not in the unnatural glow of multiple screens.

* Drink real water from a real glass, between meals and at meals.

* Include your kids (and spouse) whenever possible in the making, setting, and cleaning of dinner.

* Store food and leftovers in glass jars and generally reduce the amount of plastic in the kitchen.

* Be sure to shower the chef with compliments and always offer to help clean up.

* Remember the formula for sugar: 4 grams equals 1 teaspoon. This also makes a handy math lesson for your kids.

* Make it a nonnegotiable rule that everyone tastes everything . . . every time it is served.

* Teach your kids table manners, and model them.

* Treat your family table with respect and love. Light candles, use cloth napkins and dinnerware.

* Try to have regular meal times and enforce attendance.

* Express gratitude on a regular basis. Practice builds the gratitude muscle.

* It's never too late to make new friends and there's no better place to find them than at your local farmers' market. That is where I met Jessica Harris (see her picture on page 169) this past summer. I was behind the table at my friend's farm stand, selling arugula and mushrooms, and she was in front of the table buying them. We chatted. It turns out she is a food historian who has written 12 books (most recently, *Beyond Gumbo*) and makes her own hootch! A perfect new friend for me. Jessica is a fount of great advice, including the suggestion on page 168. Definitely a do!

— *Don't* —

* Worry about dishes not coming out right. You *can't* fail! It's just one meal and you get to try again tomorrow.

* Buy food containing high fructose corn syrup, artificial sweeteners, or refined sugars. Wean yourself off of diet drinks.

* Drink your fruit from a carton.

* Drink soda or juice (unless you really need the heaping teaspoons of sugar).

* Cling to unrealistic standards for what constitutes a meal. A sweet potato, a salad, some hummus and raw veggies . . . that's a great dinner!

* Bring phones or computers to the table. No exceptions for mom or dad.

— *Do* —

* And most of all, **DO** stay informed!

We live in a world where everything changes so quickly, sometimes for the better (it is easier to find organic produce), but sometimes for the worse (almost all processed foods are made with GMOs, some of which is forbidden in other countries, and yet here we don't even label them).

The only way you can rejoice or protest is if you have knowledge. Join an environmental group, read the news, watch movies like *Fed Up, Forks Over Knives, GMO OMG,* and *Food, Inc.* Follow a few Twitter feeds like Mark Bittman (@bittman), Michael Pollan (@MichaelPollan), EWG (@ewgtoxics), Michele Simon (@MicheleRSimon), NRDC (@NRDC), and Kristin Wartman (@kristinwartman). Follow some cutting-edge doctors like David Kessler (@DavidAKesslerMD), Mark Hyman (@markhymanmd), Yoni Freedhoff (@YoniFreedhoff), Wendy Sue Swanson (@SeattleMamaDoc), Dr. David Katz (@DrDavidKatz), Dr. Harvey Karp (@DrHarveyKarp), Dr. Nicole Avena (@DrNicoleAvena), Andy Bellatti, MS, RD (@AndyBellatti), Center for Science in the Public Interest (@CSPI), and the work of Dr. Robert Lustig.

Kirstin's kitchen rules and tools

Right now you are probably saying, "rules? I don't follow rules—I am free and fantastic!" And I love that. So let's call them tricks instead. I have been cooking since I was knee-high to a cricket and have learned a few tricks that help keep the kitchen a safe, productive, and delicious place to be. Follow them now and break them later when I am not looking.

read the recipe all the way through

And I mean the whole recipe. It will only take a minute and it will give you a preview of what you need to do when: whether you should start a pot of water boiling, turn on the oven, or rush to the store for a last-minute ingredient.

get your ducks in a row

There's a fancy French term for this concept: *mise en place* (put in place). To be a truly efficient cook, you'll want to prepare all of your ingredients and tools beforehand so they are ready for you to grab and incorporate without delay. This might seem like an extra step, but you'll be grateful you did it.

★ Ready your measuring spoons and cups and a few bowls for the prepped ingredients. Get out your pot and skillet, and oil the baking sheets if needed. Later you won't have to knock around the kitchen with dirty hands and goggly eyes looking for them.

★ Chop and measure all the ingredients in the recipe.

★ Line up the prepped ingredients in the order in which they are written on the recipe, because that is usually the order in which they will be used (see photo opposite). And if by chance you forget to add an ingredient, it will be right there on the counter saying, "Yoo-hoo (Laurie)! What about me?"

follow the yellow brick road

A recipe is like a road map. If you follow it, it will guide you safely to the right destination. If you don't, things can run amok. So when you finish a recipe for the first time, consider if you'd take a few different turns next time—more spice, perhaps—or maybe some basil. (Write it on the recipe so you'll remember when you come back to it.) Eventually you can toss the map and improvise cooking your way to new horizons. But the first time, follow the map.

wash well

Stay clean and healthy. Wash your hands with soap and hot water. Wash your cutting boards with soap and hot water—not once, but many times while cooking. Rinse your produce. Wipe down your sink and counters regularly. While you're at it, wash behind your kids' ears. All of these measures (well, except the last one) will help you minimize risk of bacterial exposure.

You need to be especially careful of touching other surfaces after handling raw meat of any kind. Whether it be a knife, a spoon, cabinet knobs, garbage can lid, or phone—all need to be fastidiously cleaned with soap and water once they have come in contact with meat. Those germs are dastardly and invisible, so always assume they are there until you scrub them away.

Finally, wash the dishes as you go. I know it's no fun, but a counter cluttered with dirty dishes will clutter your mind and put a damper on your creativity.

know a few recipes by heart

Make sure they are healthy, simple, and beloved. Tomato sauce is a good one, as are beans on toast, garlic greens, vegetable soup, a simple roast chicken breast, or a quick curry. Teach them to your kids so that no matter where in their lives they are, they will always be able to improvise and whip up something fast, healthy, and delicious.

know your timing

Prepping times

No matter if you are a beginner or a seasoned pro, following a recipe the first time just takes longer. Everything must be read, then re-read. A new ingredient needs to be sniffed, poked, then prepared in an unfamiliar way, and you have to consult the recipe at every turn. But the next time you can just skim the recipe, and by the time it has become a favorite you will know it by heart.

Cooking times

Ovens tend to fib and say they are one temperature when they are not. Some stove burners are super hot and scorch your garlic in seconds, while others are just plain wimpy. Whether you live on a mountain top or by the sea, there are so many environmental factors that influence cooking time. So get to know

your stove and oven, check your beans long before we say they will be done, and flip the vegetables because they are golden, not because we say so.

be safe

Fire! Knives! Boiling cauldrons! All are useful kitchen tools and only risky if not handled right. So log onto YouTube and watch some kitchen safety videos with your kids. Knife skills, kitchen hygiene, and what to do in case of a stovetop fire are much more easily learned when watched.

Food safety is also a matter of cooking certain foods to the right temperature. Visit foodsafety.gov to learn about how to cook your food to the right temperature and keep you and your family safe. And check a Web site like stilltasty.com to see if leftovers are safe to eat.

put kids in charge (of some things)

Before you tie back your hair and put your aprons on, be thoughtful as to which cooking tasks you assign your kids. Your 15-year-old may be a lovable klutz and still in need of some coaching with a butter knife, while the 12-year-old may be capable of cooking a three-course dinner (so long as he has help lifting a hot pot safely). Only you know your kids well enough to firmly set limits—which you will know only after cooking with them many times—so cook often and learn together.

taste! taste! and yet again . . . taste!

That is the only way food will taste good. Taste often, and adjust the seasonings as you go along.

be fearless

It's just cooking! We all have flops. I still "rename" things all the time when they go awry (it was banana bread and now it's sticky banana pudding—ta da! See page 69).

But even more often, I promise, you will cook something delicious, make someone feel loved, and make them smile while nourishing their bodies with real, good homemade food. The more you cook, the faster and more intuitive it will become. The more you learn about how to pick your ingredients, the better everything will taste. A simple dinner made with a few good ingredients and love is 1,000 times better than a stressful fancy feast. So aren't you lucky? Because you can make a simple dinner!

and finally, have fun!

Cooking is fun. Really! It should be a creative, playful, and generous interaction with your family. Turn up the music, light candles, and kick off your shoes. Kids are naturally drawn to the kitchen—first of all, it's where *you* are and it's a room full of magical potions, machines that whirr, and sweet things to be tasted. So bring them in and be patient, so that someday you can send them out in the world capable of cooking for themselves—and happy to do so. Just please, oh please, don't ever call cooking a chore. Hoeing a potato field is a chore. Cooking is an adventure.

cooking with all five senses

Once you start touching, listening, smelling, and thoughtfully tasting the food you are cooking, from pea pod to pot to plate, that's when you really start cooking.

– See –

We tend to first experience food with our eyes. We pick an apple according to its ideal shape and color. Pancakes form tiny bubbles to let you know they can be flipped. The roasted chicken is golden so it may well be ready. A pleasingly plated meal is far more appetizing than one that is simply plopped in its place. As you are cooking, you should not stop at seeing things, but fully experience food and cooking with all of your senses . . . .

– Hear –

Next time you cook, listen to the difference between the crackling splatter when you add something to the hot pan and the soft bubbling sound produced as it simmers. Notice that as a pan dries out, it will start hissing—a sound that, when you recognize it, will warn you that your dinner is about to burn. Once you are familiar with these sounds, you will know, even if your back is turned to the stove, that it is time to lower the heat, or add a little liquid. Your ears can save you before your nose tells you it's too late.

– Touch –

Touch is an important tool in every aspect of cooking, so wash your hands often and cop a feel. Touch while you shop: The most perfect-looking peach might be rock hard and not ready to be bitten. You won't know until you touch it. Touch the greens before you throw them in your basket—they should be so firm they squeak. Don't be afraid to toss salads, knead dough (or kale), and fold batters with your hands (they are clean, right?), which are the most elegant and efficient tool you have.

Touching—not just with your hands, but also with your mouth—allows you to experience a mix of textures. On its own, our Sweet Potato (Miso) Soup (page 117) is a lovely soup. But top the silky soup with crispy quinoa, a dab of cold yogurt, maybe a few pomegranate seeds that go pop, and you have a bowl of contrasts—hot-cold, crunchy-smooth, sweet-tart . . . every bite is surprisingly different.

– Smell –

Let your nose guide the way when you shop. Taking a whiff of the strawberries before you put them in your cart will reveal if they are sweet (they smell like strawberries) or not (no smell at all). Smell the asparagus—if it is fresh, it will have a bright grassy smell, and if not, it will smell like a wet dog. The fish shouldn't smell fishy; it should smell like the sea. The spices and herbs should clearly announce who they are when you inhale their fragrance; if they don't, they won't flavor your food either.

Your amazing nose can recognize 10,000 scents and will often connect you to a place or time far away. The tart-sweet smell of apples takes me instantly home to Denmark. The smell of browning onions may bring you back to your childhood kitchen. Also to keep in the back of your mind when you are cooking: A kitchen that smells like chicken soup or cinnamon cookies can give an intangible boost to someone who needs comforting.

– Taste

The taste of your cooking depends largely on two things: how fresh and flavorful your ingredients are (never how fancy or expensive), and how the interplay between the five tastes unfolds in your mouth. This is simpler than it sounds. Take a tiny bite from a spoon, tilt your head and say "Hmmm, what do I need more of: sweet? sour? salty? bitter? umami*?" There is no right or wrong here. This is *your* kitchen, so add whatever it needs to make it taste how *you* prefer. If you are in doubt, take a spoonful of what you are cooking and add the teensiest smidge of what you think might be missing to the spoon and taste it. *Now* what do you think?

Balancing flavors will help almost any recipe. A little salt will help tame the bitter in your greens (try a piece of raw kale and another with a sprinkle of salt—see what happens to the bitterness?). A touch of sweetness will mellow out the fiery flavor of a curry. Even your apple crumble will be better if the sweetness is brightened with a squeeze of lemon and a touch of salt. As in all matters of life, it is good to be thoughtful, then balanced.

Also known as the fifth taste, umami is a Japanese term that refers to "savoriness"–that depth of flavor you notice in roasted mushrooms, a long simmered chicken stock, or Parmesan cheese.

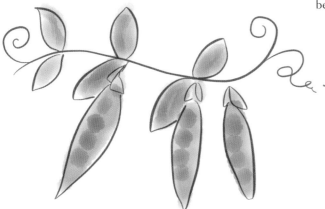

a few of our favorite kitchen tools

A few of these essentials, like pots and knives, can be pricey, but it's worth investing in quality pieces. A good heavy-bottomed skillet will never have to be replaced (and, since they do last forever, they can be found inexpensively at garage sales and flea markets).

Most of these tools, like measuring cups and baking sheets, are best shopped for at restaurant supply stores, where they are sturdy, inexpensive, and built to be used with joy and reckless abandon.

* One 5- to 8-quart enameled cast-iron pot with a lid, also called a Dutch oven. Perfect for stews, soups, braises . . . even to bake bread in. If you can only have one pot, this is it.

* 3 stainless steel pots with lids. We always suggest heavy-bottomed pots, as they distribute heat evenly and prevent food from burning. They will also last much longer than thin, dentable pots.
    * 1 large 10- to 12-quart pot for boiling pasta and making chili or soup for the whole neighborhood
    * 1 medium 2- to 4-quart pot for soups, grains, and sauces
    * 1 small 1-quart pot for small jobs like boiling an egg

* 1 medium and 1 large heavy cast-iron skillet: They go from stovetop to oven and even out to the table with good grace. Care for them well and someday your grandchildren will be using them. You can buy them "preseasoned," or you can rub a new unseasoned skillet with cooking oil and put the skillet in the oven at 350°F for 1 hour. That will give it its first "nonstick seasoning." Seasoned skillets should just be washed with hot water—never soap or harsh abrasives that remove the seasoning. Once they are wiped dry, rub them with a little oil.

* 3 knives. All you need are a chef's knife, a small paring knife, and a serrated bread knife. They can be very old or very new, as long as they feel comfortable in your hand and are kept sharp! A dull knife is like a dull friend—it will bring you down.

* A simple measuring spoon set, from a ¼ teaspoon to 1 tablespoon

* A dry measuring cup set. A plain metal set that ranges from ¼ cup to 1 cup will do fine—stay away from cute and quirky measuring sets, which often don't have accurate measurements.

* A 4-cup glass liquid measuring cup (like the simple Pyrex ones you grew up with)

* A big clean wooden cutting board. It's a beautiful surface to chop on, easy on your knives and eyes. Wash it with hot water several times during cooking, and at the end of the day rub it with a sliced lemon, or a tablespoon of vinegar and a sprinkle of baking soda, let it foam for a few minutes, then rinse with hot water so it's fresh for the next day.

* A smaller plastic cutting board (that fits in the dishwasher). Use this board only for meats and fish so you guarantee there is no cross-contamination of bacteria.

* Simple metal bowls. You can get these at the restaurant supply store. They are cheap, light, come in all sizes, and last so long that your grandchildren will be banging on them someday.

* Wooden spoons. Perfect for stirring soups and scraping out the last bit from a bowl. Wood is better looking and more durable than plastic.

* A Microplane grater. We are grateful for this tool that grates garlic, lemon zest, nutmeg, and cheese with elegance and ease.

* Offset spatula. A long thin spatula set on an angle—it's our favorite tool for flipping with finesse.

* Spring-loaded tongs. For whenever your fingers are too short or delicate, these are a helping hand.

* Immersion blender. Invaluable for making dressings and blending soups right in the pot.

* Tiny spoons for tasting. It is so important to taste your food as you are cooking it, but taste too much and you will be full and the pot empty, so tiny tastes are perfect.

* 2 or 3 baking sheets with rims. They are cheap and useful, not only to bake cookies or sweet potato fries on, but also as a quick lid for a big pot, as a platter for all your prepped ingredients, and even, when covered with a nice napkin, as a tray to bring someone breakfast in bed.

* A large ovenproof baking dish. Large enough to hold a chicken or casserole, nice enough to go from the oven to the table.

* Plenty of clean dish cloths. They dry dishes, wipe up spills, keep your counters clean, and are much "greener" than paper towels.

. . . and of course whisks!

herbs, spices, and strange ingredients

Strangers are only strange until you say hello, and then you wonder how you ever lived without them. So here is a quick introduction to ingredients that might be unfamiliar but will soon become dear friends in the kitchen.

sweeteners

honey

Raw honey is a natural sweetener made by bees from floral nectar. It is highly nutritious with significant amounts of vitamins and minerals. It is also antiviral, antibacterial, and antifungal, making it a healing substance. Buying local honey helps support the bees (and beekeepers) in your community, and also gives your honey a sprinkle of local pollen, which might help ward off allergies. Pasteurized (regular) honey has lost most of it nutrients and some wicked companies are even adding corn syrup to their cute honey bears, so raw is the way to go. Honey has lasted for thousands of years in Egyptian tombs, so it will probably survive in your pantry as well.

maple syrup

Not just for pancakes! Made from the sap of sugar maple trees, it's great for savory dishes that need just a hint of sweetness, like vinaigrettes or chili. And it's lovely in desserts and drinks. Maple syrup is an excellent source of the trace mineral manganese and a good source of zinc. When shopping for syrup, note that Grade B is better than A because it contains more minerals; just make sure the bottle is 100% pure maple syrup and not just maple-flavored syrup.

Unopened bottles of maple syrup can be stored in a cool dry place, but once they are opened they should be kept in the refrigerator.

sauces and pastes

dashi

A Japanese broth made with dried bonito and kombu seaweed. It is used for soups, sauces, and marinades (see page 115).

fish sauce

A favorite ingredient of ours! Yes, it smells pretty funky, as it's made by fermenting fish—often anchovies—in a brine, but just a dash of it gives depth and "bass" (that unami flavor) where it's needed. It is irreplaceable in Vietnamese and Thai dishes, but its usefulness doesn't stop there. Is your tomato sauce lackluster? Add fish sauce! Need anchovies for your Caesar salad? Fish sauce! Need a surprise for dessert? Fish sauce! (Just kidding.) Typically you can find it in the Asian section of larger supermarkets. If there are several brands, pick a lighter-colored one with less sodium.

Tofu

Hoisin

Coconut Milk

Rice paper Wrapper

Fish sauce

Miso

Ginger

Tahini

Red & Green Curry

Honey

Bonito Flakes

Kombu

Rice Vinegar

hoisin sauce

You may have had hoisin sauce along with your mu-shu pork or Peking duck. This sauce is very aromatic with a multitude of sweet and spicy flavors. It's great in stir-fries, but also good as a dip or a spread in wraps. You can find hoisin sauce alongside the soy sauce in most supermarkets or in Asian markets. It will last forever in your fridge.

miso

This delicious, healthy soy-based paste is useful to have in your fridge for soups, marinades, and dressings. See page 114 for more information on this amazingly versatile ingredient.

rice vinegar

A mild-flavored vinegar made from fermented rice, rice vinegar is interchangeable with rice wine vinegar (though they are made differently). Seasoned rice vinegar, with added sugar and salt, can be used in recipes calling for rice vinegar, though you may wish to adjust the seasonings. If you can't find rice vinegar, substitute apple cider vinegar or white wine vinegar.

tamari and soy sauce

Both are made from fermented soybeans and can be swapped for each other. However, there are differences. Soy sauce originated in China and tamari is Japanese. Tamari is generally richer flavored and less salty than soy sauce, making it a gentler choice, especially when used in dressings and dips. Both soy sauce and tamari can contain wheat gluten, but wheat-free versions of tamari are available in most health-food stores.

Thai curry pastes

These are delicious flavor bombs packed into jars. The most common are red, yellow, and green. All three are made from chiles, but the green one (often the spiciest!) is herbaceous with fresh cilantro, kaffir lime leaf, and basil; the red one typically has chili powder, galangal (Thai ginger), and lemongrass, and

the yellow curry contains lemongrass, turmeric, cumin, and coriander. Usually found in the Asian section of the supermarket or in Asian markets, these pastes last for a year in your fridge.

tofu

What? You don't care for tofu? Tofu is a beautiful, nutritious thing, so keep trying it. First of all, it is amazingly versatile and adaptable. Sauté it and it can become crunchy and crisp; toss it with a marinade and it soaks up the flavors; add it to a smoothie and you have just added a silky punch of protein. Best of all, no matter how you serve it, this heart-healthy, cancer-fighting ingredient provides many essential nutrients. It's packed with protein and ounce for ounce contains fewer calories and fat than meat; at 2 to 3 dollars a tub, it's much cheaper as well. Because it's made from soybeans, tofu is also high in iron and zinc and is a great source of calcium and B vitamins. Talk about food as medicine!

what is tofu?

Tofu is made from soy milk that is heated and curdled, then drained and pressed into the shape and firmness needed.

how to buy it

It's usually in the produce or dairy section of your supermarket. Try to buy organic to ensure it has not been made from GMO soybeans.

silken tofu

This usually comes in shelf-stable cartons and doesn't need refrigeration until after it is opened. It comes both soft and firm, and is very smooth, making it good for desserts, spreads, and smoothies.

tub tofu

The most common kind you'll find in the super-market, it comes in a water-filled tub in different firmnesses—soft, firm, and extra firm. We prefer extra firm for stir-fries, as it holds together well.

baked or pressed tofu

Available in small blocks, it's very firm and often flavored with Asian spices or smoked. It's ready to eat and great in sandwiches, chopped into salads, or used in stir-fries . . . even just popped in the mouth as a snack.

how to freeze it

This is a great way to store tofu. Not only does it last for months, but it also gives it a "meatier" texture. Drain it first, pat it dry, and wrap it well.

fresh flavors

fresh ginger

Ginger, the rhizome of a semitropical plant, adds a spicy-sweet flavor to both savory and sweet dishes. Ginger should be peeled before using. The easiest way to do this is to scrape off the thin skin with a spoon (however, if the ginger is very fresh and the skin thin, no one will notice if you don't peel your ginger before chopping it).

Ginger stays fresh for 2 or 3 weeks in the refrigerator when wrapped loosely in a paper towel. It also freezes well (especially convenient if you mince it first), which means you can stock up on it and avoid having to use dried ginger (which is best suited for gingerbread houses).

zest

The very outermost part of any citrus fruit is called zest, and it is packed with citrus aroma, without the tartness or moisture. If you want to add a boost of citrus flavor to any dish, add the zest as well as the juice. Try adding lemon zest to shortbread cookies, vinaigrettes, and sauces. To zest any citrus, scrub the fruit well, then use a fine grater or Microplane to remove only the yellow part of the skin; the white part is quite bitter, so leave that behind.

onions

As you might notice, we use onions so often in our recipes that Laurie's daughter once called us "onion people." Although different types of onions can usually be used interchangeably in a pinch, it's good to know how they differ.

yellow onions

A great all-purpose onion, these are the onions we usually cook with. Pungent when raw, they cook down to a sweetness that fills your kitchen with the scent of home-cooked dinners.

white onions

A bit stronger with thinner skin and flesh, these are often used in Southwestern and Mexican dishes.

red onions

Milder flavored with a beautiful pink hue that gets even pinker when exposed to an acid such as a vinaigrette, red onions are great in salads and stir-fries, where their gentle flavor and color are assets.

sweet onions

"Sweet" onions, such as Walla Wallas, Vidalias, and Maui, are the sweetest of all, with less bite than regular onions. This makes them perfect for salads, sandwiches, and grilling. They are a bit more perishable than regular onions and should be refrigerated.

shallots

Shallots are smaller and more sophisticated than onions. You can swap shallots for onions in a recipe, just bear in mind that shallots do have a distinctive flavor that is a little sweeter, with a hint of garlic and a French accent.

Scallions
sliced

Yellow onion
chopped

clove →
Garlic
head →

pressed

Red onion
diced

Shallots
minced

White onion
sliced

Leeks
sliced

Chives
chopped

leeks

Though these are related to onions, leeks have their own distinct flavor. They are harsh and fibrous when raw but, once cooked, become soft and delicate, like a mild onion with a hint of grassy sweetness. Leeks can be very sandy, so it pays to rinse them well twice—once before you slice, and then once again after.

garlic

In our kitchen, if a recipe calls for two garlic cloves we add five, but you may have different sensibilities, so feel free to see amounts of garlic as suggestions only. To peel a garlic clove, pull it out of the bulb, place it on your cutting board, and cut off the root end. Then lay a large chef's knife flat on the clove and press the knife hard with the heel of your palm to crush, then pull the peel off. You can also use a small heavy object like a paperweight to crush garlic—a perfect job for your older kids.

chives and scallions

Chives are tall, grasslike, and the milder of the two; scallions look like onion tops. They have a mild onion flavor and can be used from top to bottom, raw or cooked. The two can be swapped for each other, but just make sure when using scallions instead of chives that you mince them well, as they are a bit stronger.

herbs

All our recipes call for fresh herbs. The flavor and beauty of a bright vibrant herb just can't be compared to that of a dried one. Luckily most can be found year-round in supermarkets. Even better, if you have a windowsill or a bucket of earth you can call your own, herbs can be easy to grow as houseplants and are a great way to introduce kids (and perhaps yourself) to the rewards of growing your own. We suggest herbs to use in certain dishes, but if you hate cilantro and you happen to have parsley or basil, by all means make the choice that is right for you.

tender herbs

These are usually best used raw or added toward the end of cooking a dish.

Get them fresh, make sure they smell sweet and bright and that their leaves are vigorously green on springy stems. Try to buy them in bunches rather than plastic "clam packs," but if you must buy them in a pack, make sure that the ones hiding on the bottom are also fresh (and gently ask the produce manager to find alternatives to plastic packaging).

how to store

Tender herbs prefer to be treated kindly—too cold (the refrigerator) or too hot (a sunny windowsill), and they turn droopy or black. Treat them like flowers in a glass of water and they can stay fresh for days in a cool spot on your kitchen counter or as a centerpiece on your dinner table. They might even reward you by sending out roots—in which case, plant them in a pot and call it your farm.

basil

Depending on the type, basil has leaves that can range from tiny to huge and from bright green to a beautiful purple. Basil has a green, sweet, slightly peppery scent and flavor. Use basil raw or cooked wherever you need an aromatic boost of summery green. Blend it into soups and sauces, chop it into thin ribbons and toss it with your salad. A tomato without its friend basil is sad. Pesto without basil is just nuts (actually, that's not true—try parsley or kale pesto, page 239).

cilantro

Cilantro has green jagged leaves on tender stems. It has a very distinctive fragrance and flavor that is fresh, citrusy, and brings flair to any dish it lands upon. Most of the world loves cilantro in great amounts; however, for some people cilantro tastes like soap. So whenever you cook for the cilantro adverse, put it on the side or replace it with basil, mint, or even parsley, because they *will* know if you

try to sneak it in. Cilantro loves to mingle with Asian and South American dishes. When cilantro goes to seed, the seeds plucked are called coriander (also the name cilantro goes by when it travels abroad).

dill

Soft, delicate, feathery leaves belie the grassy citrusy punch of this herb. If you are looking to give a dish a Northern European vibe, this is the herb you should chop. It is delicious in eggs or with potatoes, beautiful draped onto fish; torn into salads, it adds a bit of surprise to each bite.

mint

The sparkly herb! Sweet, fresh, and slightly bracing, it's a taste we're all familiar with. Fresh mint comes in different shapes and slightly different flavors. The most common types—spearmint and peppermint—can be used interchangeably. Fresh mint is lovely in desserts and paired with fruit and beverages, but don't stop there. Savory dishes such as roasted vegetables, soups, salads, and stir-fries all benefit from a handful of mint.

parsley

Bright and earthy tasting, parsley should be used freely and with joy. It comes both as the robustly flavored "Italian" flat-leaf parsley and the milder curly parsley. Which you use is a matter of your preference; just be sure to be generous. Not only does it taste bracingly fresh, but it adds vitamins K, C, and beta-carotene (which converts to vitamin A) to anything you toss it into. Add parsley to salads, make into a salad (tabbouleh), or use it instead of basil for a pesto that stays bright green.

"twiggy" herbs

These herbs are a brawny bunch, all of them eager to have their opinions heard. So start with a little before you add a lot, and add them early in the cooking process so the flavors can mellow out a bit. If you are feeling rustic, you can throw in the whole twig

without chopping it; just remove it before serving. As with tender herbs, pick these herbs while they are green, fresh, and sweet smelling.

how to store

Wrap twiggy herbs loosely in a paper towel, place them in a plastic bag, and store them in the warmest part of the refrigerator; one of the compartments in the door works perfectly. Don't rinse or wrap the herbs tightly as the trapped moisture may cause them to mold. If you end up with too much, these herbs are easily dried. Just wrap the ends with a rubber band and hang them in a dark dry place for a week or so, then store them in an airtight container.

oregano

The warm, balsamic, and aromatic flavor of oregano makes it the perfect addition to Mediterranean and Mexican cuisines. It has small grayish green leaves and small white or pink flowers. Oregano is not timid; a little goes a long way. It is the perfect herb to sprinkle on pizzas, fish, and into tomato sauce.

rosemary

Sweet, strong, and pine-scented, rosemary twigs have leaves that look like deep-green pine needles with silver-white undersides. Everyone loves them roasted with potatoes, vegetables, or chicken. Try adding a tiny bit of rosemary to bread, shortbread cookies, or a citrusy dessert.

sage

Can you say sage without thinking about the flavor of turkey and stuffing? Sage is a child of many shapes. Its beautiful leaves can be spear-shaped or large and round. It can be dark green with white stripes or . . . sage green. Try sautéing the leaves in a little olive oil or butter to crisp them up and toss with pasta or grains. Add them to roasted dishes, including squashes and potatoes. Slip whole leaves under the skin of poultry—this is both beautiful and will perfume the whole bird.

thyme

Thyme is sweetly perfumed, slightly citrusy, and the softest spoken of these twiggy herbs, so it can easily be paired with more delicate flavors such as shellfish, poultry, and sweet vegetables like carrots and corn.

spices

Grab any jar from your spice cabinet, close your eyes, and take a whiff. If you can't tell whether it is sage or cinnamon, throw it away, friend. Spices have a shelf life of about a year, so unless your kitchen is a cafeteria, don't buy in bulk. To get the maximum flavor out of your spices, buy them whole and grind them in a coffee grinder, or pound them wirh a mortar and pestle.

allspice

Aptly named, allspice tastes a bit like cinnamon, pepper, and clove mixed together. It comes in whole dark seeds, the size of peas, or ground. It might make you think of Christmas sweets and apple pie, but try adding a pinch to your meatballs or tomato sauce for a delicious Middle Eastern touch.

cardamom

The Queen of Spices. No other spice more completely captures the essence of the exotic. It has a warm, honeyed, intoxicating flavor with hints of orange blossoms, clove, and pepper. Each pod contains 10 to 15 small, dark, sticky seeds. You can purchase cardamom in pod form, as whole seeds, or powdered. It is used both in sweet and savory cooking. Just be mindful that it is a generous spice and a tiny pinch goes a long way.

chile powder

Typically this spice is made out of a single type of ground chile. Check the ingredient list to see what kind of chile was used and make sure no other ingredients were added. Not to be confused with . . .

chili powder

A spice mix of ground chiles and other spices such as cumin, pepper, sometimes cinnamon, coriander, and salt. Usually the label notes whether it is spicy or not.

cinnamon

You know cinnamon: It is the quintessential sweet aroma of bakeries, buns, and homemade cookies. There are several kinds, all made from the fragrant inner bark of an evergreen tree. Ceylon cinnamon (true cinnamon) is light and sweet with papery bark. The cinnamon you probably have in your rack right now is cassia, which is not true cinnamon; it is a bit bolder with a warm spicy flavor (in its whole form, the bark is very uniform, unlike the papery flakiness of a true cinnamon stick). Both have not only the ability to make things taste sweeter than they actually are, but also help reduce blood glucose, making it a perfect spice to use when curbing sugar consumption.

coriander

Coriander is the seed of cilantro, but it doesn't taste like its mom at all. It is perfume-y with a dash of citrus. It comes both as whole little round seeds or ground. Often paired with cumin, it adds a little exotic mystery. Use it in chilis and curries or sprinkle the crushed seeds on meat or fish, or even into sweet/savory dishes like chutneys and applesauce.

cumin

A loud "manly" flavor, cumin mellows and becomes cozy and warm once cooked, so if you have time, it is good to briefly "toast" the spice in a dry skillet before using it. It comes both as whole small oblong seeds or ground. Indispensable in Indian, North African, and South American cooking, this is a spice that belongs in every rack. Toss in a bit of cumin when sautéing onions and garlic for lentils, beans, or a vegetable stew; or add it to curries, braises, and marinades. You can even gently fry cumin seeds to add a crunch to your soup.

Chili powder

Cardamom

Vanilla bean

Turmeric

Allspice

Bay leaves

Coriander

Chile

Smoked paprika

Cinnamon

Cumin

Indian curry powder

A rich flavorful mix of Indian spices. One curry powder can be quite different from another, ranging from mildly spiced with cumin, coriander, and cinnamon to fiery hot with chiles and pepper. Garam masala is a "warm" tasting curry blend often used in North Indian cooking. Go on an Indian market adventure, sniff around, and find one or two you like. Start with a teaspoon and add more until you are happy. Of course, curry powder is used to make curry dishes, but it is also great sprinkled into sautéed greens, mixed with salad dressings, rubbed onto chicken, and tossed with toasted nuts.

vanilla

Vanilla is one of the world's most expensive spices! And no wonder—it's the long seedpod of an orchid flower that is so persnickety that each flower needs to be pollinated by hand. Once picked, the vanilla pods (or beans) are usually either sold whole or as vanilla extract and can bring a touch of heaven to anything you bless it with. (Beware of artificial "vanilla flavoring"—it is made of some very strange stuff.)

To use a whole bean, split it lengthwise, then use the back of your knife to scrape out the thousands of tiny seeds that perfume the pod. You will end up with roughly ½ teaspoon of potent vanilla seeds, which you can fold into your recipe. Don't throw away the pods! Either blend them with sugar in a food processor to use for sprinkling in or on baked goods, or fill a small bottle with vodka, and pop in a pod. Slowly, and in the most lovely way, the vanilla pod will transform the vodka into your very own homemade extract.

salt

Salt is an amazing mineral. It keeps us alive, and when sprinkled thoughtfully will make everything, even desserts, taste better. But too much salt can be a disaster—not just for your heart but for the palate, too. It is very hard to fix an oversalted dish (you have to add other ingredients to dilute the salty flavor). So while cooking, taste often and add a pinch of salt at a time; but don't wait until the very end, because then you will only be seasoning the surface. Taste carefully and consider a splash of lemon or some fresh herbs to make your dish taste perfect. Salt is a flavor amplifier, so use it wisely.

Since salts vary in size and saltiness, it helps to get to know one well. Keep it in a bowl on your counter and use it as your "house salt." It is also helpful to grab a 3-finger pinch of salt and measure it. If it's ½ teaspoon, then you know when a recipe calls for 1 teaspoon, it's two of your pinches.

kosher salt

A coarse salt with a light, flaky texture that is less likely to stick to your fingers when you pinch it. This is *our* "house salt," which we keep out in a bowl at all times and use for everything from pasta water (which we salt to taste like the sea) to roasting a chicken.

sea salt

This delicate salt is made by evaporating seawater. Since it contains the minerals from the sea it derived from, sea salt comes in different hues and flavors. Depending on how it was dried, it can vary from granular to beautiful flakes and crystals. Since good sea salt can be quite pricey, we like to use it to finish a dish, like sprinkling over a salad or on raw vegetables so its shape and flavor can shine.

olive oil

Our favorite oil to use in the kitchen, olive oil is one of the main reasons the Mediterranean diet is so healthy. (Among other health benefits, olive oil offers protection against heart disease by controlling LDL, or "bad" cholesterol, levels while raising HDL, or "good" cholesterol, levels.) However, olive oil comes in many different forms, so here is a quick breakdown.

regular, pure, or light olive oil

Best for higher heat cooking like sautéing or when you need a neutral-flavored oil. This olive oil is usually the least expensive. Since it comes from the bottom of the barrel, it has to be refined and filtered to remove both the bitter flavors and acid content. This means a lot of the flavors we love have been lost, and it is not as nutritious. However, since it has been purified, it has a higher smoke point than extra virgin olive oil, so it is good to use in the pan or oven. By the way, "light" does not mean "low fat"—it refers to color and flavor.

virgin olive oil

Virgin olive oil is produced when olives are pressed, with hardly any further manipulation or processing—hence the term "virgin." This milder flavored olive oil is good for marinades, everyday salad dressings, pestos, and for roasting.

extra virgin olive oil

This is a high-quality olive oil, since it comes from the first pressing. It is delicious just as it is, so is perfect for dipping bread, in salad dressings, and for drizzling on dishes after they have been cooked.

cold-pressed olive oil

Cold-pressed olive oil is the most precious olive oil of all. Usually this means the farmer used the best olives, which were cold-pressed with care to make sure that all the flavors and health benefits remain intact. This is the olive oil you use when you really want to showcase it, so use it in cold or room temperature dishes, for dipping, drizzling, and dressings that have just been gently whisked. Or use it to drizzle on hot dishes like pasta, fish, and vegetables after they have cooked.

how to store it

Olive oil (as all unrefined oils) loses its health benefits and flavor and becomes unpleasant when stored in a light or warm spot. So keep it in a cool dark place and it will stay fresh for months. If you like to keep it on hand, pour it into an opaque bottle and pop on a pouring spout.

other oils

Every day new cooking oils seem to gain favor. Coconut oil was evil at one point, now it is great . . . and tomorrow it might be bad again. Take new information with a big grain of salt, and remember that though our bodies need oil, it is a fat and so should be consumed in moderation.

for high-heat cooking (like stir-fries)

When cooking oil starts to smoke (conveniently called "the smoke point"), it can lose some of its nutritional value, gain some unhealthy traits, and give food an unpleasant taste, so it is good to know which oils are best suited cooking and which are better for using cold.

For frying: Peanut, rice bran, unrefined avocado, and cold-pressed (untoasted) sesame oil are all good choices, because they stand up well to the heat.

For sautéing: Many oils are ideal for sautéing, including avocado, canola, coconut, grapeseed, olive, cold-pressed (untoasted) sesame, high-oleic safflower, and sunflower oils.

for drizzling

When it comes to making dressings or for drizzling onto raw vegetables and on food after it has been cooked, you're looking for great flavor. For this purpose, unrefined nut or seed oils like walnut, hazelnut, pistachio, and flaxseed oil, both roasted and raw, are fantastic. Not only are these oils full of warm nutty flavors, they are also good for your heart, rich in monounsaturated fats, vitamin E, and omega-3 fatty acids. All these oils are delicate, so they are best used without being cooked and should be stored in the fridge after opening.

start your day right

fresh, fruity summer porridge

makes 6 servings

PREP TIME: 15 minutes   CHILL OUT TIME: overnight

Summer porridge? It may sound like an oxymoron, but this hearty mix of raw oats, yogurt, and fresh fruit is cool and tangy. Spoon it into pretty glasses or mason jars, pop them into the fridge, and let chill overnight so the oats soften and all the flavors get to know each other. The next morning, enjoy breakfast in the sun, or just tuck a jar to go into your pocket—or into little hands—if time is tight.

1 cup old-fashioned rolled oats (not "instant")

3 cups plain yogurt (whole or low-fat) or kefir

3 tablespoons honey or maple syrup

2 large apples (not peeled), grated

1 cup mixed fresh fruit, such as sliced kiwi or strawberries, raspberries, blueberries, or blackberries (save a little extra for garnish)

1 Combine the **oats, yogurt, honey, apples,** and **mixed fruit** in a bowl, making sure that the apple is completely folded into the yogurt ❓.

2 Divide the porridge evenly among six 8-ounce glasses or mason jars, cover tightly with wrap or lids, and refrigerate overnight. Have a good night's sleep.

3 The next morning, as the sun rises, garnish the porridge with more fresh fruit and call the troops to breakfast.

 why ❓ 'cause . . .

The acid in the yogurt prevents the apples from turning brown.

 play ✳ with it

✱ Add 1 tablespoon flax or chia seeds for health.

✱ Toss in a handful of nuts for power.

✱ Add a pinch of cardamom or cinnamon or dash of vanilla for joy.

warm, cozy winter porridge

makes 22 servings

PREP TIME: 15 minutes   CHILL OUT TIME: overnight   COOKING TIME: 10 minutes

Let's stop slurping sweet gluey porridge powder from an instant package. Instead, say rise and shine to crunchy, fruity, whole-grain, fill-up-your-belly, homemade porridge. Make a batch of porridge mix on a weekend and you'll have enough for a couple of days. To save time in the morning, start it the night before. Next day, just slide the pot on the stove, put out a few toppings your family can mix and match, and get ready to go out and meet the world with energy and sunshine. Porridge can be invited for dinner too—cheap and cheerful, it's perfect for a meatless Monday!

2 cups steel-cut oats (Bob's Red Mill is toasted and doesn't need to be cooked as long)

1 cup brown rice cereal (the kind for hot porridge—like Bob's Red Mill Creamy Brown Rice)

1 cup pre-washed quinoa (like Ancient Harvest)

½ cup golden flaxseeds

½ cup chopped almonds

¾ cup finely chopped dried apples (or other favorite dried fruit)

¼ teaspoon salt

Milk or nut milk (optional)

Simmer: To cook in liquid over low heat, keeping the bubbles tiny, giggling, and just beginning to break the surface.

1 Combine the **steel-cut oats**, **brown rice cereal**, **quinoa**, **flaxseeds**, **almonds**, **dried apples**, and **salt** in a large bowl and stir to mix. Spoon into a pretty glass jar, cover, and store in the fridge. Label the jar "Breakfast for My Champions."

2 The night before you want to serve the oatmeal, measure out ¼ cup of the mixture for each serving into a lidded pot. Add 1 cup water or milk per serving (use milk or nut milk instead of water to make it creamier and add protein). Bring to a **simmer** and cook for 4 to 5 minutes. Remove from the heat, cool, cover, and chill in the fridge until the sun rises.

3 To serve, heat the porridge in a saucepan over medium heat until heated through (add a little milk or water to loosen it up if you need to), about 5 minutes. Meanwhile, make yourself a pot of tea and put spoons, bowls, and porridge toppings (see below) on the table. Sing out "Breeee-akfast!"

play  with it

* Add a dash of spice: cinnamon today, cardamom and ginger tomorrow.

* Top with chopped fresh fruit or berries, maple syrup, applesauce, hemp seeds, chia seeds, or toasted nuts.

seeds of power granola

makes 12 servings
PREP TIME: 20 minutes   BAKING TIME: 30 minutes

This recipe uses some of the healthiest nuts and seeds around to give you a superpower leap on your day. Resist the temptation to stir this mix until it's cool; leaving it alone when it's warm will result in more of those irresistible clusters. If you listen, you will hear that it snaps, squeaks, and purrs as it cools. Serve with milk or yogurt and fresh berries, or eat it by the handful, straight out of the jar.

3 cups old-fashioned rolled oats (not "instant" or "quick cooking")

1 cup ground flaxseed meal

1 cup unsalted raw sunflower seeds

1 cup unsalted raw pumpkin seeds

1 cup sliced almonds

1 cup unsweetened flaked coconut (or shredded if you can't find flaked)

½ cup maple syrup

½ cup olive oil or nut oil, such as hazelnut, coconut, or walnut

½ teaspoon salt

1 Preheat the oven to 325°F. Rub a little oil on 1 large baking sheet or 2 smaller ones.

2 Combine **all of the ingredients** in your biggest bowl and toss with your hands until all the seeds and nuts have gotten to know each other well.

3 Spread the granola on the baking sheet(s) and bake for 15 minutes. Check to see if the edges are beginning to darken, and stir the granola gently with a spoon. Continue baking until golden and toasty, about 15 minutes.

4 Let cool completely. Then crunch away. The granola can be stored, covered tightly, in the fridge for at least 2 weeks.

kids  in charge

Gather, measure, and toss the ingredients in a big bowl.

Customize the granola with their choice of flavorings and mix-ins.

play with it

★ Before baking, add 1 teaspoon vanilla, cinnamon, or ginger.

★ After baking, toss in dried fruits such as cherries, raisins, or chopped apples.

★ Amp up the power with 1 cup of chia, sesame, or hemp seeds; add to the mix before baking.

yogurt-fruit-granola-yogurt parfaits

makes 1 serving
PREP TIME: 10 minutes prep for each serving

Just look at the nutritional label on a store-bought cup of fruit yogurt (28 grams of sugar—that's 7 teaspoons!) and you will want to start making your own version immediately. Anybody with smarts knows that a sugar-loaded breakfast is actually dessert—not a great way to start the day. (Who are those kooky manufacturers who take a perfectly nutritious food like yogurt and completely mess it up?!) Your version will be full of calcium-rich Greek yogurt, fresh fruit, and honey. Real breakfast—not a weird crazy dessert.

¼ cup Seeds of Power Granola (page 59) or your favorite low-sugar, store-bought variety

⅔ cup plain Greek yogurt (whole or low-fat)

1 teaspoon honey

½ cup chopped fresh fruit, such as berries or apples

In a nice looking clear glass, sprinkle a bit of **granola**, add a dollop of **yogurt**, then a drizzle of **honey**, then **fruit**, then granola . . . You get it! Keep layering until all your ingredients are used up.

play with it

* Stir a dash of vanilla or cinnamon, cardamom, and orange zest into your yogurt.

* Replace the granola with toasted walnuts.

three ingredients, that's it!

homemade nut butter

makes 1½ cups

PREP TIME: 5 minutes   PROCESSING TIME: 10 minutes

Nut butters are so easy to make (three ingredients!), and the process that turns crunchy nuts into creamy butter is magical! Have your kids watch while you make this, then toast some bread and get out the strawberry preserves. Peanuts, hazelnuts, almonds, cashews, and macadamia nuts, as well as sunflower seeds, all make delicious butters. Get nuts from the bulk bins if you can; they are usually the freshest.

2 cups unsalted dry-roasted  nuts or seeds (you can leave the skins on)

2 tablespoons canola oil or a nut oil, such as coconut or hazelnut

A pinch of salt

1 Combine the **nuts**, **oil**, and **salt** in a food processor and process (on high if your processor has speeds) until the nuts are coarsely chopped. If making crunchy nut butter, remove 2 to 3 tablespoons of the nuts at this point. Using a rubber spatula, scrape down the sides.

2 Continue to process until the nuts become a coarse meal. Stop and scrape down the sides. Then process until the nuts pass through pasty Play-Doh stage and they suddenly relax, lie down, and become a creamy butter, about 8 minutes (yes, 8)* or more. Call your kid tasters over to judge it.

3 Add any flavorings (see below) and process until incorporated. Fold in the reserved chopped nuts, if using, for chunky style.

4 Scrape the nut butter into a jar with a tight fitting lid. Label it homemade! It will keep in the refrigerator for up to 1 month.

Watch that the machine does not overheat; if it does, turn it off and allow it to cool down. Also, sometimes you will come across a crazy bunch of nuts that seem to never get "buttery," but they will!

why  'cause . . .

Toasted nuts are not only easier to digest than raw, but they take less time to process into nut butter. If you only have raw nuts on hand, toast them at 300°F until they start to become golden, about 15 minutes, before processing.

play  with it

Incorporate these at the very end:

* 1 tablespoon honey or maple syrup

* A sprinkle of cinnamon and vanilla

* A little melted dark chocolate, or Laurie's favorite: a pinky-size piece of peeled fresh ginger and a dash each of vanilla and maple syrup

kids k in charge

* Come up with nut butter combos (cashew, honey, and vanilla . . . or almond, macadamia, and maple syrup).

* Fold the reserved crunchy nuts into the creamy butter for chunky nut butter.

* Scoop the nut butter into the jar or jars.

* Design a label and give as gifts!

two-minute teacup eggs

makes 1 serving
PREP TIME: 15 to 20 minutes   COOKING TIME: 2 minutes for each serving

Kids can turn a few fresh ingredients into an omelet in just 2 minutes. Put out the components and let everyone assemble their own teacup eggs. Pop the cup into the microwave to make your own little "omelet." P.S.: Eggs are not just for breakfast—they make perfect little lunches and dinners, too!

2 eggs

Olive oil, for the teacup

2 tablespoons milk

Assorted groupings of chopped and grated toppings (your favorites, as long as they cook quickly):
Swiss cheese, corn kernels, tomatoes, and fresh basil
Ham, cheddar, and sliced scallions
Fresh mozzarella, pesto, and peas
Roasted peppers, jack cheese, and cooked kale or spinach

Salt and freshly ground black pepper

1 Give everyone **2 eggs** and a ceramic teacup (a small mug or ramekin is fine too).

2 Rub the inside of the teacup with a little **oil** on a paper towel. Crack the eggs into the cup, and with a fork, gently beat the eggs until they are golden yellow. Mix in the **milk**.

3 Let everyone make their eggs taste the way they want by adding as many (or as few) **toppings** as desired. Just don't fill the cups more than three-fourths full (or they will messily overflow when heated up).

4 Microwave one teacup at a time on high for about 45 seconds. Caaaarefully remove the cup with an oven mitt (or have a big helper do it—the cup will be very hot), and give the eggs a gentle stir, then put it back in and microwave until the eggs have puffed up and are no longer runny, about 45 seconds (more or less depending on your microwave). Add salt and pepper to taste.

cook's **🔑** tip

You can also bake these in ramekins in a 350°F oven. Place them on a baking sheet in the center of the oven and bake until eggs are golden and puffy, 15 to 20 minutes.

blueberry oat pancakes

makes 16 (4-inch) pancakes
PREP TIME: 20 minutes   COOKING TIME: 15 minutes

Here's what's in pancakes made from a standard store-bought mix: bleached flour, thiamin mononitrate, sugar, dextrose, partially hydrogenated soybean oil, salt, wheat gluten, defatted soy flour, corn syrup solids, soy lecithin, mono- and diglycerides, soybean oil, and lactic acid.

And here's what's in *these* pancakes: almonds (packed with protein, fiber, vitamin E, calcium, magnesium, potassium, and monounsaturated fats that keep you healthy and full longer); blueberries (rich in fiber and antioxidants); and oatmeal (with cholesterol-lowering fiber, magnesium, zinc, and phosphorus—it's also gluten free). Happy pancakes or sad pancakes? Your choice!

1½ cups milk of your choice
(cow, goat, almond, soy, flax . . .)

3 eggs

1 tablespoon maple syrup or honey

1½ cups almond flour*

1½ cups old-fashioned rolled oats
(not "instant")

2 teaspoons baking powder

1 teaspoon salt

1½ cups fresh or frozen blueberries

High-heat oil, such as grapeseed, for the pan

You can pick up almond flour at a health food store or make your own by pulsing blanched almonds in a food processor into a soft meal.

1 Combine the **milk, eggs, maple syrup, almond flour, oats, baking powder,** and **salt** in a blender and blend on high speed until the oats are fairly smooth, about 30 seconds. Pour the batter into a medium bowl and let it rest until it has thickened slightly, 10 to 15 minutes (enough time to set the table and brew a pot of tea).

2 With a rubber spatula, gently fold the **blueberries** into the batter.

3 Heat up a griddle or skillet over medium heat. Dip a paper towel in the **oil** and carefully rub it onto the hot surface. Preheat the oven to 200°F (to keep the pancakes warm).

4 Spoon 2 heaping tablespoons of batter onto the pan for each pancake, leaving room between them to allow them to spread. When the tiny bubbles on the surface begin to pop and the edges are dry, gently flip the pancakes with a spatula (if you "fast flip" they will splatter) and cook for 2 minutes longer. Any odd-shaped pancakes naturally belong to the cook. Transfer the finished pancakes to an ovenproof platter, cover with foil, and keep warm in the oven.

5 Any leftover pancakes can be frozen (put a piece of wax paper between each before wrapping) and reheated on busy mornings.

homemade pancake mix

Make your own box of pancake mix for faster weekday pancakes! Whisk together 6 cups almond flour, 6 cups old-fashioned rolled oats, 2½ tablespoons baking powder, and 1 tablespoon salt in a large bowl. Pour into a large container with a tight-fitting lid. The mix will keep for 2 weeks in a cool pantry or for months in the fridge. To use the mix to make pancakes, just follow the Blueberry Oat Pancake recipe (opposite), replacing all the dry ingredients with 3 cups of this mix.

Makes 12 cups mix/enough for 64 pancakes or 4 Sunday breakfasts

play with it

★ Add a few tablespoons of chia or flaxseeds to the batter to boost the omega-3s (good fats) and fiber.

★ Spice things up with a dash of cinnamon or a teaspoon of vanilla.

★ Stir in the grated zest of an orange and a touch of grated ginger.

★ Substitute the blueberries with bananas, raspberries, strawberries, or blackberries.

banana muffins

makes 12 muffins (cakes)
PREP TIME: 15 minutes   BAKING TIME: 20 minutes

A muffin is a tiny cake! And sometimes not so tiny. Cake for breakfast? No wonder kids like muffins! *Pssst*, parents! Although these are treats, they use whole-grain flour, fruit, and unrefined sugar. And cinnamon is a trickster spice that makes sweets taste sweeter.

4 bananas (the riper, the sweeter, the banana-ier, the better)

1 egg, beaten

¼ cup melted coconut oil or any neutral-flavored oil, such as safflower

½ cup to ¾ cup honey (depending on ripeness of bananas)

1½ cups whole wheat flour

1 teaspoon baking soda

1 teaspoon ground cinnamon

½ teaspoon salt

1   Preheat the oven to 350°F with the rack in the middle. Line 12 cups of a muffin tin with liners or oil well.

2   In a large bowl, mash the **bananas** with a potato masher or fork. Add the **egg**, **oil**, and **honey** and stir to combine. Using a rubber spatula, fold in the **remaining ingredients**. Fill the muffin cups three-fourths full.

3   Bake until a toothpick inserted in a muffin comes out clean, about 20 minutes.

twist #1: bonus banana bread recipe!
Prepare an 8½ x 4½-inch loaf pan with a thin coat of oil. Pour the muffin batter into it and bake at 350°F until the tip of a knife inserted into the center of the bread comes out clean, 50 to 60 minutes. Banana bread!

twist #2: flip the flop (sticky banana pudding)
We attempted to make gluten-free muffins by replacing the whole wheat flour with almond flour. Of course, it flopped big time! With only 1 egg and no wheat, there was nothing to hold the batter together. Crestfallen but not beaten, we tasted the gooey concoction before tossing it—and it was delicious! So we spooned it into big bowls, renamed it sticky banana pudding, and served it with a grin. To make it, replace the flour with almond flour and bake in an oiled shallow baking dish (like a brownie pan) at 350°F for about 40 minutes. Serve warm. Moral of the story: Sometimes all you have to do is rename the dish!

play ✳ with it

Flavor up the batter with any of the following:

* Toasted walnuts or pecans
* A pinch of cardamom, allspice, or grated orange zest
* 3 to 4 tablespoons flax or chia seeds
* A little chopped dark chocolate or 1 teaspoon chopped candied ginger
* A handful of blueberries

peanut butter granola bars

makes 12 bars

PREP TIME: 15 minutes   BAKING TIME: 30 to 40 minutes

These are perfect for those days when you don't have time for breakfast, or want a pick-me-up on a marathon workday. Nuts, seeds, and whole grains are good for your brain and heart. We like to use a mix of slivered almonds, sunflower seeds, flaxseeds, and shredded coconut, but you can tailor this to your taste.

3 egg whites

¼ cup olive or nut oil

⅔ cup peanut or almond butter

¾ cup maple syrup

3 cups mixed raw nuts and seeds

2 cups old-fashioned rolled oats (not "instant")

1 cup white, whole wheat, or brown rice flour

¾ teaspoon salt

1 Preheat the oven to 325°F with the rack in the middle. Line a 9 x 9-inch baking pan or a regular baking sheet with parchment paper.

2 Combine the **egg whites**, **oil**, **nut butter**, and **maple syrup** in a big bowl and stir together until thoroughly incorporated. Add the **nut** and **seed mix**, **oats**, **flour**, and **salt**. Using your hands, mix the dough really well until it sticks together ❓.

3 Firmly pat the dough flat into the baking pan or shape into a 9-inch square on the baking sheet. Bake until golden, 30 to 40 minutes. Let cool for 15 minutes. Using a pizza cutter or serrated knife, cut into small bars. The bars will keep, wrapped tightly, in the refrigerator for up to 1 week, or freeze them for future snacking.

why  'cause . . .

The egg whites and maple syrup are the glue that keep the oats and nuts happily stuck together.

play  with it

For extra crunch, put the cut bars back into the oven, turn it off, and leave them there until they are cool.

homemade jam

makes about 2 cups

PREP TIME: 15 minutes   COOKING TIME: 20 minutes

Store-bought jam is often just a big jar of candy, loaded with sugar. Making your own allows you to control just how sweet it is, and makes use of fruit at its peak. Because it is made with less sugar than store-bought, the jam will only last a week in your fridge, so pour it into a pretty jar and serve often with toast and tea.

2½ cups berries or coarsely chopped stone fruit (such as plums or apricots)

⅓ cup sugar

Juice of ½ lemon or lime

1 Combine the **fruit** and **sugar** in a small pot and bring to a simmer over high heat, stirring. Reduce the heat to medium and simmer until the fruit is soft, about 10 minutes. Using a potato masher or fork, mash about half the fruit until you have a chunky puree.

2 Return the jam to a slow simmer, cooking until the juices have reduced and thickened, about 10 minutes. Add the **citrus juice** to taste.

3 Let cool slightly, then transfer to a jar with a tight-fitting lid. Refrigerate up to 1 week, or freeze in a freezer-safe container for future toast.

play  with it

* Add a little vanilla extract after flavoring with citrus juice.

* Plums and cinnamon are happy together.

* Orange zest and ground cardamom make everything better.

* Peaches love a little grated fresh ginger.

danish stone-age bread

makes 1 large loaf

PREP TIME: 10 minutes   BAKING TIME: 1 hour

There's not even a speck of flour in this high-protein, fiber-packed, omega-3–rich bread. And you can throw it together in just 10 minutes, in just one bowl. Adapted from a recipe for *stenalderbrød* made famous by Kong Hans, a restaurant in Copenhagen, this is a bread to keep you full of energy all morning long. It's delicious on its own, or thinly sliced, toasted, and served with homemade jam and goat cheese. You can easily swap out the nuts and seeds called for here with your favorites; just keep the total to 6 cups, with more seeds than nuts.

But aren't nuts and seeds fattening? Sure they are, if you eat them in copious amounts. But if you have a few slices of this bread toasted for breakfast, or throw some seeds and nuts into your salad, you will be filled with slow-burning nutritious fuel, so you won't be tempted by the nonfat sugary snacks that leave you hungry for one more.

5 eggs (or 10 egg whites to keep it cholesterol free)

⅓ cup olive or nut oil

1½ teaspoons salt

1 cup unsalted raw sunflower seeds

1 cup raw sesame seeds or hemp seeds

1 cup raw whole skin-on hazelnuts or walnuts

1 cup unsalted whole almonds

1 cup unsalted raw pumpkin seeds

1 cup flaxseeds

1 Preheat the oven to 325°F with the rack in the middle. Line the bottom and sides of a 9 x 5 x 3-inch loaf pan with parchment paper or grease it with oil.

2 Whisk together the **eggs**, **oil**, and **salt** in a large bowl. Add the **remaining ingredients** and stir thoroughly to combine. Press the batter firmly into the loaf pan. Smooth the top with the back of a spoon so there won't be any runaway nuts in your house.

3 Bake until the bread sounds hollow when thumped on the bottom, about 1 hour. Take the loaf out of the pan and let cool completely before slicing.

play  with it

* Lightly toast the seeds and nuts first.

* Toss in ½ cup dried cherries or blueberries, ¼ cup goji berries, a pinch of cardamom or cinnamon, and/or a little grated orange zest.

no-knead bread

makes 1 loaf

PREP TIME: 30 minutes   RISING AND BAKING TIME: about 14 hours
(don't be scared; you're just sitting around while it's doing all the work)

Baking your own bread is a beautiful thing. And baking bread that requires no kneading is even more beautiful. Baker Jim Lahey of Sullivan Street Bakery in New York showed the world that with just a tiny bit of yeast and 1 day of rising, you could bake a crazy-good loaf of fresh crackling bread. If you are new to bread making, shaping the bread for the first time may be messy—just keep going! In fact, every family should appoint one person as their official family baker who knows this recipe by heart.

Olive oil, for greasing

1½ cups all-purpose flour

1½ cups whole wheat flour, plus more for dusting

½ teaspoon instant yeast

1¼ teaspoons salt

1½ cups warm water

1 Rub a large, nice looking bowl (to channel your great-grandmother) with **olive oil** and set aside. In another bowl, combine the **flours**, **yeast**, and **salt**. Add the **warm water** and, using your hands, mix together until well combined. The dough will be unruly and sticky, but that's the way it likes to be.

2 Transfer the dough to the oiled bowl, flip it over to coat with oil all over, and cover with plastic wrap. Let the dough rest quietly for at least 12 hours (and no more than 18) in a warm room.

3 Line a large bowl with parchment paper coated with a little olive oil. Lightly dust a work surface with whole wheat flour. Plop the dough out onto the work surface and with very wet hands grab the dough and fold it onto itself twice. Turn the dough over so that it is seam-side down and the top is smooth and tight. Tuck the ends of the dough under to make a nice, taut surface. Transfer the loaf to the parchment-lined bowl, seam-side down, cover, and let it rest for 2 hours.

4 Thirty minutes before the 2 hours are up, place a 6- to 8-quart heavy pot with a lid (like cast-iron) into the oven and preheat the oven to 450° to 500°F degrees, depending on how high your oven goes. After 30 minutes, carefully remove the heated pot from the oven and set it on a heat-proof surface. Grab the 4 corners of the parchment paper to lift the dough out of the bowl and lower it along with the parchment into the pot.

5 Cover and bake for 30 minutes. Uncover and bake until browned, 15 to 30 minutes longer. Remove from the pot and cool on a wire rack. Be fantastically proud of yourself.

"The smell of good bread baking, like the sound of lightly flowing water, is indescribable in its evocation of innocence and delight."

—M. F. K. FISHER

play ✻ with it

* Add 1 cup mixed seeds, such as sunflower, hemp, poppy, or flax, to the flours.

* Add chopped herbs (like rosemary or thyme), chopped olives, or roasted garlic to the dough in step 1.

* Sprinkle the bread with ¼ cup seeds right before sliding it into the oven.

A Good Egg

Eggs are made (or laid) for dinner. They transform boring leftovers into something special, turn salad into supper, and add luxury to soups and stews.

Eggs are perfect for lunch, too. They can quickly be cracked into a frittata, slipped into a sandwich, or eaten cold, peeled from the shell with a little salt, pepper, and buttered pumpernickel bread.

Eggs are even fabulous for breakfast!

The egg whites are full of protein and the yolks are packed with so many of the minerals and vitamins you need to stay healthy: Vitamin A, lutein, and zeaxanthin for your eyes; iron and folate for your blood; phosphorous and vitamin D for your bones; zinc to keep your immune system strong; iodine for your thyroid.

All this in its own single-serving, compostable package.

∗ how to buy them ∗

Since chickens are so good to you, be good to them, too, and buy organic, pasture-raised eggs. The words "natural" and "cage-free" don't necessarily mean what they say unless they are attached to the word "organic."

If you can, support your local chicken farm or farmers' market by buying the eggs there. The eggs will be fresher and you can look the farmer in the eye and say thank you.

∗ how to store them ∗

Eggs usually come in a perfectly good crate for storage. Just leave them in there; they will be safe and won't lose moisture. Kept in a cold spot in the back of the fridge, they will last well beyond their expiration date.

However, if you intend to bake with your eggs, leave them on your counter to warm up. When a recipe calls for room-temperature eggs, it is not kidding—cold eggs can cause the curdling of batter, lumpy loaves, and other cake catastrophes.

To check if an egg is still good or not, submerge it in a bowl of water. If it sinks to the bottom and lies down, it is fresh (great for poached eggs); if it stands upright on the bottom, it is still usable (good for hard-boiled eggs). If it floats, toss it . . . far!

boiled eggs

makes 6

PREP TIME: 10 minutes   COOKING TIME: 5 to 12 minutes

If there is a beautiful half-moon egg on your salad, is it not what your fork reaches for first? If there is a soft-boiled egg on your breakfast tray, is that not where your toast point dips before it even says hello to the jam?

6 large eggs

1   Place the **eggs** in a medium lidded pot and cover them with 1½ inches cold water. Bring to rolling boil (big bubbles) over high heat.

2   Once it is boiling, immediately remove the pot from the heat, cover, and start your timer. For soft-boiled eggs, let them sit for 5 minutes. For hard-boiled eggs, let them sit for 12 minutes.

3   Transfer to a colander and rinse under very cold water.

4   To peel a hard-boiled egg, tap the egg on its side, then gently roll it around using the palm of your hand to press down on it. The shell should come off easily. Hard-boiled eggs kept in their shells will keep in the fridge for up to 5 days.

poached eggs

makes 6

PREP TIME: 10 minutes   COOKING TIME: 3 to 5 minutes

Poached eggs are one of the quickest ways to add protein to any meal. Slide them onto a plate of grilled asparagus and drizzle with a tart vinaigrette, let the egg settle into a bowl of beans or greens, or top a tossed salad with one and call it dinner.

Salt and freshly ground black pepper

2 tablespoons light-colored vinegar ❔

6 large fresh eggs ❔

1 Fill a medium pot with 2 inches of water **salted** like the sea and add the **vinegar**. Bring it to a boil over high heat.

2 Meanwhile, prepare the **eggs** for their future by cracking each of them into its own teacup.

3 Reduce the heat so the water is not quite boiling, just confidently simmering. Gently slip each egg into the water and immediately cover the pan with a tight-fitting lid (if your pan doesn't have a lid, improvise with a pizza pan or baking sheet). Turn off the burner and turn on a timer.

4 Don't peek! until . . .
  * For runny yolks, leave the eggs poaching for 3 minutes.
  * For medium-firm yolks, 4 minutes.
  * For firm yolks, 4½ minutes.

5 When the eggs have reached your preferred firmness, use a slotted spoon to carefully lift and drain each egg. Season to taste with salt and pepper and serve hot.

why  'cause . . .

* Vinegar helps the egg whites hold together. Choose a light-colored vinegar so it won't discolor the eggs.

* When poaching eggs, it helps if they are very fresh; the whites will hold together better when dropped into the water.

fried eggs

makes 1 or 2

PREP TIME: 5 minutes   COOKING TIME: 3 to 5 minutes

Olive oil or butter, for the pan

1 or 2 eggs

Salt and freshly ground black pepper

1 Heat up a cast-iron or other heavy-bottomed skillet over high heat. Drizzle enough **olive oil** or melt enough **butter** to lightly coat the bottom.

2 Crack the **eggs** and gently slip them into the skillet. Immediately reduce the heat to low.

3 For sunny-side up eggs, cook until the whites are completely set and the yolks begin to firm up. For over-easy eggs, flip them gently and cook for a just a moment longer; for over-hard, flip and cook until the yolks are no longer runny, 30 seconds or so longer than over-easy. Season with salt and pepper.

twist: crispy eggs!

Follow the recipe for Fried Eggs but ignore the words "lightly," "gently," "slip," and "low." Instead, slick the pan generously with the butter (or olive oil if you are virtuous). Fry the eggs over medium-high so they crackle, puff, and spit. Flip and cook until the eggs are crisp and deeply golden on both sides. Season with abandon, using salt, pepper, and hot sauce.

scrambled eggs

makes 4 to 6 servings

PREP TIME: 2 minutes   COOKING TIME: 5 minutes

Poor scrambled eggs! They get awakened so roughly by being scrambled and they return the favor by becoming bouncy, dry, and tough. Today wake them up gently and they will rise softly, to be tender and glossy.

8 eggs

½ cup milk (whole, fat-free, whatever you have)

Salt and freshly ground black pepper

Olive oil, for the pan

1 Whisk together the **eggs** and **milk** in a bowl until they are one. Season with **salt** and **pepper**.

2 Heat a heavy-bottomed skillet over medium-low heat. Drizzle **olive oil** into the pan to coat the bottom.

3 Pour in the eggs. Don't stir! Let the eggs cook until the bottom starts to set (stiffen), about 1 minute.

4 Using a heat-resistant spatula, gently push one edge of the eggs into the center of the pan, while tilting the pan to allow the still-liquid egg to flow in underneath. Repeat with the other edges, until there's no liquid left.

5 Turn off the heat and continue gently stirring and turning the egg until all the uncooked parts become firm. Stir gently and keep the curds as large as possible.

play ❋ with it

* Add fresh herbs (such as chives, dill, parsley, or cilantro) to the egg mixture.

* Fold in a little feta, tomatoes, and basil.

* Add 1 teaspoon soy sauce, scallions, and bean sprouts.

frittata

makes 4 to 6 servings
PREP TIME: 15 minutes   COOKING TIME: 15 to 20 minutes

A frittata is a fancy name for an open-faced omelet, but without the flip and fold. It's actually much easier than an omelet, so if you mess up, you don't have to pretend you changed your mind and made a scramble instead. (What! You haven't done that?)

8 eggs, gently beaten

2 tablespoons grated Parmesan cheese (optional)

¼ teaspoon salt and a pinch of freshly ground black pepper

2 tablespoons olive oil

2 tablespoons diced onion

2 to 3 cups chopped vegetables, such as red bell pepper, kale, asparagus, tomato, or zucchini

Note: I can't tell you how many times I have put the skillet on the counter to cool down and accidentally grabbed the hot handle. Learn from my pain: Leave a potholder or cloth draped over the handle to remind you that it's hot!

1 Whisk together the **eggs**, **Parmesan** (if using), **salt**, and **pepper** in a medium bowl.

2 Preheat the broiler with the rack in the middle of the oven.

3 Heat a large broilerproof pan over medium-high heat and add the **oil** to the pan. Add the **onion** and cook until softened, about 2 minutes. Add the **chopped vegetables** and cook until tender, about 5 minutes.

4 Add a little more oil to the pan if it's dry. Pour the egg mixture over the vegetables, reduce the heat to medium-low, and stir once with a heat-resistant spatula. Cook until the egg mixture begins to set, 4 to 5 minutes.

5 Place the pan under the broiler and broil for 3 to 4 minutes, until lightly browned and fluffy. Slide the frittata from the pan and cut into wedges.

play ✽ with it

* Add 1 tablespoon chopped soft herbs such as basil, dill, or parsley to the egg mixture.

* Top with ½ cup cubed cheese (feta, goat, or Swiss are all tasty) before broiling.

* Use black beans, peppers, and corn and serve topped with guacamole, salsa, and a sprinkle of cilantro.

* Top an asparagus frittata with smoked salmon, chives, and a dollop of Greek yogurt.

purple power smoothies

makes 2 or 3 servings

PREP TIME: 15 minutes

Who has time to make a breakfast that is healthy, full of vitamins, fiber, and protein? You do! When you keep a few ingredients on hand, it's easy to start the day off right with a tasty power shake to feed the body, warm the heart, and free the mind from snack attacks until it's time for lunch.

2 cups milk (dairy, nut, grain, or soy)

1 banana

1 cup frozen blueberries

1 to 2 teaspoons ground cinnamon, to taste

1 to 2 tablespoons ground flaxseed meal for big kids and adults, ½ to 1 teaspoon for little kids

¼ cup peanut or almond butter without any additives like sugar

Pour the **milk** into a blender and top with the **remaining ingredients**. Blend until creamy and smooth.

play ✳ with it

Add a small handful of spinach or kale, blend well, and all you will taste is a new vigor for life.

the green genie

makes 2 or 3 servings
PREP TIME: 15 minutes

Once you blend all these ingredients together, the spinach will *poof* disappear. Your eyes will see green and your mouth will taste fruit, but your body will thank you for the generous dose of iron, antioxidants, and minerals the spinach delivers. Just like that.

1 cup unsweetened almond milk

1 orange, peeled, halved, and seeded

1 kiwifruit* (or ½ banana), chopped

½ green apple*, cored and chopped

1 or 2 dates, pitted

1 cup spinach

3 ice cubes (optional)

*If they're organic, you don't have to peel them—just wash well.

Pour the **milk** into the blender and top with the **almond milk, orange, kiwi, apple, dates,** and **spinach**. Add 3 **ice cubes** if you like it cold. Blend until creamy and smooth. Drink and roar.

play ✳ with it

Add 1 tablespoon flax or chia seeds, a bit of grated orange zest, and a splash of vanilla.

a date with chocolate breakfast shake

makes 2 or 3 servings
PREP TIME: 15 minutes

Unsweetened cocoa powder (try to find fair trade and organic!) is packed with vitamins and antioxidants—its flavonoids increase blood flow and oxygen to the brain, helping you think up bright ideas. Dates are chock-full of fiber, vitamins, minerals, and antioxidants to keep your energy up so you can actualize the bright ideas.

2 cups very cold unsweetened milk (dairy or nut)

1 banana, cut into chunks and frozen

2 tablespoons unsweetened cocoa powder

4 dates, pitted

¼ cup nut butter of choice

A big handful fresh spinach (you won't taste it but you will go forth as Popeye) or chopped kale

Pour the **milk** into the blender and top with the **remaining ingredients**. Blend until creamy and smooth.

play  with it

Add 1 tablespoon flax or chia seeds, a sprinkle of cinnamon, or a splash of vanilla—just for happiness.

lunches to stay and go

super hippie wrap!

makes 4 wraps
PREP TIME: 20 to 30 minutes

Oh, those hippies were onto something! Something powerfully good happens when you mix avocados with carrots, sprouts, and sunflower seeds. On their own, each is delicious, but wrapped up together, it's true love, man.

About ½ English cucumber

½ cup hummus, homemade (page 145) or good-quality store-bought

4 whole-grain wraps or large flour tortillas

1 avocado, cut into 8 thin wedges

A squeeze of lemon or lime juice

1 cup grated carrots (unpeeled if organic)

1 cup fresh sprouts (your favorite kind)

¼ cup unsalted raw sunflower seeds

1 With a vegetable peeler, cut the **cucumber** into a handful of wide strips and set aside.

2 Spread the **hummus** onto each **wrap** to within ¼ inch of the edge. Press 2 pieces of **avocado** onto the bottom third of each wrap and drizzle with a bit of **citrus juice** (to keep the avocado green). Top the avocado with **carrots**, cucumber, **sprouts**, and **sunflower seeds**. Tightly roll up the wraps, then wrap with wax paper or foil.

cook's 🥄 tip

How to "peel" an avocado: Start with a ripe avocado, which is one that gives slightly when squeezed. Cut it in half lengthwise around the pit, then twist the halves to separate. Remove the pit by sliding the tip of a small spoon gently underneath it and lifting it out. Using a large serving spoon, scoop out the flesh in one piece and slice.

kids **k** in charge

★ Peel and peel and peel the cucumber into wide strips.

★ Slice the avocado with a table knife.

★ Arrange the vegetables on the wrap.

hoisin veggie wrap

makes 4 wraps
PREP TIME: 20 minutes

A whole-grain tortilla, crunchy vegetables, and seeds, all seasoned with hoisin sauce make for *real* good fast food. Serve with extra hoisin or Sesame Sauce (page 236) on the side.

3 cups thinly sliced green cabbage or undressed bagged coleslaw mix

¾ cup unhulled raw sesame seeds

2 teaspoons toasted sesame oil

Salt

4 whole-grain wraps (8-inch)

2 tablespoons hoisin sauce, plus more for serving

One 4-inch piece English cucumber (unpeeled), seeds scraped and cut lengthwise into 8 wedges

2 carrots, grated, about 1 cup (unpeeled if organic)

4 ounces seasoned baked tofu*, sliced into long strips

You can usually find this in the refrigerated section with the regular tofu.

1 Combine the **cabbage, sesame seeds**, and **sesame oil** in a medium bowl and toss to coat. Season with **salt**.

2 Arrange the 4 **wraps** on the counter in front of you and spread 1½ teaspoons of the **hoisin sauce** on the bottom third of each wrap, to within ¼ inch of the edges.

3 Divide the **vegetables** and **tofu** evenly among the wraps, arranging them on top of the hoisin sauce.

4 Tightly roll the wrap onto itself, folding the sides in like a burrito until it is closed. Wrap with wax paper or foil.

play  with it

* Add leftover chicken to the mix.
* Give it a squeeze of lime.
* Replace the cabbage with kale or spinach.
* Use jicama instead of cucumber.

* Throw in some sliced scallions.
* Use miso paste or tahini, or both, in place of hoisin.
* Use a big leaf like collard or cabbage as a wrap.

crunchy chicken "ish" salad

makes 6 servings
PREP TIME: 20 minutes

If you are wandering down the healthy path to eating more plant-based foods, make an easy transition by incorporating plant-based "meats"—or vegetable proteins—that are found in health food stores and supermarket freezers. Newbies can ease in gently by adding them to very flavorful dishes like a chili or spicy stir-fry, or in something fresh and loudly crunchy like this "chicken" salad. (Tip: Rather than exclaiming "Can you believe this isn't chicken?!" just smile and maybe tell them later.)

12 ounces unbreaded vegetable protein "chicken" strips (like Gardein or Beyond Meat), patted dry and cut into bite-size pieces

¼ cup plain Greek yogurt (whole or 2%)*

2 tablespoons mayonnaise*

2 tablespoons diced red onion or scallions

2 tablespoons sliced almonds

2 tablespoons diced celery

1 small apple (unpeeled), cut into small dice

Juice of 1 lemon (and a bit of the zest if you want it zestier)

Salt and freshly ground black pepper

Combine **all the ingredients** together in a small bowl and toss. Taste for seasonings: More pepper? More lemon? Call in your kid taster to help decide.

To make a vegan version, leave out the yogurt and replace the mayonnaise with 6 tablespoons vegan mayonnaise; we like Earth Balance Mindful Mayo from the refrigerated section.

play with it

* Add halved grapes, 1 tablespoon mild curry powder, and a pinch of poppy seeds.

* Fold in some chopped tender herbs like dill, parsley, or chives.

kids  in charge

* Measure and stir.

* Taste the apple to make sure it is the best.

* Squeeeeze the lemon and watch that the seeds don't make it into the bowl.

kale sesame seed salad rolls

makes 4 rolls

PREP TIME: 30 minutes

These are inspired by Vietnamese summer rolls and with the healthy addition of kale. They're a great way to ensure that you don't miss out on your greens, whether you're on the go, skipping down the street, or sitting at your desk.

4 cups shredded kale (roughly one large bunch, stems removed) or cabbage

1 teaspoon toasted sesame oil

Salt

4 rice paper wrappers (8½-inch round), plus some extra for backups

½ English cucumber, cut into wide ribbons with a vegetable peeler

¼ cup peanut butter

2 carrots, grated (unpeeled if organic)

4 teaspoons sesame seeds or chopped peanuts

1 Place 2 large pieces of plastic wrap on your counter (this prevents the wrappers from sticking) and fill a large bowl with warm water.

2 Combine the **kale**, **sesame oil**, and a pinch of **salt** in a large bowl and "knead" the kale until it is silky and lightly coated in oil.

3 Quickly swish the **rice paper wrappers** in the water, shake off any excess liquid, and lay them next to each other on the plastic wrap. Blot with paper towels to soak up any excess water.

4 Dividing evenly, spread the shredded kale across the bottom third of each wrapper, leaving the edges uncovered. Top the kale with a strip of **cucumber**, a few dollops of **peanut butter**, another few slices of cucumber, and a big pinch of **carrots** and **sesame seeds**.

5 Roll up each wrapper, folding in the short sides like you would a burrito. Cut in half and serve right away, or wrap to go if eating on the run.

cook's 🥄 tip

Rice paper wrappers—round, flat, edible "papers"—are used for wrapping spring rolls. You can find them in the Asian section of larger supermarkets and Asian grocery stores. They need to be soaked briefly in hot water to become pliable.

play ✳ with it

★ Add cooked mushrooms, tofu, or shredded chicken to the kale.

★ Stir hoisin or hot sauce into the peanut butter.

★ Throw in fresh herbs such as cilantro, mint, or chives.

★ Serve with hoisin sauce or Sesame Sauce (page 236) for dipping.

kids 🄺 in charge

★ Knead the kale!

★ Be the wrap wrapper, water swisher, and water off-blotter.

★ Fill the wrappers with vegetables.

★ Sprinkle the sesame seeds.

crunchy pb&g (peanut butter and grape) wrap

makes 1 wrap
PREP TIME: 15 minutes

Wraps are the ideal on-the-go meal because you can put practically anything in them. Wrap them around fruit and peanut butter and they can be called breakfast . . . or roll them for dinner and they are a quick portable picnic to bring onto the patio, atop the roof, or out to a park bench.

2 or 3 tablespoons peanut butter (or nut butter of your choice)

1 large whole wheat tortilla or other sandwich wrap

8 grapes, red or green, finely chopped

A squeeze of orange or lemon juice

1 small banana

1 Spread the **peanut butter** onto the bottom half of the **tortilla** in the shape of a large rectangle. Press the **grapes** evenly into the peanut butter.

2 Squeeze a little **citrus juice** over the **banana** ❓. Nestle the banana into the peanut butter at the bottom of the tortilla (you might need to take a bite of the banana so it fits).

3 Tightly roll up the wrap, folding in the left and right sides like a burrito.

4 Wrap the roll in wax paper or foil. Slip it into your lunch box or knapsack.

 why ❓ 'cause . . .

Rubbing a peeled banana (or an apple, pear, or avocado) with something acidic like lemon juice will keep it from turning brown.

 play ✳ with it

✱ Replace the grapes with blueberries, raspberries, or sliced strawberries.

✱ Heat the filled wrap in an oil-coated skillet over medium heat until it is browned and crisp for a crunchy warm peanut-buttery treat. (Have a big helper assist you if needed.)

shiitake "bacon," lettuce, and tomato

s"b"lt

makes 4 sandwiches

PREP TIME: 20 minutes   ROASTING TIME: 45 minutes

Laurie grows her own shiitakes, but no matter how many she harvests, there never seems to be enough, because when roasted, shiitakes taste like bacon! They become irresistibly crisp little bacon-y slices that are perfect for a vegetarian BLT, but also make a yummy addition to soups, salads, or eggs or scattered on top of peas and beans.

8 slices great bread, toasted

Mayonnaise (low-fat, vegan, or fancy aioli)
to spread on the bread

8 crunchy lettuce leaves

1 to 2 large tasty tomatoes, thickly sliced

Shiitake Bacon (at right)

1   Spread each slice of **toast** with **mayonnaise**.

2   Sandwich the **lettuce**, **tomato**, and **shiitake bacon** between the toast pieces.

3   Cut in half. Think you are only going to eat half. Eat the whole thing happily.

Shiitake Bacon

Preheat the oven to 350°F with the rack in the middle. Line a baking sheet with parchment paper. Combine ½ **pound shiitake mushrooms** (stems discarded), 3 **tablespoons olive oil**, 1 **teaspoon soy sauce**, and **a spinkle of salt**. (If you have it, smoked salt is perfect for this.) It's good to do a bit of gentle kneading so all the mushrooms get anointed. Spread the mushrooms, in a single layer, on the lined baking sheet and roast, stirring about every 15 minutes, until golden, crisp, and irresistible, about 45 minutes. Season with a goodly grind of black pepper. Makes 4 servings (if you don't eat too many off the baking sheet).

play ✳ with it

✶   Add avocado, a few fresh basil leaves, or a bit of pesto.

✶   Use cabbage leaves as wraps instead of bread.

cannellini bean tartine

makes 4 servings

PREP TIME: 5 to 10 minutes   COOKING TIME: 20 minutes

Fast, cheap, and cheerful, this dish has all the makings of the perfect dinner for a college student. It requires just one pan and provides crunchy carbs and protein-rich tangy beans. Serve with greens on the side or on top. Make sure you get the bread good and crisp; that little bit of crunch makes a big difference.

Olive oil, for the pan

4 slices good-quality bread

½ onion, chopped

1 to 2 garlic cloves, minced (or more if you're in that kind of mood)

1 can (15 ounces) cannellini or other white beans, drained

1 cup tomato sauce (your favorite kind)

1 Heat a medium heavy-bottomed skillet over medium-high heat. Drizzle in **olive oil** to cover the bottom. Slide in the pieces of **bread** and let them sizzle on both sides until they are golden and very crisp. Remove them from the pan and transfer to a plate.

2 Drizzle a little more oil onto the pan if necessary and add the **onion** and **garlic**. Cook over medium-high heat until they soften and turn golden, about 5 minutes.

3 Add the **beans** and **tomato sauce** and simmer, stirring occasionally, until the beans and sauce are well acquainted, about 10 more minutes.

4 Arrange the toast in shallow bowls, or on a chipped plate . . . whatever you have. Spoon the beans on top.

play  with it

* Slide a fried egg on top, then shower with Parmesan cheese.

* Add lots of hot sauce or a dash of Worcestershire.

* Fold raw chopped spinach into the beans when adding the tomato sauce.

* Tuck a few cubes of aged cheddar into the sauce to melt at the last minute.

* Top the toast and beans with a salad of shredded raw kale or any greens dressed with a tart vinaigrette.

* Drizzle with balsamic vinegar or a squeeze of lemon juice.

* Toss in fresh herbs, such as parsley, thyme, or rosemary.

whole-grain quesadillas with crunchy cabbage

makes 2 quesadillas
PREP TIME: 15 minutes   COOKING TIME: 5 to 6 minutes

Here is an example of how a few humble ingredients can come together to make a delicious lunch. We've adapted *Cook's Illustrated*'s clever method of folding and flipping the quesadilla—less mess, more joy. Serve with guacamole and salsa on the side.

2 large (10-inch) whole-grain tortillas or wraps (Ezekiel sprouted grain tortillas are our favorite)

¾ cup shredded cheese, such as cheddar, Monterey jack, or a combination

¾ cup finely shredded green cabbage or undressed bagged coleslaw mix

Olive oil, for brushing

Salt

To cook: To make something delicious and nourishing with love for yourself or someone else very lucky

A cook: Someone kind, smart, and curiously attractive

1 Heat a large skillet, preferably cast-iron, over high heat. Working with one **tortilla** at a time, slide into the dry pan and cook for about 30 seconds, flipping once, until slightly golden (this makes it pliable). Transfer the tortilla to a work surface.

2 Cover half of each tortilla with **cheese** and **cabbage**. Using tongs, fold the tortillas in half and press down on them so that they stick together. Using a pastry brush, coat the tops with **olive oil** and sprinkle lightly with **salt**.

3 Heat the skillet over medium-high heat. Place the quesadillas in the skillet, oiled-side down. **Cook** until crisp, 1 to 2 minutes. Brush the tops with olive oil and carefully flip! Cook the other side until crisp.

4 Transfer to a cutting board and cut into wedges.

play  with it

* Serve with Romy's Guacamole (page 147), Salsa (page 154), and/or Hummus (page 145).

* Toss in chopped roasted chiles.

* Sprinkle on cumin or chili powder.

* Add 1 cup cooked beans or chili to the mix.

* Or, try Laurie's favorite: last night's leftover vegetables, all chopped up.

Spanish tortilla

makes 4 to 6 servings
PREP TIME: 30 minutes   COOKING TIME: 25 minutes

This is the perfect dish for anyone (but especially teenagers) to learn how to make by heart—no recipe needed, since it is essentially just a few potatoes, onions, and eggs. What's more, it's a quick, cheap, tasty, and nourishing meal no matter where in the world you are or how small your kitchen is.

9 large eggs

1 teaspoon salt

⅓ cup olive oil (not a fancy one, pure or virgin is fine)

1¾ pounds russet (baking) potatoes (4 to 5 medium), cut crosswise into ⅛-inch-thick slices (unpeeled if organic)

1 medium onion, finely diced

1 Whisk the **eggs** with the **salt** in a large bowl until golden yellow.

2 Heat a medium skillet over medium-high heat. Add ¼ cup of the **oil** and 1 slice of the **potato**. When the oil starts to sizzle around the slice, add the rest of the potatoes.

3 Reduce the heat to medium-low and cook, gently flipping the potatoes every now and then until they soften, about 5 minutes. You don't want them to brown. Add the **onion** and cook until soft, about 5 minutes. Take the pan off the heat and, with a slotted spoon, remove the potatoes and fold them into the bowl with the eggs.

4 Preheat the broiler with the rack in the middle. Wipe out the skillet with paper towels and heat over high heat; drizzle in the remaining oil to cover the bottom. Pour in the egg mixture and immediately reduce the heat to medium low  .

5 Cook until the eggs are completely set (stiff) at the edges, and almost set in the center. The tortilla should easily slip around in the pan when you give it a shake (after 6 to 8 minutes). If not, run a spatula under and around the edges to loosen it.

6 Put the pan in the oven and broil until the eggs are lightly browned and puffy, 3 to 4 minutes.

7 Slide the tortilla onto a platter and let cool if you like (you can serve it hot but it will be a little harder to cut neatly). Cut into wedges or squares and serve hot or at room temperature.

why  'cause . . .

You first heat the pan on high so when the eggs hit the pan they will instantly develop a crust, which prevents them from sticking, Then you reduce the heat to let the eggs sweetly set instead of getting uptight and burning.

play with it

* Add a little diced chorizo, chopped asparagus, sliced roasted peppers, or a sprinkle of Spanish cheese on top. Serve with aioli.

* Add a chopped clove of garlic to the onions.

soupersalads!

a vegetarian take on grandma's elixir

chicks and noodle soup

makes 6 to 8 servings
PREP TIME: 20 minutes   COOKING TIME: 20 minutes

Chickpea noodle soup is every bit as delicious and comforting as chicken soup. But since all the ingredients are basic pantry staples, it's faster to make—so that after stomping in from the rain, you can quickly have soup simmering on your stove.

Olive oil, for the pot

1 large onion, finely chopped (about 2 cups)

4 to 6 garlic cloves, minced (the more the merrier)

3 celery stalks, finely chopped

3 carrots, finely chopped (unpeeled if organic)

8 cups vegetable broth* (organic if you can)

1½ cups cooked chickpeas, home-cooked or canned (rinsed and drained)

3 tablespoons freshly grated Parmesan cheese

1 teaspoon minced fresh rosemary, thyme, or parsley or a mix of all three

Salt and freshly ground black pepper

1½ cups whole-grain elbow macaroni (or any other pasta shape)

Juice of 1 lemon (optional)

1 Heat a soup pot over medium heat. Drizzle in enough **olive oil** to cover the bottom. Add the **onion** and **garlic** and cook, stirring now and then, until soft and translucent, 5 to 6 minutes.

2 Add the **celery, carrots, broth, chickpeas, Parmesan, herbs,** and **salt** and **pepper** to taste and bring to a boil. Reduce the heat and simmer 10 minutes, skimming off any foam that floats to the top with a large flat spoon or soup strainer.

3 Add the **pasta** and simmer until it is tender, about 8 minutes. Taste the soup! Does it need a squeeze of **lemon** to make it tangier? Or how about a sprinkle more of Parmesan, pepper, or fresh herbs?

If you are using the 32-ounce "boxes" of broth, don't measure, just pour: 32 ounces = 4 cups.

play  with it

* Add ½ cup chopped tomatoes.

* Throw a few leaves of thinly sliced spinach or Swiss chard into the pot.

* Add a pinch of cinnamon and cumin while sautéing the onions for Moroccan flair.

* Add a tablespoon of mild curry for an Indian-flavored soup.

* Add eggs! Bring the soup to a slow simmer, gently slide in 4 eggs to poach with the soup for 5 minutes, spoon into wide bowls, and shower with herbs, black pepper, and Parmesan cheese.

chicken noodle soup

makes 8 servings

PREP TIME: 20 minutes   COOKING TIME: 40 minutes

What other dish warms up your kitchen, conjures your ancestors ("Hello, Grandma Minni!"), scares away colds, and brings everyone to the table? None.

1 whole bone-in, skin-on chicken breast
(1½ to 2 pounds), organic if you can

3 carrots, scrubbed and chopped
(unpeeled if organic)

3 stalks celery, chopped

2 medium onions (or 4 leeks, white and
light green parts), chopped

1 bay leaf (optional)

4 or 5 garlic cloves, finely minced
(garlic is great in cold season)

8 cups chicken broth (organic if you can)

Salt and freshly ground black pepper

1 cup of your favorite pasta
(elbows, alphabets, or stars)

3 tablespoons chopped fresh herbs
such as parsley, dill, or chives

1 In large heavy-bottomed stockpot, combine **all the ingredients except for the pasta and herbs**. Bring to a simmer over medium heat and cover. Reduce the heat to low and keep it at a gentle simmer.

2 Every now and then, skim the scum (gray foamy stuff) from the surface with a large flat spoon or soup strainer.

3 After 30 minutes, take the chicken out with tongs. When cool enough to handle, discard the skin, and pull the meat off the bones and chop or tear into bite-size pieces.

4 Add the **pasta** to the pot and simmer until it is tender, 8 to 10 minutes. Return the chicken to the pot and add the **herbs**.

5 Taste to make sure it has enough seasonings. Serve and feel well.

cook's tip

Homemade stock of any kind will last for 2 to 3 days. Stock from a can or carton will last for 4 to 5 days. Because of the lining in the can, canned stock should to be transferred to a glass container.

play with it

★ Add a little lemon zest or a squeeze of lemon juice.

★ Toss in some chopped fresh zucchini, a handful of fresh spinach, or escarole.

★ Swirl in a spoonful of tahini or a dollop of pesto.

★ Add a dash of hot sauce, a cup of chopped tomatoes, and a little oregano.

★ Use cooked quinoa or pearled barley in place of the pasta (just remember they both need to cook longer than pasta, so add them earlier or precook them).

a bold and tangy cold fighter

tomato red pepper soup

makes 6 to 8 servings
PREP TIME: 15 minutes   COOKING TIME: 25 minutes

Tomato soup is rainy-night soup; add red pepper, which is loaded with even more antioxidants and vitamin C, and it becomes helpful at warding off colds. Drop a spoonful of cooked quinoa into each bowl, perhaps a poached egg (page 79), and a sprinkling of parsley, then light a flock of candles, and call it a soup-supper by the fireside.

Olive oil, for the pot

1 large onion, chopped

2 garlic cloves, chopped

1 can (28 ounces) good-quality diced tomatoes with their juices

1½ cups roasted red peppers, drained and chopped (from a jar or home roasted)

4 cups chicken or vegetable broth (organic if you can)

Salt and red pepper flakes

1 Heat up a soup pot over medium heat. Drizzle in enough **olive oil** to cover the bottom. Add the **onion** and cook until soft and translucent, 5 to 6 minutes. Add the **garlic**, stir for a moment, and when the garlic is warm and fragrant, add the **tomatoes**, **roasted peppers**, and **broth**.

2 Cover and simmer for 20 minutes. Using an immersion blender or standard blender (working in batches and filling the blender only half full to avoid a soup explosion), puree until very smooth.*

3 Now comes the important part: Taste it! Does it need **salt**? Perhaps some **red pepper flakes** for a little kick? Maybe a little more broth or water if it has thickened too much?

For a silky-smooth soup, pour the soup through a fine-mesh sieve to remove the tomato and pepper skins. Use a soup ladle to push the mixture through.

cook's tip

How to roast peppers:

1. Preheat the broiler with a rack about 6 inches from heat. Slice peppers in half lengthwise and rub all over with olive oil. Place on foil or an oiled baking sheet, skin-side up.

2. Broil until the skin bubbles, blackens, and wrinkles, 5 to 10 minutes. Transfer the peppers to a paper bag and close it tight to keep the steam in (this helps loosen the skin). Once cool, peel the skin from the pepper and discard the stem and seeds.

play with it

★ Add a rind of Parmesan as the soup simmers, which adds a little "bass" to the pepper "treble" (but remove it before blending).

★ Add a sprig of fresh thyme or rosemary as it simmers.

★ Swirl in a little Greek yogurt at the end.

★ Add a tablespoon of chopped fresh ginger to the onions.

★ Garnish with toasted nuts and seeds.

tortellini pesto soup

makes 4 or 5 servings

PREP TIME: 15 minutes   COOKING TIME: 10 minutes

Noodles, broth, peas, and pesto. It doesn't get much simpler—or more flavorful—than that. Of course, you may complicate it a tiny bit (but a healthy bit!) by adding finely chopped broccoli or spinach.

Olive oil, for the pot

1 or 2 garlic cloves, chopped

4 cups tasty organic chicken or vegetable broth (if it's not tasty, your soup will be sad)

2 cups of your favorite fresh tortellini (cheese, spinach, or mushroom)

2 cups frozen peas

3 tablespoons basil pesto, homemade (page 239) or store-bought

Freshly ground black pepper

1 Heat up a soup pot over medium-high heat. Drizzle in a thin layer of **olive oil** to coat the bottom. As soon as it is hot, add the **garlic** and cook until it starts to turn golden, about 30 seconds.

2 Carefully pour in the **broth**, then slip in the **tortellini** and **peas**. Simmer for 4 to 5 minutes. Taste the tortellini for doneness, then swirl in the **pesto**.

3 Now taste! Does it need a little pepper, or a smidgen more pesto? This is your soup, so you get to decide!

 kids **k** in charge

★ Choose the tortellini flavor.

★ Measure the peas and pesto.

★ Taste the soup to make sure it is perfect.

 play ✳ with it

★ Throw in a fresh basil leaf or two.

★ Sprinkle a handful of fresh spinach or some chopped-up broccoli florets when adding the tortellini.

★ Top with a little shredded Parmesan cheese.

★ Stir in a little grated lemon zest.

a simple—and chic!—soup

mixed-grain Italian peasant soup

makes 6 servings

PREP TIME: 15 minutes   COOKING TIME: 20 minutes

The world is full of simple, fast, and delicious recipes and often they're as close as your friend's kitchen. Thank goodness for great neighbors like Monina. She gave us the wheatberry salad in our last book, *The Family Dinner*, and here she shares a soup that is cheap, delicious, and—once draped with a few toppings—as fabulously chic as she is.

Olive oil, for the pot

2 large onions, chopped

4 garlic cloves, minced

2 celery stalks, chopped

½ cup pink lentils

⅔ cup semi-pearled farro

⅔ cup pearled barley

4 cups chicken* or vegetable broth (organic if you can)

Salt and freshly ground black pepper

*Monina stores chicken carcasses in the freezer until she has 4 or 5. Then she puts them in a pot with water to cover, adds a carrot, halved onion, and garlic cloves and simmers over low heat for 3 to 4 hours to make a concentrated broth.

1 Heat up a soup pot over medium-high heat. Drizzle in enough **olive oil** to cover the bottom. Add the **onions**, **garlic**, and **celery**. Cook until the onions and celery are starting to soften and get translucent, 4 to 5 minutes. Remove them with a slotted spoon and set aside ❓.

2 If the pot is dry, add a little more oil. Add the **lentils**, **farro**, **barley**, and **broth**. Bring to a simmer and cook until the grains are tender/al dente, about 15 minutes.

3 Add the reserved onion mixture 5 minutes before the grains are done. Season with **salt and pepper** to taste and serve piping hot.

 cook's tip

Pearled grain has had part of its outer bran polished off, so it cooks in less than half the time it would otherwise. If you have whole, unpearled grains, cook them in the soup without the lentils until they are almost done (45 to 50 minutes), then add the lentils for the last 15 minutes.

 play with it

★ Add fresh herbs such as thyme, rosemary, or parsley.

★ Top with sprouts such as alfalfa, radish, or sunflower.

★ Top with chopped avocado and halved cherry tomatoes.

★ Serve with a thick slice of grainy bread.

 why 'cause . . .

Monina likes to leave a little crunch in the soup, so she removes the vegetables early and adds them back just before serving.

sweet as a pea—and delicious hot or cold

peppermint green pea soup

makes 4 or 5 servings

PREP TIME: 15 minutes COOKING TIME: 10 minutes CHILL OUT TIME: 1 hour

This sparkling, fresh, and minty soup is the brightest of greens. Serve it hot in a bowl or cold in small glasses. Drizzled with a pretty yogurt spider web (see Kids in Charge), it's a great soup to serve to guests.

Olive oil, for the pot

1 medium onion, chopped

3 garlic cloves, minced

4 cups vegetable or chicken broth (organic if you can)

3½ cups frozen or freshly shucked peas

½ cup loosely packed fresh mint leaves

⅔ cup Greek yogurt* (whole or low-fat), plus more for garnish

Salt and freshly ground black pepper

*To make a vegan version, you can substitute canned coconut milk for the yogurt.

1 Heat up a soup pot over medium heat. Drizzle in a thin layer of **olive oil**. When the oil is shimmering, add the **onion** and **garlic** and cook until fragrant and soft. Add the **broth** and bring the soup to a simmer. Add the **peas** and most of the **mint** (saving a few for garnish). Let the soup simmer for 5 to 6 minutes until hot (but not longer as the peas will lose their bright color) then remove the soup from the heat.

2 Add the **yogurt** to the pot and with an immersion blender or standard blender (working in batches and filling the blender only half full to avoid a soup explosion), puree until smooth.

3 If you want to serve the soup cold, pour it into a shallow bowl and chill it in the fridge for 1 hour or until cold. Otherwise reheat over medium heat, but don't let it boil ❓. Taste your soup! It will probably need a little **salt and pepper**. Ladle into bowls. Garnish with a dollop or spiderweb of yogurt and a jaunty mint leaf.

 why **?** 'cause . . .

If you let the soup boil, the yogurt will curdle (separate into little white bits). The soup tastes the same but is not quite as pretty; you can save it by reblending until smooth, then reheating.

 kids **k** in charge

Make a Yogurt "Spider Web"!
Thin ⅓ cup Greek yogurt with milk until it is the consistency of very thick cream. Drizzle it onto the soup in a few circles, one inside another. Then stick a toothpick into the center of the soup and drag it out through the rings, repeating back and forth. Ta-da! Beautiful!

this heartwarming pot rescues lost vegetables

Sunday soup

makes 10 servings

PREP TIME: 15 to 30 minutes   COOKING TIME: 30 to 40 minutes

Here's the perfect way to use up those vegetables languishing in your fridge. This soup is very versatile; you can use whatever vegetables you have on hand so long as you start with leeks or onions and a few garlic cloves. To make a vegetarian version, skip the sausages and add quinoa, beans, or lentils. This is your Sunday and your soup. Make it with what you have on hand . . . then serve with big pieces of toasted bread spread with good butter, and a hunk of Parmesan for grating.

Olive oil, for the pot

3 cooked Italian sausages, your favorite kind, sliced (optional)

3 leeks (white and light-green parts), chopped and rinsed thoroughly ❓

2 small carrots, chopped (unpeeled if organic)

2 celery stalks, chopped

2 big handfuls sturdy greens (kale, cabbage, or chard), chopped or torn

1½ cups chopped tomatoes, fresh or canned

4 (or more) garlic cloves, chopped

½ cup green (French) or brown lentils, rinsed

8 cups vegetable or chicken broth (organic if you can)

Salt

Vinegar, any type (optional)

Red pepper flakes (optional)

1 Get out your big Sunday soup pot and heat it over medium-high heat, then drizzle in enough **olive oil** to cover the bottom of the pot. Throw in the **sausage** (if using) and cook until nice and browned. Transfer to a plate with a slotted spoon.

2 Add the **leeks** to the pot and cook, stirring, until they have softened a bit, 5 to 6 minutes. Add the **carrots**, **celery**, **greens**, **tomatoes**, and **garlic**. Stir for a few minutes until all the vegetables have gotten acquainted and are starting to soften. Add the **lentils**, **broth**, and sausages (if using). Let your soup simmer for 30 minutes while you read the Sunday paper.

3 Taste and adjust the seasonings—does it need **salt**? A splash of **vinegar**? A few **hot pepper flakes**? Make it taste perfect for you.

 kids **k** in charge

★ Go on a treasure hunt—in the fridge!— for forlorn vegetables.

★ Tear the greens from their stems.

★ Rinse the leeks.

★ Measure the lentils.

★ Convince the grown-ups that pasta is a good addition.

 play **✱** with it

★ Add the rind of a Parmesan cheese as the soup simmers to add flavor.

★ Add a splash of wine before adding the broth and let it bubble for a moment, to boost flavor and add a little acidity.

★ Garnish with fresh herbs such as parsley, chives, or chopped dill.

 why **?** 'cause . . .

Leeks hide sand and dirt deep within their swoops and swirls. To wash it well, chop it first, then submerge in a big bowl of cold water. Let sit for a few minutes, then lift the leeks out with a slotted spoon, leaving the sand behind in the bottom of the bowl.

marvelous miso

what is this pungent paste?

Miso is a paste made mostly from soybeans, often with other grains like rice, chickpeas, or barley mixed in as well. It has a soft soy-salty flavor and a buttery texture and is a delicious way to add umami—a deeply satisfying bass note—to your dishes.

Miso is incredibly versatile. If you keep a tub of it on hand, you can easily use it to replace vegetable or meat broth in soups. It is also a tasty addition to marinades and dressings, is great spread on sandwiches and toast, and makes a great, quick hot sipping broth on a cold day.

Plus, miso is really good for you. It's a probiotic, which means it contains bacteria and enzymes that are beneficial to digestive health and that strengthen the immune system. It also provides protein, vitamin B_{12}, riboflavin, vitamin E, vitamin K, and dietary fiber.

One thing to keep in mind is that miso is more nourishing when not overheated (boiling kills all the good bacteria), so it is best just gently swirled into soups at the very end.

Look for miso paste in well-stocked supermarkets, heath food stores, and Asian markets. It is typically packaged in small tubs or bags and stocked in the refrigerated section close to the fresh tofu.

Miso is available in several stages of fermentation, ranging from white or blond miso, which is the mildest, to yellow and red miso, which have been fermented longer and are stronger in flavor. Yellow miso works best in soups, dressings, and marinades; it's a good all-purpose choice.

Depending on the grains used to make the miso, it can contain gluten. If this is a concern, read the label carefully (both Eden Foods and South River have gluten-free miso). Whenever possible, buy organic. Once you have opened a tub of miso, it will last for up to a year in your fridge.

miso soup

makes 4 servings

PREP TIME: **5 minutes**   COOKING TIME: **20 minutes**

There are only three ingredients—kombu, bonito, and miso—in this deeply satisfying broth; it's worth seeking them out, if not for the flavor alone, then for the nourishment they bring. Kombu is a wide, dried seaweed that will add amino acids and flavor your broth with the salty sea. It is found dried, in the soy sauce/seaweed section of health-food stores or Asian markets. It is also a good addition to a pot of beans or rice, adding both flavor and digestibility. Bonito flakes are fluffy pink shavings of dried, smoked bonito fish usually found near the seaweed. They will add a splash of the ocean and smoke to your broth.

1 piece of kombu*, a little longer than your hand

6½ cups cold water

1 cup loosely packed bonito flakes

6 tablespoons yellow miso paste in a small bowl (a little less if you're using red miso paste and a little more if using white)

Good kombu is covered with a fine white powdery substance. Do not wash this off! It's full of that umami flavor we love.

1 Place the **kombu** in a pot with the **water** and set over medium heat. Bring to a simmer, then immediately remove the pot from the heat. Add the **bonito flakes**, scattering them across the surface of the water.

2 Once the flakes have settled onto the bottom of the pot, pour the broth through a fine-mesh sieve into a bowl. Discard the kombu (or refrigerate to cook with rice or beans later on) and bonito. This mild broth is called dashi.

3 Spoon the **miso** into a small bowl, then add a ladleful of the dashi broth, stirring to loosen up the miso. Stir three-fourths of the mixture into the pot. Taste and add the rest if desired. Return the pot to the heat and bring to barely a simmer. Serve hot.

cook's tip

If you don't happen to have kombu or bonito in your pantry, heat up 6 cups of low-sodium vegetable or chicken broth and swirl in the miso. Soup's up.

play with it

★ Add a few cubes of tofu and a little fresh chopped spinach for an appetizer or an afterschool snack.

★ Thinly sliced scallions make everything better, and so does a little grated ginger. Just swirl them in before serving.

★ Throw a little rehydrated wakame seaweed into the pot at the very end.

★ Add steamed vegetables and cooked soba noodles to reheat in the miso broth, and dinner is ready.

sweet potato (miso) soup

makes 6 to 8 servings

PREP TIME: 10 minutes   COOKING TIME: 25 minutes

This soup is quick and easy to make and every single ingredient in it is especially healthy for you. Sweet and savory and silky, top it with toasted quinoa and it will be crunchy, too. It's a gorgeously vibrant bowl of taste contrasts!

Olive oil, for the pot

1 small onion, chopped

1 thumb-size (a big thumb) piece of fresh ginger, peeled and minced

2 garlic cloves, minced

1 medium sweet potato, peeled and cubed (about 3 cups)

6 cups water

¼ cup yellow miso paste

A pinch of cayenne pepper (optional)

1 Heat up a soup pot over medium-high heat. Drizzle in enough **olive oil** to cover the bottom. Add the **onion** and cook until it softens, about 5 minutes. Add the **ginger** and **garlic** and cook until fragrant, about 1 minute. Add the **sweet potato** and **water**, cover, and simmer until the vegetables are completely tender, about 20 minutes.

2 Add the **miso** to the soup. Using an immersion blender or standard blender (working in batches and filling the blender only half full to avoid a soup explosion), puree the soup until smooth. Taste and adjust with more **miso** and some **cayenne pepper** (if using).

3 Pour the soup into bowls. Add toppings, as below, if you care to. Enjoy the sunshine.

play  with it

* Top with "crunchy quinoa" (see page 120) for texture and protein.

* Top with a dollop of yogurt and a sprinkle of fresh cilantro and/or mint.

luscious, creamy, and elegantly understated

cauliflower (miso) soup

makes 4 to 6 servings
PREP TIME: 15 minutes   COOKING TIME: 20 minutes

This is everything you want in an elegant soup: creamy, delicious, and healthy as well. Best of all, you would never guess that it only takes a few minutes to make—and even fewer ingredients. The secret is miso paste, which is a great alternative to vegetable or chicken stock, giving your soup a rich flavor.

Olive oil, for the pot

1 medium onion, diced

2 garlic cloves, minced

1 head cauliflower (about 1½ pounds), broken into small pieces

6 cups water

6 tablespoons yellow miso paste

1 Heat up a soup pot over low heat. Drizzle in enough **oil** to cover the bottom. Add the **onion** and **garlic** and gently cook until they are soft but have not changed color, 3 to 4 minutes ❓.

2 Add the **cauliflower** and 2 cups **water**, increase the heat to medium-high, cover, and bring to a simmer. Cook until the cauliflower is very tender and can easily be mashed with a spoon, about 15 minutes.

3 Stir the **miso paste** into the soup. Using an immersion blender or standard blender (working in batches and filling the blender only half full to avoid a soup explosion), puree the soup until it is velvety and completely smooth.

4 Return the puree to the pot and stir in the remaining 4 cups **water**. Return the soup to a simmer. Taste and adjust the seasonings.

 kids **k** in charge

* ★ Pull the cauliflower apart.
* ★ Measure the miso.
* ★ Be the official taster.

 play ✱ with it

* ★ Add chopped ginger when sautéing the onions.
* ★ Top the finished soup with a sprinkle of toasted breadcrumbs, quinoa; or nuts; a drizzle of nut or olive oil; or chopped parsley or mint, or a sprig of cilantro.

 why ❓ 'cause . . .

Browning onions adds a lot of flavor and color to a dish, which is usually a good thing, but sometimes you want the onion flavor and color to only hum softly in the background. In such cases, you "sweat" the onions, which means cook them slow and low, so that they just soften and release their juices without browning.

lovin' the lentils soup

makes 8 servings

PREP TIME: 20 minutes   COOKING TIME: 45 to 55 minutes

Lentils may be dressed in a brown and dull suit, but that's just a disguise! These legumes change in your mouth: At first warm and comforting, they then fill your body superhero-style with strengthening and powerful protein so you can run like the wind and spin like a tornado.

Olive oil, for the pot

1 large onion, chopped

1 small red bell pepper, chopped

6 ounces organic turkey or vegan sausage, cubed (optional)

4 or 5 garlic cloves, chopped

6 cups chicken or vegetable broth (organic if you can)

1 cup brown lentils, rinsed

Salt and freshly ground black pepper

1 Heat up a soup pot over medium heat. Drizzle in a thin layer of **oil**. Add the **onion, bell pepper, sausage** (if using), and **garlic** and let them sizzle until everything is fragrant and starting to soften, 4 to 5 minutes.

2 Carefully pour in the **broth** and **lentils** and pop on a lid. Turn the heat down low so the soup gently simmers for 35 to 40 minutes. Taste the soup! Are the lentils cooked? Do you need a little **salt** or **pepper**? If you prefer the soup a little thicker, just let it simmer without a lid for 10 minutes more.

play with it

Make it Indian:
When cooking the onions, add 1 table-spoon grated fresh ginger and 1 heaping tablespoon mild curry powder; and instead of sausage, add 2 to 3 unpeeled cubed red potatoes. Simmer lentils and broth until tender, then stir in 1 cup thawed frozen peas. Serve with a dollop of yogurt and fresh cilantro.

soup into supper

Toppings that make it a meal

At some point, soup got demoted to lunch or even appetizer status. But picture a rustic bowl of lentil soup topped with crunchy quinoa, some sweet crisp brown onions, a drizzle of yogurt, and perhaps some leafy greens. First your spoon dips into the onions, then the soup . . . a bite of quinoa next, a bit of greens, then some tangy yogurt. . . . How is that not a perfect supper?

To turn a simple bowl of soup into a meal, it helps to add a few toppings to create interesting textures and flavors, so that each bite is varied enough to keep your taste buds interested. Here are a bunch of our favorite add-ons (all of which would be perfect on your salads, too).

Seeds
Toasted sesame, sunflower, poppy, or hemp seeds add both protein and crunch.

Nuts
Toasted slivered almonds or chopped walnuts, whole pine nuts, or chopped peanuts.

Crunchy quinoa
In a heavy-bottomed pan coated with olive oil, sauté 2 cups of cooked quinoa over medium-high heat until it is golden and crunchy-crisp, about 10 minutes. Season with salt and pepper. Store in a sealed jar and hide it (from Laurie) in the fridge. It's that good!

Crisp wild rice (for particularly fancy soups)
Pour 1 inch of oil (a type that can withstand high heat, such as grapeseed oil) into a small pot and heat over high heat. Once the oil is shimmering hot gently slip in 3 tablespoons uncooked wild rice, which will expand and puff up almost immediately. Remove the mixture with a slotted spoon and transfer to a plate lined with paper towels. Puff more rice until you have enough. Toss with salt to taste. Use immediately.

Raw fruits or vegetables
Add vibrancy and vigor with thinly sliced or diced raw cabbage; cubed apples or pears tossed with citrus; carrots peeled into long curls; radishes cut into slivers or matchsticks; fennel cubed or sliced paper-thin; raw onions cut into small dice; sliced scallions; or a fluffy mound of raw sprouts.

Croutons and breadcrumbs
Finely chop pumpernickel bread, toss with a little olive oil, and sauté; float in the soup just before serving.

Or cube or tear any bread you were about to discard, toss with olive oil, maybe a little garlic and some herbs, and toast in the oven or in a skillet until it's even better than the day it was born.

Stack and thinly slice corn tortillas into strips, toss with oil, perhaps a little chili powder and lime zest, then bake on an oiled baking sheet at 350°F for 10 minutes or until crisp.

Caramelized onions

Thinly slice 1 or 2 onions of any kind. Heat a large skillet over medium heat and coat with enough oil to cover the bottom. Add the onions in a thin layer, sprinkle with salt and pinch of sugar (this speeds up the browning). Cook, stirring now and then, until some are golden, some are dark, and most are crisp, 15 to 20 minutes. It is important to sample some, but do try to leave a few for the soup.

✳ Tangy ✳

✳ Add a dollop of yogurt, either plain or seasoned with chopped herbs and salt.

✳ Squeeze lime or lemon juice into the soup at the last moment.

✳ Swirl in a teaspoon of sour cream or a spoonful of chopped fresh tomatoes tossed with garlic, basil, and balsamic vinegar.

✳ Hearty ✳

✳ Float a spoonful of cooked grains such as brown rice, quinoa, millet, or wild rice in the bowl.

✳ Add a heaping spoonful of cooked beans.

✳ Slip in a poached egg.

✳ Broil a few cubes of Halloumi (Greek grilling cheese) until golden and soft, and float in the bowl; or sprinkle on crumbled feta cheese.

✳ Green ✳

✳ Season with mixed chopped herbs such as parsley, chives, cilantro, basil, or mint.

✳ Toss a tangle of frisée, radicchio, or watercress with lemon juice, olive oil, and season to taste. Then float it on top of a hearty soup for a contrast in temperatures and textures, and an extra boost of vitamins.

✳ Spoon in Kneaded Kale (page 122) or collards tossed with lemon and sesame seeds.

✳ Top with cubed avocado tossed with citrus.

✳ Spicy ✳

✳ Add a spoonful of salsa, green or red, roasted or not.

✳ Swirl in harissa (Moroccan spice paste).

✳ Toast cumin seeds, whole coriander seeds, or garam masala powder and scatter on top.

✳ Sprinkle in a tiny bit of turmeric or paprika (regular or smoked).

kneaded kale

PREP TIME: 15 minutes

We love kale in all its forms—the beautiful, almost black lacinato kale (aka dinosaur or Tuscan black), the frilly petticoats of Scotch kale, the flat blue-gray leaves of Russian kale, the faint aroma of roses in red kale. Kale is tough enough to withstand winter frosts, giving us the opportunity to prepare fresh greens in the dead of winter. Its toughness, however, benefits from a little tenderness before the leaves land in your bowl. If you knead the kale with a little olive oil, it will relax, become more toothsome, and turn into an altogether different leaf, open to being dressed and happy to mingle with other greens. Once kneaded, kale will keep in an airtight container or bowl in the fridge for several days. Make a big batch and use it for salads; as proud toppings for eggs, beans, or cooked grains; and to slip into sandwiches and wraps.

3 to 4 large bunches of any kind of kale (they will wilt down to about half the size)

1 teaspoon olive oil per bunch

1 Wash and dry the **kale** well (you can actually wring it dry in a towel). Remove the stems by grabbing the stem end with one hand and using your other hand to pull off the leafy part into bite-size pieces. Send the stems to compost heaven.

2 Put the kale into a large bowl. Drizzle with **olive oil**. Using both hands, knead the kale as you would dough until it is silky and tender, about 30 kneads. Use right away, or store covered for up to 4 days in the fridge.

kids **k** in charge

Kneading the kale is great for kids whose hands typically get their workouts on computer keyboards or game consoles.

a very simple kale salad

makes 1 serving
PREP TIME: 20 minutes

Simply tossed. Simply good.

1 very large handful Kneaded Kale
(page 122) per person

A pinch of salt per person

1 sliver of garlic, minced, per person

1 teaspoon fresh lemon juice per person

2 teaspoons olive or nut oil per person

Put the **kale** in a salad bowl. In a small jar, combine the **salt** and **garlic** and smash with a spoon. Add the **lemon juice** and shake vigorously. Add the **oil**, shake again. Dip a kale leaf in to taste and adjust with salt and lemon juice. Toss with the kale.

play ✳ with it

✱ Add cubed avocado and/or sunflower seeds.

✱ Substitute the olive oil with toasted sesame oil and add a dash of soy sauce and chopped ginger to the dressing. Add shiitake mushroom "bacon" (see page 96), slivered carrots, and celery to the kale.

✱ Add crumbled feta cheese, shredded mint or parsley, chopped tomatoes, and crushed pita chips.

✱ Add sliced strawberries, raspberries, or pomegranate seeds; grated ricotta salata; and toasted walnuts.

caesar kale salad with homemade croutons

makes 6 servings

PREP TIME: 20 minutes   BAKING TIME: 15 minutes

Caesar is a sneaky salad. Lurking among those crunchy spears of romaine is a heavy dressing, tons of cheese, and white-bread croutons—not exactly healthy ingredients. Here, we've swapped out romaine for our beloved kale, tossed out the white-bread croutons and added a whole wheat variety or crunchy quinoa, and cut down on the cheese—leaving you with a salad that is crisp, tasty, and not filled with junk. We also have a vegan option!

DRESSING

2 garlic cloves, minced

2 teaspoons Worcestershire sauce, Asian fish sauce, or chopped anchovies

3 tablespoons low-fat or vegan mayonnaise

Grated zest and juice of 1 lemon

2 tablespoons grated Parmesan cheese (for vegans use nutritional yeast)

1 tablespoon Dijon mustard

½ cup light-tasting oil, like virgin olive oil or canola oil

Salt and freshly ground black pepper

SALAD

6 large handfuls Kneaded Kale (page 122), from about 3 large bunches kale

2 cups Whole-Grain Croutons (recipe right) or crispy quinoa (see page 120)

¼ cup grated Parmesan cheese (for vegans, use nutritional yeast)

1　**For the dressing:** Whisk together the **garlic,** Worcestershire sauce, **mayonnaise,** lemon **zest** and **juice, Parmesan, mustard, oil,** and **salt** and **pepper** to taste in a large bowl until smooth. Dip a piece of kale into the dressing and see how it tastes. Does it need more salt? Or lemon? Make it taste how you like it best.

2　**For the salad:** Toss the dressing with the **kale, croutons,** and **Parmesan.**

whole-grain croutons

All you need to make your own croutons is some **whole-grain bread** cut into cubes, tossed with a bit of **olive oil,** sprinkled with **salt and pepper,** and perhaps some minced **garlic** and **Parmesan cheese.** Spread onto a baking sheet and bake at 400°F until golden and irresistibly crunchy, about 15 minutes.

quinoa salad

makes 6 servings

PREP TIME: 20 to 30 minutes   COOKING TIME: 10 to 15 minutes

Wouldn't it make you happy if, every time you opened your fridge, there was a nice big bowl of nutrient-packed salad ready to eat? Make a batch or two of this salad on a Sunday afternoon and serve half of it for dinner. Then, eat the rest for lunch later in the week, layer it into wraps, or serve over a plate of greens for dinner on a warm summer night.

1½ cups quinoa (rinsed if needed)

½ cup unsalted raw sunflower seeds

½ to 1 cup chopped fresh parsley

½ cup dried berries, like raisins or blueberries*

2 celery stalks, chopped

2 carrots, chopped (unpeeled if organic)

8 kale leaves, stems removed, thinly sliced

¼ cup olive oil

¼ cup fresh lemon juice

1 teaspoon salt

Some dried fruit, especially berries, often have sugar added to them (and many contain sulfites), so look at the label and get dried fruit with as little or no added sugar and other nasty additives as possible. Brands that are 100-percent organic are more reliable.

1 Bring a large pot of salted water to a boil. Add the **quinoa** and return to a boil. Cook until al dente, as you would pasta, 10 to 11 minutes. Drain well and spread on a baking sheet to cool, about 15 minutes.

2 Meanwhile, combine **all the remaining ingredients** in a large bowl and toss.

3 Add the cooled quinoa and toss. Taste! Does it need more lemon juice? More salt? A few more dried berries? Taste and add until the salad is tart and sweet, crunchy and very good. (By the way, not sure how this happens, but the flavors in grain salads sometimes flutter away after a day or so, so just re-taste and adjust for the mysterious disappearance.)

 kids **k** in charge

★ Rinse the quinoa.

★ Measure the sunflower seeds.

★ Toss everything together.

★ Squeeze the lemons.

★ Be the official taste testers.

carrot, walnut, and apple salad

makes 4 to 6 servings

PREP TIME: 15 minutes

Sweet, tangy, and crunchy, all in one bright mouthful.

4 cups grated carrots, about 8 carrots (unpeeled if organic)

2 apples (unpeeled), cut into small cubes

½ cup walnut halves, toasted

½ cup crumbled mild feta cheese (optional)

¼ cup fresh lemon juice

1 teaspoon salt

Toss **all the ingredients** straight into your salad bowl, then toss again. Taste! Does it need more lemon juice? More nuts? Make it perfect for you!

why  'cause . . .

Toasting nuts brings out their best qualities: fragrant, intensely nutty, and crisp. Beware when toasting, however. The moment you turn your back on them, they'll laugh at you and burn!

In the oven: Spread the nuts in a single layer on a baking sheet. Toast in a 350°F oven until golden and fragrant, 7 to 10 minutes.

In a skillet: If you just need to toast a handful of small (like pine nuts) or chopped nuts, heat up your heavy bottomed skillet on high heat. Add nuts to the pan and immediately turn off the burner. Stir the nuts once or twice and let sit for a few minutes.

play  with it

Add:
* Toasted sesame or sunflower seeds
* A sliced scallion
* Cubed baked tofu
* Shredded cabbage (purple would be pretty), kohlrabi, or kale

simple bright green salad

PREP TIME: 10 focused minutes to shop, 30 minutes to wash and dry

Just greens, simple greens, tossed with something tart, salty, and a little oil . . . often that is all you need to complete a plate. If you always have a big bowl of prepped greens on hand, it will also be one of the fastest dishes you can make. Grab some greens, toss with dressing, and you're done! When you shop for greens, use all of your shopping senses. Look for lettuces that strut. Give them a gentle squeeze: They should feel crisp, smell fresh, and look green. They should even sound fresh, squeaking at your squeeze, not limply sighing.

GREENS (MIX AND MATCH)

Bright green varieties, like Bibb, romaine, or watercress

Arugula

Red oak leaf

Some kale and Swiss chard

Any endive, curly or not, red or green

Baby spinach, baby beet greens, and turnip tops

DRESSING

Your Family's House Dressing (page 137)

1 Fill a big bowl with very cold water. Remove any yellowing or blemished leaves. Pull the lettuce leaves from the cores, and submerge all the **greens** in the water, swishing them about. If the water becomes very dirty, lift the greens out of the water, drain the water (into nearby petunia pots), and repeat the bath.

2 Dry the greens in a salad spinner or pat them dry with a kitchen towel. Pull tough stems from kales and chards.

3 Line a large container with a clean kitchen towel, arrange the greens in it, and cover tightly. Refrigerate for up to 2 weeks.

4 When you're hungry for a salad, take a plateful of greens from the container, toss with Your Family's House Dressing, and dig in.

kids  in charge

* Pick the greens and pull the leaves apart.

* They are naturally expert washers and spinners!

* And they can be the tossers, too.

play  with it

Add:

* Fresh herbs such as chervil, chives, dill, cilantro, and mint.

* Edible flower petals such as nasturtiums, chive blossoms, and marigold petals.

rainbow salad with carrot miso dressing

makes 4 to 6 servings
PREP TIME: 30 minutes

Next time you're at the grocery store, send your kids on a treasure hunt for colorful vegetables. You don't have to stick to the ones in this recipe; just try to include a variety of colors on your plate. Every color contributes different essential nutrients for fighting cancer and heart disease, boosting immunity, reducing inflammation, and maintaining your organs in tip-top shape. The deeper the color, the richer the antioxidant levels, but that's no reason to stay away from lighter foods. Challenge yourself to eat the whole rainbow!

2 carrots, chopped (unpeeled if organic)

1 cup chopped red cabbage

1 tomato, chopped

1 cup chopped broccoli

1 yellow bell pepper, chopped

1 cup chopped jicama, cucumber, or green cabbage

Carrot Miso Dressing (at right)

Arrange the **carrots, cabbage, tomato, broccoli, bell pepper,** and **jicama** on a plate and serve with the dressing on the side.

carrot miso dressing

This dressing is good on just about everything. Not only does it make a fine dip for vegetables, but it is excellent drizzled on a simple green salad or poached fish or chicken and makes a great sandwich or wrap spread.

In a blender, combine **2 carrots** (coarsely chopped), ¼ **small red onion** (coarsely chopped), ⅓ cup **lime juice** or rice vinegar, **2 tablespoons toasted sesame oil**, 3 tablespoons yellow or red **miso paste**, 1 tablespoon chopped fresh **ginger**, ¼ cup **water**, and **salt** and **pepper** to taste. Blend until smooth. Add more water if you want it thinner. Taste and adjust the seasonings. The dressing will keep, tightly covered, in the fridge for 1 week. *Makes 1½ cups.*

a chopped salad

makes 6 servings
PREP TIME: 20 to 30 minutes

A chopped salad makes everyone happy. Each bite has all sorts of flavors and textures. It is so good it barely needs a dressing: good olive oil, a bit of tartness, some salt and pepper at most. Do improvise with the vegetables. Just try to cut everything the same size and use equal amounts so no one vegetable gets to yell too loud, all of them just humming in contented harmony. You can double or triple the recipe and store it, undressed, in an airtight container in the fridge for at least 4 days. It comes in very handy for lunches, light dinners, and afterschool snacks.

1 cup cooked chickpeas, roughly chopped

1 small head romaine lettuce, chopped, or 3 cups Kneaded Kale (page 122)

1 cup diced celery

1 cup diced tomatoes

1 cup diced red cabbage

1 cup seeded and diced cucumber (no need to peel)

1 cup chopped carrots (unpeeled if organic)

1/1/1/1 Vinaigrette (page 138) or whatever dressing makes you happy

Combine **all the ingredients except the dressing** in a big lovely salad bowl, toss. Add the **dressing**, toss again to coat all the ingredients, then call us all over for lunch.

play **✱** with it

Add:

* ✱ 1 cup cubed extra-firm tofu cubes
* ✱ 1 large avocado, diced
* ✱ 1 cup chopped jicama
* ✱ ⅓ cup diced red onion
* ✱ A few sunny hard-boiled eggs (page 178)
* ✱ ½ cup olives, roughly chopped

* ✱ ½ cup chopped fresh basil, dill, or parsley
* ✱ Feta cheese, crumbled
* ✱ 1 cup cooked grains like wheatberries, quinoa, or farro
* ✱ 1 can tuna or salmon, drained and flaked with a fork

perennial plate's farro salad

makes 4 to 6 servings

PREP TIME: 30 minutes   COOKING TIME: 30 minutes

Daniel Klein is the chef behind *The Perennial Plate* (theperennialplate.com), a wonderful documentary series on the web dedicated to sustainable and adventurous eating. He, along with his wife, Mirra Fine, produce great stories about local food around the world. Daniel is one of the best chefs we know. He's so good, in fact, that Laurie asked him to prepare her wedding supper. Happily, he said yes! Daniel wanted to write a recipe for something that almost always gets thrown away unnecessarily: beet greens.

FARRO

4½ cups water

1 tablespoon salt

2 garlic cloves, smashed

2 sprigs of fresh thyme

1 sprig of fresh rosemary

1½ cups pearled farro

SQUASH

1 large delicata squash, cut crosswise into ¼-inch-thick rounds (leave the seeds in!)

Olive oil, to taste

1 tablespoon ground coriander

Salt and freshly ground black pepper

2 tablespoons honey

SALAD

Juice of 1 to 2 lemons (about 3 tablespoons)

1 tablespoon honey

⅓ cup olive oil

1 cup minced beet greens (from one bunch of beets), stems removed, or your favorite greens or herbs

¼ cup minced shallot or red onion

½ cup smoked ricotta, ricotta, or feta cheese

1 **For the farro:** Combine the **water**, **salt**, **garlic**, and **herbs** in a large pot and bring to a boil over high heat. Reduce the heat to medium-low and bring to a simmer. Add the **farro** and cook to al dente, about 10 minutes. Drain the farro and discard the herbs and garlic. Let cool to room temperature.

2 **For the squash:** Preheat the oven to 400°F. Line a baking sheet with parchment paper.

3 Toss the **squash** rounds with **olive oil**, **coriander**, and **salt** and **pepper** to taste. Arrange on the baking sheet. Heat up the **honey** in the microwave, then brush it over the squash, avoiding the seeds in the center. This will speed up the caramelization of the squash without burning the seeds. Roast until golden brown, about 20 minutes. Set aside. These can be served hot or at room temperature.

4 **For the salad:** Whisk together the **lemon juice**, **honey**, and **olive oil** in a small bowl. If the **beet greens** are especially bitter, pour some of the vinaigrette over them and set aside for 1 hour before serving. At least 20 minutes before serving, combine the greens and the farro in a large serving bowl. Drizzle the dressing over and toss to coat. Arrange the squash over the greens and sprinkle the **shallots** and **ricotta** on top.

your family's house dressing

makes 1⅓ cups

PREP TIME: 5 minutes

⅓ cup good-quality vinegar of choice (balsamic, red wine, white wine, apple cider)—whatever you have, as long as it tastes good

1 teaspoon salt

1 garlic clove, minced, or 3 tablespoons minced shallot

1 cup flavorful olive oil or nut oil (hazelnut or walnut), or a combination of the two

1 Combine the **vinegar**, **salt**, and **garlic** in a 16-ounce mason or other jar and shake until the salt has dissolved. Add the **oil** and shake and shake again.

2 Taste it on a salad leaf. Does it need more salt? A little more vinegar? Adjust to your family's taste. The vinaigrette will keep, tightly covered, in the fridge for up to 1 week.

play  with it

* Add chopped soft herbs such as chives, basil, tarragon, or parsley.

* Add a dollop of Dijon mustard and a drizzle of honey.

* Replace vinegar with lemon or lime juice.

* Add chopped walnuts or hempseeds.

you'll never buy store-bought again

house dressings

There is really nothing good about prepared salad dressings: They taste like old socks, are made with funky ingredients like sugar and chemical preservatives, and they're just not worthy of your beautiful greens. It takes only 5 minutes to make your own dressing and about that much time to teach your kids how to pull it together. Help them get it right every time by drawing the measurements in lines on a 16-ounce mason jar and designating it as the family salad dressing jar; this helps little cooks get the ratio of oil to acid right.

1/1/1/1 salad with vinaigrette

makes 1 serving
PREP TIME: 2 minutes

Kirstin's favorite dressing is quick, light, and measured directly into the salad bowl—no jar or shaking necessary. For this dressing you can get out your best vinegar and finest olive or nut oil, since this is where they will all shine. The ingredients below are per person; just multiply times the number of people you are serving.

1 pinch of salt

1 teaspoon vinegar or lemon juice

1 tablespoon of your best oil (olive, hazelnut, walnut . . .)

1 very large handful salad greens

Get out your big salad bowl, add the **salt** and **vinegar** and whisk them together. (If you want you can throw in a bit of minced garlic and fresh herbs.) Swirl in the **oil**. Toss in the **greens**. Taste. Serve.

cook's tip

Since these dressings have very few ingredients, the flavor of both the vinegar and oil is important. They should be so good that when you taste them on a piece of bread with a little salt you say . . . mmm, tasty.

farm dressing

makes 1¼ cups
PREP TIME: 10 minutes

This dressing brings out the best in fresh produce from the farmers' market or vegetable garden. Just drizzle it over the crunchiest and most colorful vegetables you can find that you've laid out on a pretty platter. Serve with thick slices of whole-grain bread, cubes of good cheese, and maybe a few hard-boiled eggs—peeled, quartered, and sprinkled with salt and pepper. Sit somewhere you can watch the sunset and crunch together in contented silence.

¾ cup Greek yogurt (whole or low-fat)

2 tablespoons mayonnaise, preferably low-fat

2 tablespoons chopped tender herbs
(whatever you have—basil, chives, parsley)

2 teaspoons white wine vinegar or fresh lemon juice

2 tablespoons minced shallot or red onion

Salt and freshly ground black pepper

Whisk together **all the ingredients** in a bowl until smooth. Taste and adjust the seasonings. Drizzle over vegetables.

play  with it

Add some Southwestern heat with a dab of chopped chipotle chile in adobo, or a dash of cayenne pepper.

snacks and drinks

vegetable carpaccio

PREP TIME: 15 to 30 minutes

Looking for a quick afterschool snack? A gorgeous, over-the-top appetizer fit to serve your fancy friends? A colorful, crunchy, fresh, insanely healthy, beautifully simple dish? Here you go! Take a walk with your kids through the produce aisle and find any seasonal vegetables that catch your eyes. Some vegetables we typically eat cooked are delicious raw, too!

Carrots

Kohlrabi

Sugar snap peas

Zucchini

Sweet potatoes

Broccoli stems (Don't throw them out! Cut off the tough outer skin and eat the inside.)

Parsnips

Turnips

Cucumbers

Cauliflower

Fresh herbs

Freshly squeezed lemon or lime juice

Salt and freshly ground black pepper

Edible blossoms (like nasturtiums, squash blossoms, borage), optional

Peel any **vegetables** with a thick skin. Using a very sharp knife, vegetable peeler, or mandoline, slice the vegetables very thin. Serve either the simple or fancy way (see below).

The simple way to serve:

Lay the vegetable(s) on a platter, and serve with the citrus juice and salt or farm dressing (page 139) in little bowls on the side.

The fancy way to serve:

Choose vegetables in different colors, textures, and shapes. Gently toss with plenty of citrus juice, salt, and pepper. Arrange them on a platter, wooden board, or individual plates. Top with fresh herbs and edible blossoms.

popcorn

makes about 10 cups
COOKING TIME: 10 minutes

Do we really need a recipe for popcorn? Well, when was the last time you had hot popcorn, not from a microwave, made without chemical ingredients, GMO corn, bright colors, or strange fats? When was the last time you made it from scratch?

2 tablespoons peanut, grapeseed, or other high-heat oil

½ cup organic popcorn kernels

½ teaspoon salt

1 Place the **oil** in a large heavy-bottomed pot over medium-high heat. Toss in 5 **corn kernels** and cover. When the kernels pop, pour in the remaining kernels, add **salt**, and cover.

2 Shake the pot every 15 seconds. For the first minute, not much will happen. But get ready! The kernels will begin to pop furiously; continue shaking. Lift the lid away from you a tiny, tiny crack, to let out any steam in the pot. Continue shaking until the popcorn stops-a-popping, 4 to 5 minutes. Remove the pot from the heat and carefully lift lid. Catch any wild flying corn.

3 Toss in any flavorings from below. Pour into a large bowl. Enjoy the movie.

play  with it

Toss your popcorn with:

* 2 tablespoons real butter, melted

* A grated clove of garlic sautéed with 2 tablespoons olive oil

* A sprinkle of seeds like sesame, hemp, and chia

* A dash of Bragg liquid aminos or soy sauce

* A pinch of truffle or garlic salt

* Chili powder and lime juice

* Chopped fresh herbs like chives, dill, and thyme

* 2 tablespoons Parmesan cheese

romy's guacamole

makes about 2 cups
PREP TIME: 15 minutes

It's green and delicious. And maybe it is—but maybe it's not—avocado (see Play with it).

3 soft-ripe avocados

1 tablespoon chopped fresh cilantro or oregano

1 garlic clove, minced

2 tablespoons chopped red onion

Juice of 1 lime, or to taste

Salt

Combine the **avocado**, **cilantro**, **garlic** and **onion** in a bowl and mash with a potato masher until smooth and creamy. Season with **lime juice** and **salt** to taste.

play with it

To make peacamole or edamole: Replace the avocado with 3 cups thawed green peas or shelled edamame. Put them into a food processor and whir until smooth. Add the remaining ingredients. Season to taste.

cook's tip

Does an avocado pit keep my guacamole green? Nope! Well, yes it does, but only right where the pit is covering the guacamole. The key is to keep air from touching the guacamole, so lay a piece of wax paper, a flat plate, or a thin layer of salsa directly onto the guacamole. The lime or lemon juice will also help prevent the avocado from oxidizing too quickly.

hummus

makes 2½ cups
PREP TIME: 15 minutes

A dip that is good for you? Oh yes it is! Blend chickpeas or (for a bright green hummus) edamame with sesame tahini and you have a protein-packed dip that's rich in omega-3s and fiber. Add a lot of lemon juice and garlic too, and you have a dip that will make any vegetable happy to be dunked.

¼ cup tahini paste

¼ cup fresh lemon juice

¼ cup water

2 tablespoons olive oil

1 small garlic clove

¼ teaspoon ground cumin

1 can (15 ounces) organic chickpeas, drained, or 1½ cups thawed shelled edamame (green soybeans)

Salt

Parsley, olive oil, paprika, and cumin, for garnish (optional)

1 Combine the **tahini, lemon juice, water, garlic, olive oil,** and **cumin** in a blender and blend away until frothy, white, and creamy.

2 Adding them a handful at a time, blend the **chickpeas** or **edamame** with the tahini mixture until it is the consistency of Greek yogurt. Add **salt** to taste.

3 Swirl the hummus into a shallow bowl. Garnish with **parsley,** a drizzle of **olive oil,** and a sprinkling of **paprika** and **cumin,** if desired.

way better than store-bought. way.

baked tortilla chips

makes 4 to 6 servings

PREP TIME: 5 minutes   BAKING TIME: 15 to 17 minutes

Tortilla chips were invented to use up leftover tortillas in a glorious way. Baking them instead of frying gets you that dippable crunch without all the fat and with much more flavor than the store-bought kind.

2 teaspoons olive oil, plus a bit more for the baking sheets

10 corn tortillas (The thinner the tortilla, the crisper the chip.)

A sprinkle of salt

1 Preheat the oven to 400°F. Rub 2 baking sheets with **oil**.

2 Stack the **tortillas** and cut them in half, then into quarters. Transfer to a bowl and toss with the 2 teaspoons **oil** and the **salt**.

3 Spread the chips out on the baking sheets, but don't let them overlap as this will prevent them from crisping up. Bake for 10 minutes, turn over with a spatula and, if you need to, rearrange the darker ones to the center of the baking sheet. Bake until they crisp up, about 7 minutes longer. For the crispest chips, turn off the oven and leave the chips in there until they cool.

play * with it

Before baking, toss with chili powder, a dash of garlic powder, and a touch of cumin.

wafer-thin slices of deliciosity

oven sweet potato wafers

makes 2 or 3 servings
PREP TIME: 10 minutes   BAKING TIME: 20 minutes

Crisp on the outside, tender in the center—these chips make for a delicious afternoon snack or side dish. Call it a chip, but know it is a vitamin-packed, fiber-full vegetable.

1 tablespoon plus 1 teaspoon olive oil

1 medium organic sweet potato (unpeeled), scrubbed and thinly sliced (as thin as you can!) into rounds on a mandoline* or by hand

A pinch of salt

*If you are using the mandoline, pleeeeasse take care of your fingers—that last stump of potato isn't worth a stump of your finger!

**Since the sweet potatoes bake so briefly, the oven temperature is important. If your oven runs hot or cold, just keep an eye on them and take them out when golden.

1 Preheat the oven to 400°F** with the racks in the middle and bottom half. Rub each of 2 baking sheets with ½ teaspoon **oil** (don't use parchment paper as this will prevent crispiness).

2 In a medium bowl, toss the **sweet potato slices** with the remaining 1 tablespoon oil and the **salt**, making sure they are evenly covered .

3 Spread the slices out on the baking sheets. Try not to let them overlap, as this will prevent them from crisping up. Bake for about 10 minutes . . . do not walk away! These little chips need your full attention just for a few minutes more (or else they get too dark). Take the baking sheets out and flip the chips with a spatula; if you need to, rearrange the darker ones to the center of the baking sheet. Bake until they crisp up, about 7 minutes longer. Eat warm, as they soften as they cool.

play with it

★ Before baking, toss with chopped fresh rosemary or mint.

★ Add a dash of smoked paprika and garlic powder when you toss with the oil.

★ After baking, give them a squeeze of fresh lime and a sprinkle of chili powder.

why  'cause . . .

The oil conducts heat, making sure they bake evenly. If they are baked without oil they will become dry and rubbery.

seedy crackers

makes 40 or more crackers, and be sure to let everyone know YOU made them

PREP TIME: 30 minutes   BAKING TIME: 30 minutes

You don't have to be crackers to make your own: Just mix a quick dough, roll it out on parchment paper, cut, and throw the whole sheet into the oven. If you really *like* fiddling with dough, you can cut it into shapes like . . . fishy crackers. Our version isn't filled with artificial colors and flavors.

2 cups mixed seeds (like sesame, pumpkin, and flaxseeds), plus more for sprinkling

2 cups whole wheat (or white whole wheat) flour

½ cup olive or nut oil

1 tablespoon baking powder

1 teaspoon salt, plus more for sprinkling

1 cup water

kids in charge

* Measure the seeds.
* Mix all the ingredients together.
* Roll out the dough.
* Poke pretty patterns with a fork.
* Cut the crackers.

play with it

* Use poppy, hemp, or chia seeds.
* Add spices to the dough, such as 1 teaspoon smoked paprika, curry powder, or turmeric.
* Add 2 teaspoons crushed whole cumin or fennel seeds.
* Add ¼ cup Parmesan cheese for cheesy crackers.
* For shiny crackers, brush with a little beaten egg white before baking.

1 Preheat the oven to 350°F with the racks in the middle and bottom half.

2 Combine the **seeds, flour, oil, baking powder,** and **salt** with the **water** in a large bowl and mix with a wooden spoon or your hands until you have a shaggy soft dough. Divide the dough into 2 balls.

3 Tear off 2 pieces of parchment paper the size of your baking sheet. Put a dough ball onto each piece of parchment and top each with a large piece of plastic wrap. With a rolling pin (or empty wine bottle if that is what you have), roll the dough balls out into rectangles. They should be as thin as a lasagna noodle (that's thin, friend!) and almost the size and shape of the parchment paper.

4 Remove the plastic wrap and poke the dough all over with the tines of a fork. With a pizza cutter, knife, or cookie cutter, cut the dough into rectangles, squares, diamonds, or shape of your choice. Don't pull the crackers apart. Sprinkle with extra seeds and a little salt as garnish. Slide each parchment paper with the crackers onto baking sheets.

5 Bake for 20 minutes. Remove any crackers at the edges that are golden, flip the rest of the crackers with a spatula, breaking them at their seams, and bake until they are lightly golden, about 10 minutes longer. Transfer to a rack to cool (they will crisp up as they do). Store in an airtight container in the fridge for 2 weeks or in the freezer for a 2 to 3 months.

kale chips

makes 4 to 6 servings

PREP TIME: 15 minutes   BAKING TIME: 20 to 25 minutes

As good for you as they are addictive—and a great way to start the little ones loving kale.

2 tablespoons olive or grapeseed oil, plus a little more for the baking sheets

2 bunches kale or collards, washed and thoroughly dried, ribs removed, and leaves torn into bite-size pieces

A sprinkle of salt

1 Preheat the oven to 300°F. Coat 2 or 3 baking sheets with **oil**.

2 Combine the **kale** and 2 tablespoons **oil** in a large bowl and massage the oil into the leaves, making sure every bit is covered.

3 Arrange the kale in a single layer on the baking sheets and bake for 20 to 25 minutes, flipping the kale now and then with tongs and turning the baking sheets or switching racks if the kale starts to brown too quickly in spots. The kale will go dark green and crispy; do not to let it brown. Sprinkle with **salt**.

play * with it

★ Mix a little grated garlic into the olive oil.

★ Toss with Japanese seaweed salt.

★ Sprinkle with sesame seeds.

★ Add a little chili for spice.

tomato bruschetta

makes 4 to 6 servings
PREP TIME: 20 minutes

Eve is what you might call a picky eater, but in an unexpected way: She refuses to eat anything that isn't real. Eve started cooking "as soon as possible," her mom says. Now, at the well-seasoned age of 11, she regularly hands her mother shopping lists with ingredient requests for her latest dishes. (True story.) When Eve seeks out new recipes, often with unfamiliar ingredients, she discovers that she loves foods she had previously refused to eat. Take tomatoes: She hadn't eaten them until she saw a recipe for bruschetta. Now tomato bruschetta is in regular rotation. Late summer is the season to really enjoy tomatoes. Collect a variety of colors—yellow, green, and red—then dice them and serve with thin slices of toasted bread for a richly hued afternoon snack (toss what's left into pasta or on fish for dinner, or fold them into your eggs for breakfast).

3 cups chopped tomatoes, the very sweetest you can find

2 garlic cloves, sliced

¼ cup fresh basil leaves, torn into small pieces, a few leaves saved for garnish

½ cup good-quality extra virgin olive oil

2 tablespoons balsamic vinegar

Salt and freshly ground black pepper

Grilled or toasted bread

1 Combine the **tomatoes, garlic,** torn **basil, olive oil, vinegar,** and **salt** and **pepper** to taste in a large bowl and toss to combine. Taste! Add more vinegar, salt, or olive oil if you think it needs it.

2 Cover and let stand at room temperature for 30 minutes. Serve spooned over grilled bread slices.

it's a dip. it's a sauce. it's a topping!

salsa

makes 2 cups
PREP TIME: 20 minutes

Serve this with eggs, in tacos, on soup, and around chips. It's fresh, vibrant, and good for you, too!

2 tablespoons minced red onion

Juice of 1 lime

½ teaspoon salt

1 to 2 small garlic cloves, minced

1 pound tomatoes, diced

Dash of Worcestershire sauce (optional)

2 tablespoons chopped fresh cilantro leaves

½ small jalapeño pepper, seeded and minced (optional)

Combine the **onion**, **lime juice**, and **salt** in a medium bowl and let sit for a few minutes ❓. Add the **garlic**, **tomatoes**, Worcestershire (if using), **cilantro**, and **jalapeño** (if using). Taste and adjust the seasonings.

why ❓ 'cause . . .

This will take some of the bite off the onions.

zzzz . . .

sleepy time tea

makes enough for twenty 6-ounce cups
PREP TIME: 15 minutes   STEEPING TIME: 5 minutes

Sip this soothing herbal tea from a nice big mug after dinner. You can find the herbs in a well-stocked health food market, or if you are lucky to have a garden, you can grow and dry them yourself.

1 tablespoon dried lavender blossoms
(for happiness)

½ cup dried mint leaves
(for grace)

½ cup dried chamomile
(for peace)

1 tablespoon fennel seeds
(for health)

2 tablespoons dried rose petals
(for beauty)

1 Combine the **lavender blossoms, mint leaves, chamomile, fennel seeds,** and **rose petals** in a 2-cup lidded jar. Store in a cool dark place.

2 For a serving, bring 1 cup water to a boil. Remove from the heat. Add 1 tablespoon tea mixture and steep for 5 minutes. Strain, blow, and sip.

real mint tea

makes 1 serving
STEEPING TIME: 5 minutes

If you have a small patch of land, even if it's as small as a pot on a windowsill, grow some mint. It's hardy enough to withstand the blackest thumb and enlivens everything it touches, especially a cup of water.

2 large sprigs of fresh mint with 10 to 15 leaves on each

1 cup boiling water

Honey (optional)

Crush the **mint** between your hands and inhale deeply, then stuff them into a mug. Pour the **boiling water** over them and let seep for 5 minutes. Remove the mint if you must. Swirl in a bit of **honey** if you care to. Sip thoughtfully.

hop on this pop

Add the freshest ingredients to soda water for naturally sweet and tangy treats.

Cucumber Lime Pop

Makes 1 serving

PREP TIME: 5 MINUTES

Ice cubes

3 slices cucumber

2 to 4 fresh mint leaves

1 tablespoon honey

1 teaspoon fresh lime or lemon juice

¾ cup (6 ounces) sparkling water

Put a handful of **ice**, the **cucumber slices**, **mint leaves**, **honey**, and **lime juice** in a large jar or cocktail shaker, cover, and shake hard. Add **sparkling water**. Taste! Add more lime or honey, if you like. Pour into a glass and enjoy.

play with it

* Add a splash of vanilla.
* Garnish with mint leaves and slices of cucumber.

Vanilla Maple Cream Soda

Makes 1 serving

PREP TIME: 5 MINUTES

½ teaspoon vanilla extract

1 tablespoon maple syrup

¾ cup (6 ounces) sparkling water

Ice cubes

Combine the **vanilla**, **maple syrup**, and **sparkling water** in a tall glass. Stir, add **ice** to fill, and sip.

Watermelon Cooler

Makes 1 or 2 servings

PREP TIME: 10 MINUTES

1 cup cubed seedless watermelon

6 fresh mint leaves

Ice cubes

½ cup (4 ounces) sparkling water

1 Combine the **watermelon** and **mint** in a blender and blend until smooth. Pour into 1 or 2 glasses filled with **ice**, top with the **sparkling water** and serve.

2 Slurp

play  with it

* Add a sliver of ginger to the blender for spice.
* Add a squeeze of lime for sparkle.

Ginger Pop

Makes 4 servings

PREP TIME: 10 MINUTES

¼ cup chopped and peeled fresh ginger

1 cup tap water

¼ cup honey

Juice of 1 lime

Ice cubes

3 cups (24 ounces) sparkling water

Combine the **ginger**, 1 cup **water**, **honey**, and **lime juice** in a blender and blend for 30 seconds. Strain through a sieve. Pour the ginger syrup into 4 large glasses filled with **ice**, top with the **sparkling water**, and serve.

play with it

* Add a little vanilla extract.
* Add some grated lime or orange zest.
* Add hot water instead of sparkling water for a wintertime tea.

. . . also try hazelnut, cashew, or macadamia nut milk

almond milk

makes 4 cups

PREP TIME: 15 minutes   SOAKING TIME: 8 hours

If you have nuts and 15 minutes to spare, you can have the freshest and most flavorful almond milk in town. Use nut milk as you would regular milk: on your cereal, when you bake, or in your Purple Power Smoothie (page 84).

1½ cups almonds, hazelnuts, cashews, or macadamias (you can even use sunflower or hemp seeds), soaked overnight in water to cover

A pinch of salt

4 cups water

1 Drain and rinse the **nuts** and transfer to a blender. Add the **salt** and 2 cups **water** and blend until the almonds have become frothy and completely smooth, 3 to 4 minutes. Turn off the blender and add the remaining 2 cups water.

2 Strain the milk through a nut milk bag* into a bowl, forcing the liquid out, a movement curiously similar to milking a cow. If you don't have a bag, pour the milk through a strainer lined with cheesecloth. Do not throw the precious pulp away!**

3 Pour the milk into a jug and store, covered, in the refrigerator. Use within 4 days. Give it a shake before drinking.

If you plan to make lots, nut milk bags make both the milk and the process run smoother. You can find them in health food stores and online.

**Leftover almond pulp can be folded into muffin and pancake mixes or dehydrated and used for baking.*

play  with it

Add:

★ A date or three for sweetness.

★ A pinch of cinnamon—to help regulate blood sugar, for its antimicrobial properties, and because it will make you happy.

★ A splash of vanilla extract.

★ A tablespoon or two of honey.

★ A touch of turmeric, for its anti-inflammatory talents and it sunny yellow hue.

diiiiiiiner!

Sunday dinner, fast and easy enough to make Monday through Friday

weekday roast chicken with lemon and garlic

makes 4 to 6 servings

PREP TIME: 20 minutes   ROASTING TIME: 50 minutes to 1 hour

Roasted chicken and potatoes that are fragrant with garlic and lemon . . . on a weeknight? Yes! Your butcher is the key to making this speedy version of the weekend staple. Ask him or her kindly to butterfly the chicken (or see directions below), so it can roast faster by lying flat on the baking sheet. Buy an organic chicken whenever possible—they're happier, healthier, much tastier, and worth every extra cent. The earlier you salt the chicken (even as far as a day or 2 in advance), the moister and more flavorful it will be. You can also cheat and get a kosher chicken, which has already been salted.

   The beauty of this recipe is that it only requires your attention for a few minutes. Lay the chicken on a bed of potatoes, garlic, and lemons and pop it in the oven. After that, you can leave it alone while you call your kids to set the table, make a salad, and catch up on your family's day.

One 3-pound chicken, preferably organic and free-range, butterflied (see Cook's Tip)

Salt

Olive oil for the baking sheet, plus 1½ tablespoons for the bird

1 pound small potatoes* (unpeeled), halved or quartered

8 garlic cloves (unpeeled)

1 lemon, cut crosswise into ¼-inch-thick slices

Try purple potatoes, which are the healthiest of all due to their antioxidants!

1 Sprinkle the **chicken** with 2 teaspoons **salt** as soon as you get it home.

2 Preheat the oven to 450°F. Grease a rimmed baking sheet with **oil**.

3 In a large bowl, toss the **potatoes** with 1 tablespoon of the olive oil, a goodly sprinkle of salt, the **garlic**, and the **lemon slices**. Arrange them on the center of the baking sheet and slide it into the oven for a few minutes.

play with it

★ Before roasting, rub minced garlic and chopped fresh herbs such as rosemary, thyme, or sage all over the chicken. Scatter any leftover herbs on the baking sheet.

★ Add parsnips, carrots, sliced squash, slicded sweet potatoes, or turnips along with the potatoes. Replace the lemon slices with oranges or limes.

★ Just before serving, toss fresh arugula with the hot potatoes.

4 Meanwhile, pat the chicken dry with paper towels . Rub all over with olive oil and, if you did not do so earlier, sprinkle with 2 teaspoons of salt.

5 Remove the potatoes from the oven and arrange the chicken on top of them, tucking any stray potatoes and garlic under the chicken to prevent them from burning. Roast until the juices run clear when the joint between thigh and the drumstick is pricked with a knife, or when a meat thermometer inserted in the thickest part of the thigh reads 165°F, 40 to 45 minutes. Transfer the chicken to a cutting board to rest and return the potatoes to the oven to crisp up, 5 to 10 minutes more.

6 Cut the chicken in half along the breast, then cut each breast in half and divide the legs into thighs and drumsticks. Arrange the potatoes on a platter, top with the chicken pieces, and squeeze a few of the roasted lemon slices over it all.

 why  'cause . . .

This is such a small step but an important one. Whenever you roast or fry anything, be it vegetable or beast, drying the surface will help it get crisp quicker and more evenly.

why  'cause . . .

Right when meat (any kind of meat) comes off the heat, the juices inside are under pressure to get out. If you cut into it right away, the juices will escape; however, if you let the meat rest for just a few minutes, the juices remain in the meat and keep it moist.

cook's tip

How to butterfly a chicken: Place the chicken, breast-side down, on a cutting board. Starting at the tail end, cut along one side of the backbone with kitchen shears or a sharp knife. Turn the chicken (still breast-side down) and cut along the other side of the backbone. Save the backbone in the freezer for stock. Flip the chicken over and open it like a book. Press firmly on the breastbone to flatten.

balsamic chicken with grains and greens

makes 6 servings

PREP TIME: 20 to 30 minutes   COOKING TIME: 1 hour

Here is a saucy chicken for you! With both greens and grains, this is a one-pot dinner you can just slide onto the table with a bright salad and a crunchy whole-grain baguette.

12 boneless, skinless chicken thighs ❓, trimmed of fat

Salt and freshly ground black pepper or red pepper flakes

2 teaspoons chopped fresh thyme

Olive oil, for the pot

1 medium onion, thinly sliced

8 ounces mushrooms (button, shiitake, or your favorite), sliced (about 3 cups)

6 garlic cloves, chopped

3 tablespoons balsamic vinegar

2 cans (14 ounces each) diced tomatoes with their juices, or 3½ cups chopped fresh tomatoes

1 cup pearled barley

3 cups chopped greens, such as kale, chard, or collards

Braise: To slowly cook something partially submerged in a flavorful liquid.

1 Preheat the oven to 350°F and position the rack in the lower third.

2 Toss together the **chicken**, ½ teaspoon **salt**, and the **thyme** in a large bowl. Set aside.

3 Heat a Dutch oven or large ovenproof pot over medium-high heat. Drizzle it with enough **olive oil** to coat the bottom. Add the **onion, mushrooms,** and **garlic** and cook until golden and fragrant, about 10 minutes. Add the **vinegar** and let sizzle for a minute. Add the **tomatoes** and **barley** and bring to a simmer. Season with **salt** and **black pepper** or **pepper flakes** to taste (it will taste quite tart but the flavors will mellow down as they cook).

4 Gently bury the chicken thighs in the pot, add enough water to just cover the chicken (about 1 cup), and return to a simmer. Slide the pot into the oven and **braise,** uncovered, for 20 minutes. Remove the pot from the oven and fold in the **greens**; add more water if it seems dry. Cover the pot and return to the oven to braise until the barley is tender, about 20 minutes. Taste! . . . Does it need a final splash of balsamic to brighten the flavor? Some salt or pepper flakes?

play ✳ with it   why ❓ 'cause . . .

* Once you have added the chicken to the pot, stir in 1 tablespoon each capers and mustard.

* Garnish with plenty of parsley.

Why the thigh? When you cook chicken slowly in a lot of liquid, it tends to dry out (strange but true), which is why it is wise to use dark meat, which is naturally moister. And besides, a chicken is not just a breast.

"After you have done all the cooking, the most important thing is to eat it in good company, even if you are by yourself. I set the table every night—water glass, wineglass—and I sit down. Frequently it's just me. I do it for myself."

—JESSICA HARRIS,
COOKBOOK AUTHOR

chicken adobo

makes 6 servings

PREP TIME: 15 minutes   COOKING TIME: 50 minutes

It can't get much simpler than this: Sauté onions, garlic, and ginger until they are sweet and golden, add 3 more ingredients, and simmer while you start a pot of rice and toss a salad. This is a perfect example of how, when you balance flavors—sweet (onions and garlic), tart (vinegar), salty (soy sauce), and a bit of spice (ginger)—you end up with a dish that is perfectly irresistible.

Grapeseed or other high-heat oil, for the pot

6 to 8 garlic cloves, smashed

3 inches fresh ginger, thinly sliced lengthwise

1 small onion, sliced

One 3- to 4-pound chicken, preferably organic and free-range, cut into serving pieces

½ cup reduced-sodium soy sauce

½ cup seasoned rice vinegar (or ⅓ cup apple cider vinegar mixed with 1 teaspoon honey)

½ cup water

Asian chili sauce (optional)

1 Heat a large heavy-bottomed pot over medium-high heat. Add enough **oil** to cover the bottom. Add the **garlic**, **ginger**, and **onion** and cook until golden and fragrant, 2 to 3 minutes. Add the **chicken**, **soy sauce**, **rice vinegar**, and **water**.

2 Bring to a boil, reduce the heat to medium-low (isn't your house starting to smell good now?), pop on a lid, and simmer for 30 minutes, giving it a good stir now and then. Uncover and simmer for 15 minutes more to allow the sauce to reduce a bit. Taste! What do you think: A little more vinegar? Perhaps some **Asian chili sauce**? Or how about more soy sauce?

play ✱ with it

★ Add a bay leaf and a pinch of red pepper flakes to the pot when you add the water.

★ Garnish with thinly sliced scallions, chopped cilantro, or chives.

★ If you have a pot large enough, double the recipe and freeze half for a busy night.

a crispy quinoa (yes quinoa!) crust

crunchy chicken strips

makes 6 servings

PREP TIME: 20 minutes   BROILING TIME: 10 minutes

By now, we hope you have said "no" to processed nuggets and fingers. Instead, how about taking some real chicken, tossing it with real eggs, a little tangy mustard, and a crunchy quinoa coating? No weird ingredients, no funky chicken parts, just real chicken, real simple, real good. Serve with Farm Dressing (page 139) or Homemade Ketchup (page 238) for dipping. A Caesar Kale Salad (page 125) and sweet potato would also be nice.

1¼ pounds boneless, skinless chicken breasts, preferably organic and free-range

Salt and freshly ground black pepper

¾ cup quinoa (rinsed if needed)

1 cup flour (any kind: wheat flour, rice flour, gluten-free baking flour . . .)

2 eggs

1 tablespoon mustard (your favorite kind)

½ cup grated Parmesan cheese

1 tablespoon olive oil

cook's tip

If there are days you prefer to use bread-crumbs instead of quinoa, use 1½ cups, and rather than broil the chicken, bake on an oiled baking sheet for 20 minutes at 350°F.

play with it

★ Spice them up with a few dashes of hot sauce added to the eggs.

★ Go the herby route by adding chopped chives, parsley, or thyme to the quinoa mixture.

★ Make them tangy and add a squeeze of lemon to the eggs and the grated zest to the quinoa mixture.

1 Cut any fatty bits off the **chicken** and if a breast has a "tender" (the extra strip under the breast), cut it off as well. Slice each chicken breast length-wise into 3 or 4 thick strips, about 2 fingers wide. Drop them (and the chicken tenders) into a bowl, toss with 1 teaspoon **salt**, and pop into the fridge.

2 Cook the **quinoa** in a pot of salted boiling water until tender, about 12 minutes. Drain extra well.

3 Get out 3 shallow containers. Put the **flour** in one. Lightly beat the **eggs** with **mustard** in the second. In the third container, toss the quinoa with the **Parmesan** (and any extra ingredients—see Play with It!), then taste to see if you would like to add **salt** and **pepper**.

4 Dip each chicken strip first into the flour so it is white, shaking off the excess, then into the egg (it is helpful to use tongs for this) so it is yellow, then press it hard (hard!) into the quinoa so it gets completely coated on both sides.

5 Preheat the broiler with a rack about 6 inches from the heat. Drizzle the **olive oil** onto a rimmed baking sheet. Slide it into the oven to heat it (this helps to achieve a crispier crust). When the baking sheet is hot, remove it from the oven and place the strips on it. Using tongs, flip them over so that the strips are coated on both sides with oil.

6 Broil the chicken until golden, about 5 minutes. Flip over and broil 5 minutes more or until the chicken loses its pink color.

chicken sausage with caramelized onions, broccoli, and cheesy grits

makes 4 to 6 servings
PREP TIME: 20 minutes   COOKING TIME: 30 minutes

Imagine an Italian grandma gazing out over the Tuscan hills, stirring a big copper pot of simmering polenta, then serving it on a big white platter smothered in sausages, slowly caramelized onions, and bitter greens, all topped with melting cheese and home-canned tomatoes. Now imagine making this dinner yourself, but in only 30 minutes! Polenta is a fancy Italian word for grits, which spells comfort for many of us. Even Grandma will be happy to sit down at your table for this flavorful dinner.

2 cups milk (dairy or unsweetened nut or soy)

2 cups water

1 cup quick grits (not instant)

1 teaspoon salt

A few grinds of black pepper

Olive oil, for the pot

4 medium Italian-style chicken sausages (organic, free-range, like Applegate) or vegetarian sausages

2 medium onions, sliced

2 garlic cloves, finely chopped

1 large head broccoli, finely chopped

3 cups tomato sauce with no added sugar

½ cup grated cheddar cheese
(the sharper it is, the cheesier it will taste)

play with it

* Add a sprig of rosemary to the grits; remove before serving
* Shower the finished dish with fresh herbs.
* Pass Parmesan and hot sauce at the table.
* Swap kale, spinach, or chard for broccoli.

kids  in charge

Pull the broccoli apart, peel the broccoli stem, and crunch on the tender heart.

1 Bring the **milk** and **water** to a gentle boil in a large heavy-bottomed pot. While whisking constantly, add the **grits** in a slow stream. Stir in the **salt** and **pepper** and reduce the heat to medium-low. Continue stirring, while humming cheerfully, until the grits thicken up, about 4 minutes. Keep warm over very gentle heat.

2 Heat a large heavy skillet over medium heat. Drizzle in enough **olive oil** to thinly cover the bottom. Add the **sausages** and cook until golden and cooked through. Transfer to a cutting board and slice them thickly on an angle, or into bite-size pieces. You can even leave them whole. Put them aside.

3 Wipe out the skillet, heat over medium-high heat, and add 2 tablespoons olive oil to it. Add the **onions** and cook until they caramelize and the edges are crispy, about 10 minutes. Add the **garlic** and **broccoli** and cook until the broccoli is just tender, 4 to 5 minutes.

4 In a small pot, heat the **tomato sauce** to a simmer.

5 Fold the **cheddar** into the grits. You want the consistency of soft porridge, so if you need to thin them out a bit, add a little milk. Taste the grits for seasonings. When they don't need a thing more, pour them onto your big Thanksgiving platter, top with the sausages and a mess of onions and broccoli. Serve with the tomato sauce on the side.

just plain chicken

makes 6 servings (plus leftovers for lunch)

PREP TIME: 10 minutes   ROASTING TIME: 35 to 40 minutes

When asked, our friend Michele, a mom of 4, said "I just want a recipe for plain chicken." Sometimes that's all you want, no fussing and mussing. The problem is that unless you know a couple of tricks, a plain chicken breast can end up plain old boring and dry. You never want that. So for when you want chicken that is moist, with crisp skin, chicken that you can serve immediately with a salad, or shred for tacos, or cube for lunch salads, or do whatever it is you do with plain, juicy, tasty chicken . . . here are a couple tricks.

★ It makes a huge difference what kind of chicken you buy. Buy good, fresh, organic chicken. It's better for you, it tastes better, and it's better for the bird! You never buy funky fruit do you? So why buy funky chicken?

★ Keep the bones in and the skin on. Both will keep the chicken moister. You can always remove them later.

★ Salt the chicken as far in advance as possible . . . a great trick for both moist and flavorful roasted chicken.

2 whole bone-in, skin-on chicken breasts (about 1½ pounds each)

Salt and freshly ground black pepper

Seasonings of choice: see Play with It! (below)

1 Pat the **chicken** dry with paper towels and sprinkle each with ½ teaspoon **salt**.

2 Preheat the oven to 450°F and position the rack in the middle.

3 Pat the chicken dry with paper towels and sprinkle with **pepper** and **seasonings** of choice. Set the chicken breasts on a baking sheet, skin-side up.

4 Roast until the juices run clear when poked with a knife, or when a meat thermometer inserted in the thickest part reads 160°F, 35 to 40 minutes. Transfer chicken to cutting board and let rest for 5 minutes. Cut each breast through the middle from top to bottom, then crosswise into halves or thirds.

play  with it

Before roasting:

★ Sprinkle with finely chopped garlic, lemon zest, and thyme.

★ Sprinkle with finely chopped garlic, rosemary, and sage.

★ Rub the chicken with a little olive oil or butter.

★ Roast the chicken on a bed of thinly sliced potatoes or sweet potatoes.

★ Roast the chicken on a bed of thinly sliced onions, olives, and sliced lemons drizzled with olive oil.

After roasting:

★ Rub with a little herb butter.

★ Squeeze with a goodly amount of lemon.

★ Drizzle with a balsamic or mustard vinaigrette.

★ Serve with a side of fresh salsa, on a bed of bitter greens dressed with a mustardy dressing, or on a platter of creamy lentils or beans.

a vibrantly healthy little present

gift-wrapped fish

makes 4 servings
PREP TIME: 30 minutes   COOKING TIME: 35 minutes (divided)

This fish is a gift: Did you know that black cod has almost as many omega-3s as salmon? Add super healthy shiitake mushrooms and some greens and your body will be thanking you. The packages can be made in advance, then popped in the oven while you steam a little rice or quinoa.

Olive oil, for the baking sheet

2 to 3 cups shiitake or button mushrooms, stems discarded, thinly sliced

4 teaspoons toasted sesame oil

¼ cup plus 1 teaspoon reduced-sodium soy sauce

2 garlic cloves, minced

1½ pounds skinless black cod, salmon, or other mild fish, pin bones removed (have the fishmonger do this for you)

8 asparagus, woody ends snapped off, thinly sliced crosswise or lengthwise

2 bunches baby bok choy, thinly sliced

¼ cup seasoned rice vinegar (or 2 tablespoons white wine vinegar or lime juice mixed with a dab of honey)

play with it

* Feel free to use other vegetables; slice them thinly so that they cook quickly. Grated carrots or sweet potatoes, thinly sliced peppers, and cabbage all work well.

* Add 1 teaspoon chopped fresh ginger to the mushrooms.

* Slip some fresh herbs such as chopped chives, cilantro, or mint into the package.

* For a touch of Thai flavor, add 1 tablespoon coconut milk to each package.

* Pass Asian chili sauce if you care to.

1 Preheat the oven to 450°F with the rack in the middle. Grease a baking sheet with a thin coat of **olive oil**. Tear off 4 pieces of foil, each about the size of a dinner plate, and fit each into 4 wide soup bowls.

2 Toss together the **mushrooms** with 2 teaspoons of the **sesame oil**, 1 teaspoon of the **soy sauce**, and the **garlic** in a medium bowl. Spread them on the baking sheet and pop them in the hot oven to roast until golden, about 15 minutes. Remove them but leave the oven on. Meanwhile, cut the **fish** into cubes. Into each foil-lined bowl, place the **asparagus**, top with the fish, then the **bok choy**.

3 When the mushrooms are done, add them to the bowls. Whisk together the **rice vinegar**, and the remaining ¼ cup **soy sauce** and 2 teaspoons **sesame oil** and drizzle over the fish, dividing it evenly. Tear and lay a second piece of foil on top of the fish and crimp the edges into an airtight seal.

4 Transfer the packages, seam side up (without the bowls), onto 2 baking sheets and bake for 15 to 20 minutes. Take the packages out and peek into one: The fish should flake easily when a knife is inserted into it.

The fancy way to serve:
Carefully open each packet and, using a spatula, transfer the contents to individual plates. Pour the juices from each packet over each plate and serve immediately.

The festive way to serve:
Place the packet directly on a dinner plate and let guests open their own gifts.

looks like a restaurant dish, feels like home

miso-glazed black cod

makes 4 servings

PREP TIME: 45 minutes   BROILING TIME: 6 to 8 minutes

Fancy chefs make this fancy fish in fancy restaurants, but it's so easy you can make it in your own kitchen. Sweet, savory miso glaze is good on almost any fish, so if salmon or mahi-mahi are your favorites, go ahead and use them instead. The fish gets better if you can marinate it overnight, but if all you have is 30 minutes, you will still be very happy. Serve with steamed vegetables and a bowl of rice.

4 pieces (6 ounces each) skinless black cod fillet*

⅓ cup white miso

⅓ cup maple syrup or honey

⅓ cup mirin**

1 tablespoon grated fresh ginger

1 tablespoon toasted sesame oil

Grapeseed or other high-heat oil, for the baking sheet

* Like salmon, black cod has a row of pin bones that run through the middle of each fillet; ask your fishmonger kindly to carefully remove them for you, or you can remove them yourself with tongs after cooking.

**Mirin is sweetened rice wine and can be found in the soy sauce section of the supermarket.

1 In a bowl large enough to hold your **fish**, whisk together the **miso, maple syrup, mirin, ginger,** and **sesame oil.** Put the fish into the bowl and with a spoon, completely cover it with the marinade. Cover the bowl with a plate and marinate in the refrigerator for at least 30 minutes or overnight—the longer the tastier.

2 Right before dinner, preheat the broiler with a rack about 6 inches from the heat. **Oil** a baking sheet.

3 Lightly shake off any excess marinade clinging to the fish and place the fillets in the center of the baking sheet. Broil until the glaze is dark and shiny and you feel no resistance when you poke a knife into the fish ❓, 6 to 8 minutes.

why ❓ 'cause . . .

This is the easiest way to tell if fish is done: If there is some resistance and the fish does not easily flake apart when poked with a knife, just pop it back under the broiler for another minute or two.

salmon coconut curry with vegetables

makes 4 to 6 servings

PREP TIME: 30 minutes   BAKING TIME: 25 minutes

Fish is so good for you! If you can have it once or twice a week, you will be adding important omega-3s and protein to your diet. This beautiful dish deserves good company. Prepare everything earlier in the day, then bake once the guests arrive. Scatter on fresh herbs if you care to. Serve with rice, a squeeze of lime, and a side of Thai chili sauce. Leftovers last up to 3 days in the fridge. Stir-fried together with rice it makes a perfect lunch.

4 to 6 pieces (6 ounces each) skinless salmon fillet (wild Alaskan salmon if you can get it)

Salt

2 carrots, julienned or grated in long strips (unpeeled if organic)

1 cup snow peas or sugar snap peas, topped and tailed, strings removed

1 zucchini, cut into matchsticks or cut with a julienne peeler

Grapeseed oil, rice bran oil, or other high-heat oil

3 scallions (white and green parts), chopped

2 garlic cloves, chopped

1 to 3 tablespoons red Thai curry paste*

1½ cups chopped fresh tomatoes or 1 can (14.5 ounces) diced tomatoes, drained

2 tablespoons fish sauce

1½ cups coconut milk

play ✳ with it

★ Add 1 tablespoon chopped fresh ginger to the scallions and garlic.

★ Garnish with fresh lime, chopped fresh cilantro, mint, or chives.

★ For a vegetarian curry, substitute 3 cups tofu for the salmon and throw a few extra vegetables into the curry sauce; simmer on the stovetop for 10 minutes, until the vegetables are cooked.

1 Preheat the oven to 450°F and place a rack in the middle of the oven. Season the **salmon** pieces with a big pinch of **salt**, cover, and refrigerate.

2 Toss together the **carrots**, **peas**, **zucchini**, 1 tablespoon **oil**, and a pinch of salt in a large bowl. Set aside.

3 Heat a medium skillet over medium-high heat. Drizzle in enough **oil** to coat the bottom. Slip in the **scallions** and **garlic** and cook until they begin to wilt, about 30 seconds. Add the **curry paste** and sizzle for a moment; add the **tomatoes**. Increase the heat to medium-high and simmer until the tomatoes begin to break down, 5 to 6 minutes. Whisk in the **fish sauce** and **coconut milk**. Taste and adjust the flavors by adding a little more curry or fish sauce. Take the pot off the stove.

4 Lightly oil a large ovenproof baking dish and arrange the salmon pieces in it so they are not too cramped. Top each piece of fish with a pile of the vegetables, then pour the curry sauce around the fish. Cover the dish with foil or an upturned baking sheet. Bake for 20 minutes (and start a pot of rice or quinoa). Poke a knife into the center of a piece of salmon. If it flakes easily apart, it is done, if not, bake for another 5 minutes.

Thai curry paste can be mild or very hot, depending on the brand, so start with a little, then continue with reckless abandon. If you don't have access to Thai curry paste, you can use 2 to 3 tablespoons of Indian curry powder instead. The flavor will be different, but still delicious.

a fast and flavorful way to pop your omegas

salmon cakes

makes 4 to 6 servings (about 12 small patties)
PREP TIME: 20 minutes   COOKING TIME: 40 minutes

Salmon (preferably wild and sustainably caught) is easy to find in a can, which is a good and inexpensive way to ensure that you always have a quick, omega-3–rich salmon dinner in the pantry. But best of all, these crunchy cakes are delicious! Bonus: This is actually two recipes in one. Before you add the eggs, you can serve the quinoa/salmon mixture as a salad on a bed of greens, or use it as a filling for wraps. Slip any leftover salmon cakes into a whole wheat wrap with cucumber, lemon, and shredded cabbage for lunch.

½ cup quinoa (rinsed if needed)

1½ cups water

3 cans (6 ounces each) water-packed salmon, drained and bones (if any) removed

Grated zest and juice of ½ lemon (or more to taste)

2 tablespoons mustard

½ small onion, minced

Salt and freshly ground black pepper

2 eggs

1 cup panko, whole wheat, or gluten-free breadcrumbs

Olive or grapeseed oil, for the baking sheet

Cucumber Yogurt Sauce (page 237)

play with it

To the salmon mixture, add:
* Chopped fresh herbs, such as parsley, dill, or chives
* Minced veggies, such as celery, peppers, corn, or capers

why 'cause . . .

This is a neat trick whenever you are oven "frying." A hot baking sheet will get your food sizzling to crispness much quicker. The food will also absorb less oil, and be less likely to stick.

1 Preheat the oven to 400°F and position the rack in middle. Place a baking sheet in the oven to preheat ❓.

2 Combine the **quinoa** with 1½ cups **water** in a pot. Simmer over medium-high heat for 20 minutes. This will result in quinoa that is softer than usual, helping to hold the cakes together. Drain thoroughly and let cool.

3 Mash the **salmon** with a fork in a medium bowl. Add 1 cup of the cooled quinoa, the **lemon zest** and **juice**, **mustard**, and **onion** and mash together. Taste the mixture: If it needs **salt** and **pepper** or a little more lemon, add it now. Push the mix a little to the side of the bowl so you can crack in the **eggs** and lightly beat them in the empty space. Then fold everything together.

4 Put the **breadcrumbs** in a shallow bowl. Plop a dollop of the salmon mixture (the size of a golf ball) into the breadcrumbs and roll it around so it gets completely covered. Fish out the ball and form it into a little ½-inch-thick patty. Set it aside on a plate and repeat with the remaining salmon mixture.

5 Coat the heated baking sheet with **oil**. Quickly arrange the patties on the baking sheet, leaving a little space between each one. Bake for 10 minutes, flip, and bake until golden and crisp, about 10 minutes more. Serve warm with the **sauce**.

crunchy roasted fish

makes 4 to 6 servings

PREP TIME: 15 minutes   ROASTING TIME: 15 minutes

Fish that crunches loudly, is baked rather than fried, and is ready in a jiffy . . . this is not a fish tale!

Olive oil, for the baking sheet

2 eggs

1 garlic clove, grated, or 1 teaspoon garlic powder

1 tablespoon Dijon mustard

½ teaspoon salt

1½ cups panko breadcrumbs

2 tablespoons grated Parmesan cheese

6 fillets (6 ounces each) mahi-mahi or other mild fish*

Lemon wedges, for serving

Check Monterey Bay Aquarium's seafoodwatch.org for a list of sustainable fish.

1 Preheat the oven to 475°F and position the rack in middle. Rub the **olive oil** all over a baking sheet and pop it in the oven to heat.

2 Crack the **eggs** into a bowl and beat in the **garlic**, **mustard**, and **salt**. In a shallow bowl, toss the **panko** with the **Parmesan**.

3 Pat the **fish** very dry with a paper towel , then turn each piece in the eggs until completely covered in egg. Now press the fish firmly into the panko, making sure each side is covered in breadcrumbs.

4 Arrange the fish on the hot baking sheet. Roast until golden brown, flipping half way through the cooking time, about 16 minutes. If the fish is not yet golden, put it under the broiler to color for just a moment, watching it carefully. Serve with **lemon wedges** and . . . Crunch!

why  'cause . . .

Eggs can't stick to wet fish (and fish is always wet) . . . and without eggs the breadcrumbs won't have anything to hang on to . . . so dry that fish well, and it will be all crunch.

play with it

★ Add freshly chopped herbs such as chives and parsley to the panko mixture.

★ Whisk grated lemon zest or hot sauce into the beaten eggs.

★ Serve with Farm Dressing (page 139).

lasagna in a cup! say what? (a recipe for big kids)

ravioli cupcakes

makes 12 "cupcakes"

PREP TIME: 30 minutes   BAKING TIME: 20 minutes

If you think about it, a ravioli is already a mini-layered lasagna. All it needs is some vegetables, sauce, and cheese, and another layer of the same, then . . . ta-da! A ravioli cupcake lasagna.

3 tablespoons olive oil

½ medium onion, diced

2 garlic cloves, minced

8 ounces frozen spinach or kale, thawed and squeezed dry

24 large vegetable ravioli (round ones fit best into muffin tins)

1 egg, lightly beaten

½ cup grated Parmesan cheese

4 cups of your favorite tomato sauce, store-bought or homemade (page 210)

1½ cups grated melting cheese, such as mozzarella, Fontina, or Monterey jack

1 Line 12 cups of a muffin tin with foil liners. Preheat the oven to 400°F and position the rack in the middle. Bring a big pot of salted water to a boil.

2 While waiting for the water to boil, heat up a skillet over medium heat. Drizzle in 2 tablespoons of the **olive oil,** and throw in the **onion** and **garlic.** Let them sizzle until golden, 3 to 4 minutes. Add the **spinach** and cook the vegetables for another moment, then slip it all into a bowl and let cool.

3 Boil the ravioli for half the amount of time their directions call for. Drain them well and gently toss with the remaining 1 tablespoon **olive oil.** Fold the **egg** and **Parmesan** into the spinach.

4 Spoon 1 tablespoon **tomato sauce** into each of the 12 muffin cups. Drop a ravioli on top, top with 1 tablespoon each of spinach and **melting cheese,** then a dollop of tomato sauce. Tuck a ravioli on top, add another dollop of tomato sauce and sprinkle with melting cheese. (The rest of the tomato sauce gets heated up separately.) Slide the muffin tin into the oven and bake until hot and bubbling, about 20 minutes.

5 Heat up the remaining tomato sauce in a small saucepan and serve on the side.

kids in charge

* Squeeeeeze the spinach with your hands 'til it's dry.

* Crack the egg into a small cup and whisk it with a fork.

* Layer the lasagna and tuck the ravioli into bed.

play with it

* Use Bolognese sauce instead of the tomato sauce.

* Replace the spinach with chopped, cooked broccoli.

* Add a little fresh goat cheese or a spoonful of pesto to the spinach.

cook's tip

On lazy days, skip the muffin tins and just layer the ingredients in a baking dish.

college students, this one's for you

one-pot pasta

makes 6 to 8 servings
PREP TIME: 10 minutes   COOKING TIME: 8 to 12 minutes

Dear student: In just 20 minutes and with only one pot to clean, you can have a family-dinner–size pasta dish to feed your friends and enough leftovers for a few more meals. The dried pasta is cooked *right in the sauce*, a time-saving and delicious trick Italian grandmothers use to infuse the pasta with lots of flavor. Choose a favorite rustic pasta shape that cooks in about 8 to 12 minutes (shells, penne, fusilli).

3 tablespoons extra virgin olive oil

4 garlic cloves (or more to taste), chopped

1 small onion, diced

1 can (28 ounces) diced tomatoes or 3½ cups chopped fresh tomatoes with their juices

1 bunch kale, ribs removed, chopped

2 sprigs of fresh basil, chopped, plus a few whole leaves for garnish

1 pound whole-grain (brown rice or whole wheat) pasta

Salt

About 4 cups water

¼ cup grated Parmesan cheese

Red pepper flakes (optional)

1 Heat a large-heavy bottomed pot over high heat. Drizzle in the **olive oil**. When it's hot, add the **garlic** and let it get nice and golden (this color adds lots of flavor); it will only take about 30 seconds. Add the **onion** and cook until the onion is translucent, 3 to 4 minutes. Add the **tomatoes, kale, basil, pasta, salt,** and 4 cups **water**. Bring the mixture to a boil while stirring, then reduce the heat to a simmer.

2 Cook the the whole thing for the amount of time suggested on the pasta package, giving it an energetic stir every few minutes. If it starts to look too dry, add a slosh more water (about ½ cup at a time). Once the pasta is **al-dente,** fold in the **Parmesan**. Taste! Does it need some **red pepper flakes**? A pinch of salt? Top with the fresh basil, maybe a shower of Parmesan. Enjoy!

Al dente means that the pasta still has a little chew to it. However, if you prefer mushy, make it mushy. It's your dinner!

play ✱ with it

As the pasta is cooking:
* Replace the kale with broccoli, spinach, or Swiss chard; just keep in mind that since they cook more quickly you should add them later in the cooking process. Broccoli will take about 8 minutes; the chard and spinach about 1 minute.

* Add a can of drained tuna or salmon 1 minute before the pasta is done
* Add 1 tablespoon capers, 1 teaspoon red pepper flakes, and a few chopped olives to make pasta puttanesca.

After the pasta has cooked:
* Fold in a spoonful of pesto.
* Top the pasta with a fried egg for protein.
* Drizzle with balsamic vinegar.

spaghetti and turkey meatballs

makes 6 to 8 servings

PREP TIME: 30 to 40 minutes   COOKING TIME: 45 minutes

Why make just a few meatballs when you've already got your sleeves rolled up? This recipe gives you plenty of them—half to make the kids happy at dinner tonight and enough leftovers to make you happy too: one cold right out of the fridge, another to gently reheat and smoosh into a whole wheat roll with a few pickled onions, grated cabbage, maybe some pepperoncini. . . .

3 eggs

½ cup cold water

1 tablespoon red wine vinegar

3 slices stale bread, crumbled, or 1½ cups breadcrumbs

2 pounds ground organic turkey or chicken

½ cup grated Parmesan cheese, plus more for garnish

4 garlic cloves, minced

1 small onion, minced

¼ cup chopped fresh parsley

1 teaspoon salt

8 cups of your favorite tomato sauce

Olive oil

1 pound spaghetti (try quinoa spaghetti or brown rice pasta, or even a platter of cooked grains)

 kids **k** in charge

* Stir the eggs and breadcrumbs
* Fling a noodle onto the wall: When it sticks, it's done!

 play ✳ with it

* Add 1 teaspoon each paprika and crushed fennel to the meatball mix.
* Or a flurry of red pepper flakes.
* Throw a sprinkle of parsley on the finished dish.

1 Combine the **eggs**, **water**, **vinegar**, and **crumbled bread** in a large bowl and lightly beat until it is all a smooth mush. Add the **turkey, Parmesan, garlic, onion, parsley,** and **salt** and mix well. Cover and chill in the fridge for 10 minutes to let it firm up.

2 Meanwhile, pour your **tomato sauce** into a large pot and start it simmering over medium heat.

3 Take out the meatball mixture. Rub a little **olive oil** onto your hands, grab walnut-size handfuls of the mixture, and roll them carefully into neat balls. Place them on a baking sheet about 1 inch apart.

4 Preheat the broiler with a rack about 6 inches from the heat.

5 Broil the meatballs until golden brown, turning them over once, about 5 minutes per side. Take the meatballs out. They will probably still be raw in the centers, which is okay. Carefully slide the meatballs and their pan juices into the tomato sauce. Simmer for 30 minutes, gently stirring a few times.

6 Meanwhile, bring a large pot of water salted like the sea to a boil. Cook the **pasta** according to the package directions, then drain well. Slip the pasta onto a large serving platter and toss with a drizzle of olive oil and a sprinkle of Parmesan cheese.

7 Ladle plenty of tomato sauce and meatballs on top, but make sure you put some aside for leftovers. Light the candles. Turn up Frank Sinatra.

angel hair with trees and cheese

makes 4 to 6 servings

PREP TIME: 10 minutes   COOKING TIME: 15 minutes

Here is a quick "make it by heart" dinner that you will be able to do from memory after you've prepared it once or twice. It's perfect for those nights when you have no idea what to put on the dinner table. In no time, you can cook this up, throw down a tablecloth, and merrily sing: "Diiiiinner, here you are!"

1 large head of broccoli (or 1 pound of frozen broccoli, thawed)

3 tablespoons olive oil

2 to 4 garlic cloves, sliced paper-thin (more or less)

A pat of butter (optional)

1 pound angel hair pasta

½ cup grated Parmesan cheese

Salt and freshly ground black pepper

1 Start a big pot of water boiling, and salt it to almost taste like the sea ❓.

2 Grab the **broccoli** and chop it up fine. Peel the broccoli stem and chop it up, too (yes, the stem is good!).

3 Heat up a small saucepan over medium-high heat and add the **olive oil**. Add the **garlic** and gently cook until golden. Add the **butter** (if using) and melt. Remove from the heat.

4 When the pasta water is at a rolling boil, throw both the **pasta** and broccoli into the pot, and give the pot a stir so the noodles don't stick together in a lump on the bottom. Boil until the pasta is done, 3 to 4 minutes (or however long the pasta package is telling you).

5 Drain well, toss with the garlic mixture and **Parmesan**. Add salt and pepper to taste.

why  'cause . . .

If you generously salt the water, the pasta will taste so good you can almost eat it on its own! Just imagine how much better it will taste with your sauce.

play  with it

After sautéing the garlic, add:

✱ Fresh chopped herbs, such as parsley and basil

✱ A few teaspoons of capers

✱ 1 cup cooked chickpeas

✱ Red pepper flakes

✱ A can of drained tuna

✱ A squeeze of lemon

✱ ½ cup chopped sun-dried tomatoes

when basil sleeps for the winter, parsley comes out to play

nutty winter pesto pasta

makes 3 or 4 servings
(some for now, some for later)
PREP TIME: 15 minutes   COOKING TIME: 15 minutes

This is the dinner to make for yourself when no one else is around. Fresh green herbs, tangy lemon, and crunchy almonds make that great childhood staple, pasta with butter and cheese, a bit more grown up. Toss a salad, light a candle, set the table for one, and flip through a dreamy travel magazine . . . the perfect quick dinner after a long day.

1 large handful of flat-leaf parsley
(feel free to mix in any other leafy fresh herbs, like mint, sage, arugula, or oregano)

½ cup almonds (blanched or skin-on)

2 to 3 garlic cloves

Salt

3 tablespoons olive oil

½ pound angel hair pasta

A goodly amount of grated Parmesan cheese

A pinch or two of red pepper flakes (optional)

A small pat of butter (optional)

A tangy squeeze or two of lemon

1   Start a big pot of water boiling for the pasta, salted so it almost tastes like the sea. Chop the **herbs** and put half aside. Top the remaining herbs (still on the cutting board) with the **almonds**, **garlic**, and a sprinkle of **salt** and chop them all together making a rough pesto.

2   Heat a skillet over medium heat. Drizzle in the **olive oil**, slide in the pesto, stirring and letting the almonds and garlic turn gently golden. Remove from the heat.

3   Your pasta water should be boiling by now, so throw in the **angel hair** and cook according to the time on the package. Once the pasta is done, drain and toss with the almond mixture, uncooked herbs, and **Parmesan**, **red pepper flakes** (if using), **butter** (if using), and **lemon**.

4   Taste it! You want it a little tart and pretty green, with some crunch, spice, and just enough cheesy buttery goodness to make you feel like it is the beginning of a well-deserved weekend.

 cook's tips

How to mellow garlic: For dressings and pesto, raw garlic can have a pretty sharp bite; if you want to tame it, poach it. Put the peeled cloves in a small pot with enough water to cover and bring to a gentle boil. Cook for 1 to 2 minutes.

How to roast garlic: This is the most relaxed garlic can taste. Chop off the top of a few heads of garlic and place them on a piece of foil. Drizzle olive oil over them and sprinkle with salt. Wrap them in foil and bake in a

350°F oven for 50 minutes. Use roasted garlic for pestos, mashed potatoes, as a sandwich spread, or on its own—spread on a crust of baguette with a sprinkle of salt—as a cook's treat made just for you.

15 (okay, maybe 20) minute tacos

makes 8 tacos

PREP TIME: 10 minutes   COOKING TIME: 5 minutes

Let's just take a moment here to hail cheese. Cheese is delicious. It has protein and calcium. It makes us all happy. However, we love it so much we are each eating three times more now than we did 10 years ago, and that is not healthy for our hearts (and all those cows making the cheese aren't good for the planet either—sorry cows!). So here is a cook's trick: Eat cheese, but make it matter by using small amounts of the good stuff. It packs a bigger flavor punch, so you use less and enjoy more. Here we use feta cheese, as it is often made from sheep's or goat's milk (better for the world), it is lower in fat (better for us), and it has a lot of flavor, so a little goes a long way (better for the wallet!).

3 cups shredded cabbage mixed with 1 cup shredded carrots, or 4 cups packaged coleslaw mix

1 scallion, thinly sliced

⅓ cup chopped fresh cilantro or mint (optional)

Juice of 1 lime or ½ lemon

Salt and freshly ground black pepper

2 cans (14.5 ounces each) refried beans (any color) or 3 cups home-cooked beans

8 corn tortillas

1 cup crumbled feta cheese

2 teaspoons olive oil

Romy's Guacamole (page 147)

Salsa (page 154)

1 Toss together the **cabbage** and **carrots** (or coleslaw mix), **scallion**, **cilantro** (if using), and **citrus juice** in a large bowl. Season with **salt** and **pepper**.

2 In another bowl, mash the **beans** with a fork and if you care to, add any of the "Play with It!" spices or ingredients.

Heat 2 large heavy-bottomed skillets over medium-high heat. Add the **tortillas** to the hot, dry skillet in single layer. ❓ Spoon 2 tablespoons of the beans onto half of each tortilla, sprinkle the **feta cheese** on top. Cook until the tortillas are soft enough to fold, less than 1 minute. Using tongs, carefully fold the tacos in half, press down for a moment, and flip. Cook until golden brown.

3 Take the pan off the heat and immediately drizzle each pan with 1 teaspoon **olive oil** to crisp up the tacos edges, flip once. Transfer to a plate and top the tacos with the slaw. Serve with the **guacamole** and **salsa**.

play ✳ with it

★ Add a little chili powder, cumin, or minced garlic to the beans.

★ Throw some fresh corn on with the feta.

★ Try some of those fancy new vegan taco crumbles mixed into the beans.

★ If you have leftover grilled vegetables, chop them up and fold them into the beans.

why ❓ 'cause . . .

The tacos are heated in a dry pan and oil is only added at the very last minute to crisp them up instead of sogging them down.

nice, nice brown rice

makes 4 servings
PREP TIME: 30 minutes   COOKING TIME: 35 minutes

If you can cook rice, you can make dinner. This is not really a recipe, but rather inspiration for turning a lovely bowl of rice into a customizable meal. Cook a pot of brown rice, chop up some raw vegetables, and arrange them on a platter. Then let your family add the toppings as they wish: a little carrot and some cabbage for crunch, some edamame for protein, a drizzle of this, a sprinkle of that . . . and before you know it, everyone has created their very own masterpiece. If you prep double the amount of ingredients listed below and put half aside, tomorrow you will have just the right ingredients for making fried rice! The quick recipe for that follows. Now isn't that twice as nice?

2 cups short-grained brown rice

¼ cup seasoned rice vinegar (optional)

TOPPINGS

1 cup shredded carrots (2 to 3 carrots, unpeeled if organic)

1 cup cooked edamame

1 cup shredded red cabbage

1 cup fresh or thawed frozen corn kernels

1 package (4 ounces) pressed and seasoned tofu, cut into cubes

1 cup cubed cucumbers tossed with 1 teaspoon sesame seeds

2 or 3 quartered hard-boiled eggs (page 78)

1   Bring a big pot of salted water to a boil just like you would for pasta. Pour in the **rice** and boil uncovered for 35 minutes. Drain the rice. Then return it to the pot, off the heat. Gently fold in the **vinegar** (if using), cover the pot, and set it aside to let the rice relax comfortably for 10 minutes.

2   Arrange all your **toppings** in little bowls or on a big platter and bring out your sauces (see play with it, below), give everyone their own bowl of rice, and have fun piling on the toppings!

play ✳ with it

Things to sprinkle:
* A few finely chopped scallions
* A cup of chopped peanuts
* Some toasted sesame seeds

Sauces to drizzle:
* Hoisin sauce for sweet
* Soy sauce for salty
* Peanut sauce for nutty
* Carrot Miso Dressing (page 131)
* Sesame Sauce (page 236)
* Hot sauce for the brave

twice as nice fried veggie rice!

Yield 4 servings

PREP TIME: 5 minutes   COOKING TIME: 10 minutes

This fried rice is so much better, faster—and healthier—than Chinese take-out! Leftover rice is perfect for fried rice (less sticky) so whenever you have it, just chop up 3 to 4 cups of whatever vegetables you have (cabbage, zucchini, peppers...) and you will have lunch or dinner tossed together in a flash. If you are using the vegetables from the nice rice bowl you prepped yesterday, just stir and fry, then sit down and enjoy yesterday's labor.

2 eggs, beaten

1 teaspoon soy sauce

1 teaspoon toasted sesame oil

2 tablespoons grapeseed or other high-heat oil

½ red onion, sliced

1 to 2 garlic cloves, sliced

A thumb-size piece of fresh ginger, peeled and chopped

3 to 4 cups chopped vegetables

3 to 4 cups leftover cooked brown rice

Chopped scallions or cilantro for garnish

1 Beat the **eggs** together with the **soy sauce** and **sesame oil** in a small bowl. Have at the ready.

2 Place your biggest pan or wok over high heat and drizzle in **oil** to cover the bottom. Add the **onion**, **garlic**, and **ginger** and stir-fry until the onion starts to soften, 2 to 3 minutes. Add all the **chopped vegetables** and cook until they are sizzling, 2 to 3 minutes. Throw in the rice. When the rice is good and hot, add the **eggs**. Cook, stirring vigorously, for a few more minutes until the eggs are cooked.

3 Serve topped with **sliced scallions**.

quinoa cakes

makes 4 to 6 servings
PREP TIME: 30 minutes   COOKING TIME: 45 minutes

These quinoa cakes are crispy, crunchy, tasty, perfect for meatless Mondays . . . and very adaptable! Mix them up by adding a few of the suggestions below in Play with It! And make plenty, because they freeze well and are perfect to slip into wraps and sandwiches or to pull out for dinner on a busy day. They're delicious with red pepper or yogurt cucumber sauce, but a simple tomato sauce is lovely too.

1 cup quinoa (rinsed if needed)

2 eggs

¼ cup all-purpose, whole wheat, or any gluten-free flour

3 tablespoons tahini, almond butter, or peanut butter

1 tablespoon red or white wine vinegar

1 package (10 ounces) frozen spinach or kale, thawed and squeezed dry

1 cup finely grated sweet potato (about 1 small one)

¼ cup finely diced onion

2 garlic cloves, minced

1 teaspoon salt

A pinch of freshly ground black pepper or cayenne pepper

Olive oil, for the baking sheet

Quick-Roasted Red Pepper Sauce (page 241) or Cucumber Yogurt Sauce (page 237)

1 Start the **quinoa** cooking immediately so it can cook while you are prepping the other ingredients. Combine the quinoa and 3 cups water in a pot and boil it until it is soft ❓, about 20 minutes. Drain it well.

2 Transfer the quinoa to your favorite mixing bowl. Add the **eggs, flour, tahini, vinegar, spinach, sweet potato, onion, garlic, salt,** and **pepper.** Stir, knead, and smoosh all the ingredients together until they are one tight-knit family. Cover and refrigerate for 30 minutes if you have time.

3 Preheat the oven to 400°F with the rack in the middle. **Oil** a baking sheet.

4 To shape the cakes, first wet your hands. For each patty, scoop up 3 to 4 tablespoons of the mixture with your hands and form a ½-inch-thick patty, firmly patting it so it stays together (loosie-goosies will fall apart). Arrange the patties on the baking sheet.

5 Bake until the cakes are lightly browned and crisp, flipping them over once halfway through the baking time, about 25 minutes. Serve warm with one of the **sauces.**

kids  in charge

* Squeeeeeeze the spinach dry.
* Mix, mix, mix.
* Patty-cake the quinoa cakes into shape.
* Be the official lookout for loosie-goosies.

play with it

Add:
* ½ cup chopped nuts (any kind: pine nuts and walnuts are our favorites)
* ½ cup chopped sun-dried tomatoes
* A little crumbled feta cheese
* A bit of chopped parsley, dill, or cilantro

why  'cause . . .

Cooking the quinoa a bit longer will give you softer grains, which helps the cakes stick together better.

asian dumplings in garlic broth with peas

makes 4 servings
PREP TIME: 15 minutes   COOKING TIME: 15 minutes

Dumplings are essentially gift-wrapped vegetables, so this dinner is an easy little present for your family. Simmer dumplings with ginger, garlic, and peas for a quick weeknight dinner.

Grapeseed or other high-heat oil, for the pot

5 to 6 garlic cloves, thinly sliced

1 teaspoon chopped fresh ginger

3½ to 4 cups chicken broth or vegetable broth (organic if you can)

1 tablespoon soy sauce

1 carrot, thinly sliced into coins

1 package (16 ounces) Asian vegetable dumplings

2 cups peas, any kind: snow peas, thawed frozen green peas, sugar snaps (see Cook's Tip)

3 scallions (white and green parts), thinly sliced, plus more for garnish

1 Heat up a soup pot over high heat. Drizzle in enough **oil** to cover the bottom. Add the **garlic** and **ginger** and cook until deep golden, about 1 minute (deep golden is good here, as it will flavor the broth well).

2 Add 3½ cups of the **broth**, the **soy sauce**, and **carrot**. Cover, reduce the heat to medium, and simmer for 10 minutes.

3 Just before serving, slip the **dumplings** and **peas** into the pot and increase the heat to high. Cover and cook until the dumplings are heated all the way through, 4 to 5 minutes. If the dumplings soak up too much liquid add a little more broth. Toss in the **scallions**. Taste it! Does it need more ginger? A little soy sauce? Divide among big bowls and garnish with scallions.

kids in charge

* Help find the dumplings in the grocery store. (Hint: They are usually frozen and in the appetizer section.)

* Measure the peas; if they are sugar snaps please zip off their strings (see Cook's Tip).

play with it

* Add a dab of miso paste in the beginning.

* Add a sliced red chile if you are a spicy family.

* Add Asian chili paste at the end.

* Garnish with chopped cilantro, mint, chives, or pea shoots.

* Serve with soy and hoisin sauces on the side.

cook's tip

How to string a pea or bean: Peas and larger beans have a string that runs along the top seam like a zipper. It's often tough and should be removed—a very important job for kids. Grab the tip of the pea or bean (that's where they were attached to the plant) and "zip" the string right off the pod. Sometimes there is a "zipper" on the other side of the pod that also needs to be removed.

a tangy tofu dish that even kids will love

crispy tofu and broccoli stir-fry

makes 4 to 6 servings

PREP TIME: 20 minutes   COOKING TIME: 10 to 15 minutes

Stir-fries are quick one-pan dinners. This one stars broccoli, but you can replace it with cabbage, asparagus, bok choy . . . even one of those ready-cut stir-fry mixes you can find in the produce aisle. Just be sure you have a bunch of like-minded veggies that require equal cooking time so you can fry them all up in the same hot pan.

2 tablespoons soy sauce

2 tablespoons hoisin sauce (or 2 tablespoons soy sauce blended with 2 teaspoons honey)

2 tablespoons plus ¼ cup water

½ teaspoon cornstarch

Grapeseed, untoasted sesame, or other high-heat oil, for the skillet

1 package (14 ounces) organic extra-firm tofu, cut into bite-size cubes and thoroughly patted dry

1 large head broccoli (about 1¼ pounds), broken into florets, stems peeled and thinly sliced

1 tablespoon grated fresh ginger

3 garlic cloves, minced

1 teaspoon toasted sesame oil

1 Stir together the **soy sauce**, **hoisin sauce**, 2 tablespoons **water**, and the **cornstarch** in small bowl. Set aside.

2 Heat up your largest heavy-bottomed skillet or wok over high heat. Drizzle in enough **oil** to cover the bottom. When it is very hot, add the **tofu** and cook, without stirring ❓, until golden and crisp on one side (about 3 minutes). Flip the pieces and cook until golden on 2 sides. Transfer the tofu to a plate and set aside.

3 If your pan has stuck-on bits in it, wipe it out with a paper towel. Reheat over high heat and add more **oil** to coat the bottom. Add the **broccoli** and cook, without stirring, until it browns on one side, about 3 minutes. Add the **ginger** and **garlic**, let it sizzle for a moment, then add ¼ cup **water**, cover the skillet (with a lid or pizza pan), and steam the broccoli until crisp-tender, about 1 minute.

4 Uncover and, while stirring constantly, add the soy sauce mixture and tofu to the pan. Stir-fry until the sauce has thickened, about 15 seconds. Remove the skillet from the heat and stir in the **toasted sesame oil**. Taste! Then serve immediately.

cook's 🥄 tip

Sesame oil is available both toasted and untoasted. Untoasted (cold-pressed) sesame oil is both light in color and flavor and has a high smoke point, making it ideal for high-heat cooking, as for stir-fries. Toasted sesame oil is dark in color and has a warm, nutty flavor. It is better suited for flavoring a dish than for cooking (like in dressings or drizzled onto a dish after it has finished cooking).

 why ❓ 'cause . . .

Letting the tofu sit, untouched, in the very hot pan allows the pieces to crisp up; if you move them around willy-nilly, they will never develop that delicious texture.

curried quinoa "risotto"

makes 4 to 6 servings

PREP TIME: 15 minutes   COOKING TIME: 20 minutes

Quinoa, shiitake mushrooms, sweet potatoes, broccoli, turmeric (in the curry powder)—these are among the healthiest foods you can eat. Combine them into a luscious one-pot meal, call it risotto (just to be fancy-pants about it), then serve it alongside a kale salad for the perfect weeknight dinner.

Olive or coconut oil, for the pot

1 cup (4 ounces) sliced shiitake mushrooms

½ cup minced shallots (2 medium) or onion

1½ cups diced sweet potato
(about 1 small, unpeeled if organic)

1½ cups quinoa (rinsed if needed)

1½ tablespoons hot or mild Indian curry powder

4 to 5 cups vegetable broth or chicken broth
(organic if you can)

1 cup chopped broccoli

1 can (14 ounces) regular or "lite" coconut milk

1 Heat a large pot over medium-high heat. Add the **oil** and when it begins to shimmer, add the **mushrooms** and **shallots** and cook until they begin to soften, about 5 minutes. Add the **sweet potato**, **quinoa**, and **curry powder**. Keep stirring, making sure that the quinoa and curry get nice and fragrant without sticking to the bottom of the pot, 1 to 2 minutes.

2 Carefully pour in 4 cups of the **broth** and give it a vigorous stir. Reduce the heat to medium-low, cover, and simmer for 10 minutes.

3 Add the **broccoli** and **coconut milk**, uncover and continue simmering and stirring the risotto for 5 minutes, adding more **broth** (or water) if it starts to look dryer than oatmeal porridge. Now taste the risotto; the quinoa should be saucy but still have a little crunch. Make sure it is seasoned well. Does it need a little more spice? A little more broth? Adjust so it is perfect for you.

play ✳ with it

* Add chopped ginger and garlic with the shallots.

* Sauté spinach with a little garlic and place it on top of the risotto, or just fold in a handful of raw spinach with the broccoli.

* Toast slivered almonds, sesame seeds, and curry powder in a skillet until fragrant and sprinkle on top of each bowl for crunch.

* Love the leftovers: Add an egg or two and enough breadcrumbs so the mix is the consistency of cold porridge. Patty-cake little patties, put them on an oiled baking sheet, and bake them at 350°F until crisp, about 20 minutes. Serve with a dollop of yogurt and a little mango chutney.

white bean chili

makes 12 servings

PREP TIME: 15 minutes   COOKING TIME: 40 minutes

This chili is simple and quick to make, and when topped with juicy chopped tomatoes, roasted corn, or shredded cabbage (oh, yes, you must try crunchy raw cabbage on your chili!), it's the perfect one-pot dinner for a rush-rush school night. Make enough and you also have fillings for tomorrow's tacos or lunch quesadillas (page 100).

Olive oil, for the pot

2 large onions, chopped

1 tablespoon ground cumin

2 to 3 tablespoons mild or hot chili powder, to taste

8 garlic cloves, finely chopped

2 cans (4 ounces each) mild or hot fire-roasted chiles, chopped

1 can (28 ounces) fire-roasted diced tomatoes

3 cups water

6 cans (15 ounces each) white beans*, rinsed and drained, or 10 cups home-cooked beans (see page 227)

3 corn tortillas, torn into little pieces (a secret binder and flavor)

2 tablespoons maple syrup

Salt and cayenne pepper (optional)

Toppings (see Play with It, below)

* Eden organic beans come in BPA-free cans.

1 Heat a large pot over medium heat. Drizzle in enough **olive oil** to cover the bottom. Add the **onions** and cook until they are golden, about 5 minutes. Add the **cumin**, **chili powder**, and **garlic** and cook, stirring well so they do not burn, until fragrant, 1 to 2 minutes.

2 Add the **chiles**, **tomatoes**, **water**, **beans**, and **tortillas** and bring to a gentle boil. Reduce the heat to low, cover, and gently simmer until the chili thickens, about 30 minutes, stirring now and then to prevent the bottom from burning.

3 Stir in the **maple syrup**, and taste: Does it need **salt**? Or how about making it a little spicier with more chili powder or **cayenne pepper**? Just add $\frac{1}{8}$ teaspoon at a time, as it is very hot. Serve with your favorite **toppings**. The chili keeps well for up to 4 days in the fridge (great leftovers!) or 3 months in the freezer.

 play with it

Add any of these toppings:

★ Oven-Grilled Corn (page 214)

★ Shredded cabbage

★ Shredded cheese

★ Chopped tomatoes

★ Baked tortilla chips

★ Hot sauce for ye brave

★ Greek yogurt for the mild

★ Fresh cilantro

★ A side of cooked quinoa

★ Salsa

so simple and satisfying, it's what chefs eat at home

saucy eggs

makes 4 servings

PREP TIME: 5 minutes   COOKING TIME: 10 minutes

These delicious eggs make a beautiful mess, perfect for dinner when you *think* there's nothing good in the fridge. But if you have eggs and you have tomato sauce, then you suddenly have a dinner to look forward to.

Olive oil, for the pan

4 cups of your favorite tomato sauce

4 (or more) eggs

Toasted country bread (optional)

Salt and freshly ground pepper (optional)

1 Heat up a heavy-bottomed medium skillet over medium-high heat. Drizzle in enough **oil** to cover the bottom. Carefully, but quickly, pour in the **tomato sauce** (it will splatter).

2 Once the tomato sauce is bubbling, crack an **egg** into a teacup ❓, then slip it into the sauce. Do the same with the rest of the eggs, leaving a little space between each egg.

3 Plop on a lid (a pizza pan or a big plate), reduce the heat to low, and simmer 5 minutes for soft eggs or a minute longer if you prefer hard-cooked eggs.

4 Spoon the eggs and sauce onto **toasted bread** (if desired). Add salt and pepper if needed.

why ❓ 'cause . . .

If bits of shell fall into the teacup, you can easily remove them by using a big piece of shell to scoop up the small ones. Works like a charm! (Of course, if you are feeling confident, just crack the egg straight into the pan.)

cook's 🔑 tip

One of the hottest things in the kitchen is steam. If you lift a pot lid straight up, the steam will rush out on all sides and may burn your wrist (ouch). So every time you lift a lid, don an oven mitt and always keep the edge closest to you resting on the pot, while you gently lift the opposite side a crack so the steam can escape safely. Then lift the lid like a shield between you and the steam.

play ✳ with it

★ Sauté sliced garlic or onion or both in the oil until golden, then add the tomato sauce.

★ Add a handful of greens like arugula or spinach and let them wilt into the sauce before adding the eggs.

★ Top each egg with a slice of cheddar or some other kind of assertive cheese that will melt into the sauce, making the eggs that much more lovely.

★ Shower the eggs with whatever fresh herbs you have . . . basil is good, of course, but so are parsley, chives, and mint.

★ Have some white beans? Fold them into the sauce.

★ Add cumin, a pinch of cinnamon, and a sprinkle of red pepper flakes for a Moroccan flair.

★ Yes, you can even serve them on a plate of spaghetti.

campfire hobo dinners

makes 1 serving

PREP TIME: 30 minutes (light the campfire at least 1 hour in advance)

COOKING TIME: 20 minutes in the kitchen, then 10 minutes on the fire

Here is another of our "participation dinners," but this time you get to take it outdoors! The stars of this dinner are potatoes and sausage covered with melting cheese . . . everything else is up to you and your cupboard. We offer suggestions, but use your favorite vegetables, as long as they can cook in less than 10 minutes. If you want this to be a vegetarian dinner, just include some vegetarian sausage, chickpeas, or tofu as protein. The ingredients below are per person; just multiply times the number of people you are feeding.

Olive oil, for the packet

1 medium potato, boiled in salted water until tender, then cubed

1 sausage, cooked and sliced

3 to 4 ounces cheese (sharp cheddar is good), cubed

¼ ear of corn (just snap an ear into 4 pieces)

Some sliced pickles

A few baby tomatoes

Sliced scallions (white and green parts)

½ small zucchini, sliced

Mustard for you, Homemade Ketchup (page 238) for the kids, for serving

1 Light your campfire or some coals and let burn down until glowing without large flames (like for 'smores).

2 Balance all the ingredients in bowls along a log or atop a picnic table. Oil a large piece of sturdy, heavy-duty foil with a little **olive oil**.

3 Now put your **favorite ingredients** in the center of the foil. Then wrap it all up into a little hobo package and . . . this is REALLY important, write your name on it (no one wants someone else's pickles). Put the package into the embers and . . . play some games, tell a ghost story, wait at least 10 minutes, then remove with tongs. Take a peek— the potatoes should be hot, the cheese melting, and the sausage just right. Enjoy!

4 For dessert? S'mores of course!

play with it

Add:

* Sliced roasted peppers, home-roasted (see page 106) or from a jar

* Maybe some caramelized onions

* 2 cups sauerkraut, drained well

* Make it an Indian hobo, with potatoes, chickpeas, spinach, and onions, topped with chutney and yogurt.

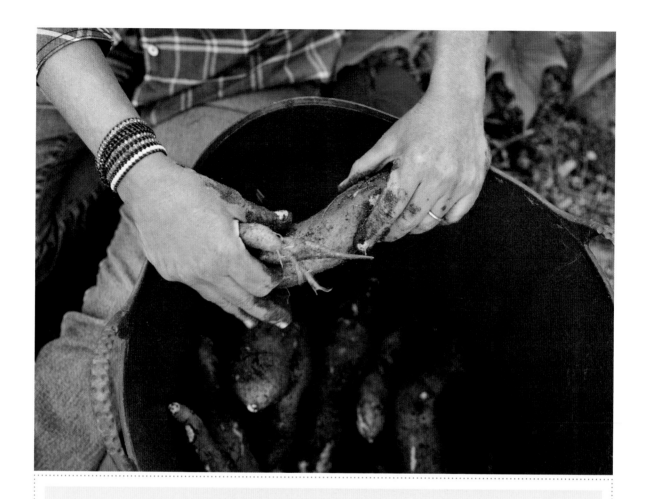

call me sweet potato

An entire weeknight dinner packed into a sweet potato

One of the important points we want to make with this cookbook is that dinner will feel a lot less intimidating when you change your attitude about what dinner is. It needn't ever be a grand production with hard-to-source ingredients. In fact, look no further than the humble sweet potato. A one-time staple of early homesteaders, it's one of the most nutritious foods to be found in the produce aisle, rich in calcium, potassium, and beta-carotene. (Buy them organic so you can happily eat the skin, which is packed with even more vitamin goodness.) Store them in your fridge for weeks!

Toss them in the oven, then make a chickpea salad from pantry ingredients, and you're done. That's dinner. In fact, bake a few as they are great cold the next day and neatly portable for lunch boxes. It's a joy to cook things that need little more than poking with a fork, popping in the oven (350°F for about 40 minutes), sprinkling with salt, and maybe dabbing with butter.

sides

good-quality ingredients make a great sauce

tomato sauce

makes 6 cups
PREP TIME: 5 minutes   COOKING TIME: 35 minutes

Homemade tomato sauce is red magic: It makes everything—even your mood—so much brighter! After just 5 minutes of prep and 30 minutes of simmering, you'll have a cheaper, tangier, and fresher sauce than anything you can get from a (corn syrup–sweetened, dried old herb–flavored) jar.

About ¼ cup extra virgin olive oil

1 medium onion, finely chopped

4 garlic cloves, finely chopped

2 cans (28 ounces each) good-quality diced tomatoes with their juices

A few fresh basil leaves

Salt

1 Heat a soup pot over high heat and drizzle in a goodly amount of **olive oil** (3 to 4 tablespoons). Add the **onion** and **garlic** and cook until the onion is translucent and the garlic is fragrant, about 5 minutes.

2 Stir in the **tomatoes, basil,** and **salt** and bring to a gentle simmer. Simmer for about 30 minutes, or until the tomatoes have started to break down and the sauce has thickened to your liking.

3 For a smooth sauce, use an immersion blender or standard blender (working in batches and filling the blender only half full to avoid a sauce explosion) and puree. Taste for seasonings.

play ✳ with it

* Add a rind of Parmesan at the beginning (remove before blending) or a sprinkle of Parmesan cheese at the end.

* Season with a splash of fish sauce or chopped anchovies, for depth.

* Sprinkle in ½ teaspoon red pepper flakes for heat.

* Drizzle in some vinegar (red or white) if the sauce is too sweet.

* Add a dab of honey if it is not.

* Add 2 tablespoons chopped fresh parsley or a spoonful of pesto.

* For a zesty puttanesca: Right before serving, add 2 chopped anchovies, 10 pitted halved Kalamata olives, 2 tablespoons chopped capers, ¼ teaspoon red pepper flakes, and 2 tablespoons chopped fresh parsley. Simmer for a few minutes and taste for seasonings.

a bowl of greens a day keeps the doctor away

sautéed greens with garlic

serves 4 to 6
PREP TIME: 15 minutes   COOKING TIME: 10 minutes

You've heard the saying, "Let thy food be thy medicine?" That goes double for dark leafy greens. Fall in love with them because they are packed with fiber and are incredibly nutrient-dense: We're talking vitamins K, C, E, and B; immunity-boosting beta-carotene, lutein, and zeaxanthin; and minerals like iron, potassium, magnesium, and calcium. They're also delicious, cheap, and available year-round. Serve these garlicky greens as a side dish, or fold them into a bowl of grains, add them to your quesadillas, mound them onto eggs, or throw a dollop of greens into your soup to supper it up.

Olive oil, for the skillet

4 to 5 garlic cloves, thinly sliced

1 large bunch kale, Swiss chard, or a combination of sturdy greens (kale, chard, frisée, or escarole), washed, ribs removed and either torn into small pieces or stacked and rolled like a cigar then cut into thin shreds (about 5 cups)

⅓ cup chicken broth, vegetable broth, or water

Salt and freshly ground black pepper

1 Heat a large skillet over high heat and drizzle in enough **oil** to cover the bottom. Add the **garlic** and cook until it starts to get golden, about 30 seconds.

2 Add the **greens** and turn with tongs so the garlic and oil are distributed among the leaves, then add the **broth** or water. Reduce the heat to medium-low, cover, and cook, until the greens are tender and the liquid has evaporated, 5 to 10 minutes. Taste and add a drizzle of oil and **salt** and **pepper**, if necessary.

 kids **k** in charge

* Wash the greens in a large bowl of water.

* Separate the leaves from the stems of the greens and tear into bite-size pieces.

 play **✳** with it

* Right before serving, add lemon zest and juice.

* Throw in a bit of red pepper flakes instead of black pepper.

* Once plated, grate on some pecorino cheese.

* Give it Asian flavors by adding a tablespoon of grated fresh ginger to the garlic, and drizzling a teaspoon of toasted sesame oil and a dash of soy sauce at the very end.

oven-grilled corn

makes 4 to 6 servings

PREP TIME: 10 minutes   BROILING TIME: 6 to 7 minutes

Use this corn to add sweetness to salads, as a delicious topping for White Bean Chili (page 201), or just serve it on its own as everyone's favorite side dish—just shuck and broil.

5 ears corn, kernels cut from cob, or 5 cups frozen corn kernels, thawed and patted dry

½ small red onion, finely diced

2 tablespoons olive oil

Salt and freshly ground black pepper

Preheat the broiler with the rack about 6 inches from the heat. Toss the **corn** with the **onion** and **oil**. Spread the corn out on a rimmed baking sheet and broil until the corn starts to sputter and some of it turns golden brown, 6 to 7 minutes. Season with **salt** and **pepper** to taste.

play with it

* Before broiling, add finely diced red bell peppers and zucchini.

* After broiling, toss with lime juice and chili powder.

* After broiling, add fresh herbs like chives or cilantro.

more peas, please!

makes 4 to 6 servings

PREP TIME: 5 to 15 minutes   COOKING TIME: 5 minutes

Is there a more perfect kitchen job for little hands than shucking peas? We think not! Plop a bowl in front of your kids and show them how to shuck: Pull off the string, open the pod, then pop a pea for you and two for the bowl; a pea for me and one for the bowl.

1 pound sugar snap peas, topped and tailed, strings removed

2 cups shucked fresh peas (about 2 pounds in the pod) or frozen peas, thawed

1 tablespoon butter, olive oil, or nut oil

Salt and freshly ground black pepper

1 Bring ½ cup water to a boil in a medium pot. Add the **sugar snaps** and shucked **peas**, cover, and boil for 1 minute, shaking the pan now and then.

2 Drain the peas, then swirl in the **butter** and season with **salt** and **pepper** to taste.

cook's tip

Once a fresh pea is picked, it loses its sweetness fast. Before you buy, ask to taste a couple. If they are starchy, smile and walk on by. If they are sweet, pick the pods that are shiny, green, and plump, then make sure to use them quickly.

play with it

★ Add grated nutmeg to the cooked peas.

★ Sprinkle the finished peas with chopped fresh herbs like mint, parsley, or chives.

blanca's garlicky green beans

makes 4 to 6 servings
PREP TIME: 10 to 15 minutes   COOKING TIME: 5 minutes

Laurie's kids looooove these beans and their friends looooove these beans. You have to try these beans!

Grapeseed, peanut, or other high-heat oil, for the pan

3 to 4 garlic cloves, minced or pushed through a garlic press

¾ pound green beans, tips pinched off

3 tablespoons soy sauce

Heat a large, heavy-bottomed skillet over high heat. Drizzle in enough **oil** to cover the bottom. Add the **garlic** and cook until it turns golden, about 30 seconds. Add the **beans** and stir-fry until they are crisp-tender, 3 to 4 minutes. Add the **soy sauce** and toss to completely coat the beans. Serve right away.

kids  in charge

* Remove all the tips from the beans
* Squish the garlic through the garlic press
* Measure the soy sauce

play with it

* Add 1 tablespoon grated fresh ginger to the garlic, or some grated orange zest.
* Toss in a few sesame seeds, too.
* Add sliced scallions or cilantro at the end.

bbb potatoes

makes 6 servings

PREP TIME: 10 minutes   COOKING TIME: 40 minutes

Crunchy and tasty, everyone's favorite side dish. Just boil, bash, and broil!

⅓ cup extra virgin olive oil, plus more for the pan

15 to 20 small organic red potatoes, scrubbed

1 garlic clove, minced

Salt and freshly ground black pepper

1 Grease a baking sheet with a thin coat of **olive oil**.

2 Boil the **potatoes** in a large pot of salted water until they can easily be pierced with the tip of a knife, 15 to 20 minutes. Drain and place on the baking sheet. Drizzle with the ⅓ cup **olive oil**, add the **garlic**, season with **salt**, and toss well.

3 Using another baking sheet or a water glass, press down on the potatoes to flatten them.

4 Preheat the broiler with the rack about 6 inches from the heat. Broil the potatoes until golden, 5 to 8 minutes. Using a spatula, turn them over and broil until golden and crispy. Season with more salt and **pepper** and serve warm.

play  with it

Mix into the olive oil before drizzling:

★ ½ teaspoon fresh rosemary or thyme

★ Grated zest and juice of 1 lemon

★ 1 teaspoon paprika

crisp roasted brussels sprouts

makes 6 servings
PREP TIME: 15 minutes   ROASTING TIME: 30 minutes

How can anyone hate the Brussels sprout? It's cute as a button, a tiny cabbage bud. Ben and Alex were picky (see page 18) and now when they cook dinner (which they do every Sunday), they roast shredded Brussels sprouts and use them in all sorts of ways—as a tasty side dish, or a frilly topping for a bowl of grains, or even tossed with pasta. Go ahead, trust the former picky eaters! The Brussels sprouts shred to a mountain, but shrink to a molehill. You can slice them in the food processor in 30 seconds or use a mandoline—almost as quick (just watch your fingers).

3 tablespoons olive oil, plus more for the pans

2 pounds Brussels sprouts, trimmed and thinly sliced

3 to 4 garlic cloves, minced

Salt and a goodly grind of black pepper

Juice of ½ lemon

1 Preheat the oven to 450°F. Oil 2 baking sheets with **olive oil**.

2 Combine the **Brussels sprouts**, **garlic**, 3 tablespoons **olive oil**, and a sprinkle of **salt** in a large bowl and toss to thoroughly coat. (Use your hands to knead it all together; the olive oil will keep them youthful looking.)

3 Arrange the sprouts in a thin layer on the baking sheets and bake, flipping once or twice, until the edges are crispy and golden, 25 to 30 minutes. Transfer to a serving bowl, add the **lemon juice** and toss. Season with more salt and **pepper** and fall in love with Brussels sprouts.

cook's tip

Shredded raw Brussels sprouts make a great salad on their own, or a crunchy addition to a mix of greens tossed with a lemony vinaigrette.

play with it

After roasting add any or all:

* 1 cup crisp unseasoned bread crumbs like panko

* ½ cup currants

* ½ cup toasted chopped walnuts

* ½ cup chopped fresh parsley or mint

* Grated Parmesan cheese

roasted cauliflower popcorn

makes 4 servings
PREP TIME: 10 minutes   ROASTING TIME: 30 minutes

A much healthier snack for movie night . . . or served on the side of weekday roasted chicken. Our advice: Double this recipe as it is likely to disappear before it makes it to the table.

1 large head cauliflower, cored and florets pulled apart into popcorn-size pieces

3 tablespoons olive oil, plus more for the baking sheet

1½ teaspoons salt

1 Preheat the oven to 450°F with the rack in the middle. Grease a rimmed baking sheet with a thin coat of **olive oil**.

2 Toss the **cauliflower** with the **olive oil** and **salt** in a large bowl, making sure that every "kernel" is evenly coated . Taste the raw cauliflower. It's already pretty good isn't it?

3 Dump the cauliflower onto the baking sheet. Roast, shaking the pan every 10 minutes, until the "kernels" are evenly browned, about 30 minutes. Taste (the cook gets all the crispy golden bits) and season with more salt if you need to.

why **?** 'cause . . .

When roasting anything, whether it is a vegetable or meat, a thin coating of oil conducts heat evenly, helping to brown and crisp, instead of shrink and wilt. It doesn't take much, just an even coating. Roast a few cauliflower bites unoiled just so you can see the difference.

play **✳** with it

★ Before roasting, add a little chopped rosemary or parsley, or toss with grated Parmesan cheese.

★ After roasting, for an Asian flair, toss with fish sauce, garlic, mint, and lime juice.

kids **k** in charge

★ Separate the cauliflower into "popcorn kernels."

★ Toss with olive oil and salt and any other additions.

★ Be the official raw cauliflower cruncher.

sliced, roasted, and totally transformed.

caramelized broccoli and cauliflower slivers

makes 4 to 6 servings
PREP TIME: 10 minutes   ROASTING TIME: 30 minutes

Slicing these vegetables thin offers more surface area to turn golden and crisp, keeping the inside tender and sweet. Whether served pure and simple, straight out of the oven, or drizzled with a vinaigrette, this is a crazy-good way to serve vegetables.

1 large or 2 small heads broccoli and/or cauliflower, cut from top to bottom into thin slices*

3 to 4 tablespoons olive oil (enough to thinly coat all the vegetables), plus more for the baking sheets

2 to 3 garlic cloves, minced

Salt and freshly ground black pepper

1 Preheat the oven to 425°F. Lightly **oil** 1 or 2 baking sheets or line with parchment paper.

2 Combine the **broccoli** and/or **cauliflower** with the **olive oil**, **garlic**, and **salt** and **pepper** in a large bowl and toss until thoroughly coated. Transfer to the baking sheet(s) and spread out so that the pieces aren't crowded. Roast until golden and tender, flipping occasionally so that the slices brown evenly, 25 to 30 minutes.

Some will crumble, that's part of the charm.

play with it

After roasting, toss the vegetables with any or all of these:

* 2 tablespoons capers, chopped

* ⅓ cup loosely packed, chopped fresh mint or parsley

* A small handful of currants or chopped raisins

* Red pepper flakes to taste

* ¼ cup toasted sliced almonds

roasted red onion flowers

makes 6 to 8 servings
PREP TIME: 10 minutes   ROASTING TIME: 1 hour

This is a beautiful side dish that you'd think grown-ups wouldn't have to share, but since they're crisp on the outside and sweet on the inside, they're pretty irresistible to kids as well.

6 medium red onions or sweet onions, such as Walla Walla, skin on and roots intact

6 tablespoons olive oil

Salt (smoked is delicious here)

Herbs—either a few bay leaves or a few sprigs of rosemary and thyme

Freshly ground black pepper

1 Preheat the oven to 350°F and position the rack in the middle.

2 Make a total of 4 vertical cuts in each **onion** to create 8 wedges still attached to the each other at the root end.

3 Drizzle a bit of **olive oil** into a small baking dish, then arrange the onions root-end down in it. Spoon the remaining olive oil into and around the onions. Sprinkle generously with **salt**, getting some into the center of the onions. Toss in the **herbs**.

4 Roast for 40 minutes. Rearrange the onions so that their petals open, and drizzle with a few spoonfuls of the caramelized onion juices in the bottom of the pan. Roast until the onions are tender on the inside with crispy bits on their outer petals, about 20 minutes longer. Season with **pepper** and more salt to taste. Serve hot or at room temperature as a side dish, or as dinner with a good cheese and a green salad.

play  with it

* Nestle a little goat cheese or Fontina into the flowers towards the end of cooking.

* After roasting, drizzle with balsamic vinegar.

* Use leftovers to glorify absolutely everything.

sweet potato fries

makes 4 to 6 servings

PREP TIME: 10 minutes   BAKING TIME: 20 to 30 minutes

A sweet potato fry is part crunchy, part silky, and all good for you! Just don't peel them—the skin contains tons of important minerals and fiber, and is the crispest part of the fry. The trick is to use skinny sweet potatoes, getting more crunchy skin on each fry. The other thing to keep in mind is that ovens are a sneaky band of liars. Though they may insist they are 400°F, they might not be, so flip a potato early to see how quickly it is browning.

3 medium organic ❓ sweet potatoes (unpeeled)

2 tablespoons olive oil, plus more for the baking sheets

Salt and freshly ground black pepper

1 Preheat the oven to 400°F. Preheat 2 rimmed baking sheets in the oven.

2 Meanwhile, cut each **sweet potato** lengthwise into quarters, then cut each quarter into wedges, keeping them more or less the same thickness so that they cook at the same rate. Transfer to a large bowl. Add the **olive oil** and **salt** and **pepper** to taste—and any fancy additions you are in the mood for.

3 Swirl a thin layer of **olive oil** onto each of the baking sheets and carefully scatter the fries evenly on both. (The key to crispy fries is ensuring that they do not touch each other . . . no cheating!) Bake until the bottoms are golden, 10 to 15 minutes. Flip them carefully using a spatula and bake until the tops are golden, 10 to 15 minutes longer.

Before roasting, add:

* 1 teaspoon curry powder
* Some crushed garlic or garlic powder
* Chopped rosemary
* A dash of chili powder

If using organic sweet potatoes, you can be sure the skin is okay to eat. Conventionally grown sweet potatoes should be peeled, as they have likely absorbed pesticides and are very possibly waxed after being harvested . . . not so good for you.

roasted sweet potato coins

Sweet and soft on the inside, caramelized on the outside—these are pure gold, perfect for dinner parties. Cut the **sweet potatoes** crosswise into ¼-inch-thick rounds. Toss them with **2 tablespoons olive oil** so they are completely covered and sprinkle with **salt and pepper** to taste. Place them on a well-oiled baking sheet. Cover tightly with foil or another baking sheet. Bake for 30 to 40 minutes at 400°. The amount of time can vary, but they should be a beautifully dark orange and very soft. Uncover, and bake for about 20 more minutes, flipping them now and then.

a wealth of hearty, rustic flavors

Laurie's pot of gold

makes 6 servings

PREP TIME: 15 minutes   COOKING TIME: 30 to 35 minutes

A hearty, rustic supper that will warm your heart and fill your stomach. Perfect on top of a plate of sautéed greens, or with a salad on the side.

Olive oil, for the skillet

4 good-quality turkey, chicken, or vegan sausages

1 to 2 medium onions (3 if you are an onion person), sliced

5 to 6 garlic cloves, finely chopped

Leaves from 1 sprig of fresh rosemary or thyme, chopped

1 can (14.5 ounces) diced tomatoes

4½ cups cooked white beans or 3 cans (15 ounces each), rinsed and drained

3 cups chicken or vegetable broth (organic if you can)

Salt and freshly ground black pepper

1 Heat a large skillet over medium heat and drizzle in enough **oil** to cover the bottom. Add the **sausages** and cook, turning occasionally, until they are golden brown and crisp, about 10 minutes. Transfer them to a cutting board and slice them into bite-size pieces or leave them whole, whatever makes you happy! Put them aside.

2 If the pan is dry, drizzle with more olive oil, then add the **onions** and cook until they are caramel colored and have little crispy edges, 10 to 15 minutes (a lovely time to practice patience). Add the **garlic** and **rosemary**, stir for a minute or two, then add the **tomatoes** and simmer for 2 or 3 minutes more. Add the **white beans** and **broth** and nestle the sausage among the beans. Bring it to a gentle simmer and cook until the sauce has thickened slightly and the beans are lovely and creamy, about 10 minutes more. Season with **salt** and **pepper** to taste and serve warm.

play  with it

* Substitute white wine or beer for some of the broth.

* Finish the dish off with a squeeze of lemon juice.

* Toss toasted breadcrumbs with Parmesan cheese and scatter on top for a crunchy topping.

* Swap out the sausage for a big handful or two of greens, such as escarole, chard, or chopped kale. Stir them into the sauce to make a beautiful, rustic stew. Top with toasted breadcrumbs and Parmesan cheese.

how to cook beans, lentils, rice, and grains

a soaking, salting, and simmering primer

Beans

Substituting beans and lentils for meat a few times a week might be the easiest, healthiest, and most cost-effective happy change you can make for your family.

One cup of beans gives you 15 grams of protein—that's a third of what an adult needs for the day—and 15 grams of fiber, which is half of the adult daily requirement. (That fiber is not only cholesterol-lowering, but also helps stabilize blood sugar levels—particularly important if you have hypoglycemia or diabetes.)

Canned beans are certainly fantastic, fast, and delicious, but wander into the dried bean section and you'll enter a beautiful world of colors, patterns, sizes, textures, and—yes—*flavors* that you won't find among the canned kind. Keep a pot of cooked beans on hand in your fridge or freezer for a protein-boosting add-on to salads soups and side dishes.

....

* how to shop for them *

Try to find fresh dried beans. That may sound like an oxymoron, but you don't want to buy a dusty bag of beans that has been lying around for ages. Old beans (a year old or more) take forever to cook—often refusing to soften at all—and aren't as flavorful. And that is a cooking tragedy.

Shop for beans ideally in the bulk sections of natural food stores or ethnic markets with a frequent turnover. Beans should appear plump and shiny. Wrinkles are the sign of a dried old bean; also check for little pebbles, which cause a dinnertime uproar if crunched on. Rinse the beans well, as they may be dusty.

....

* to soak or not to soak? *

Long soak (4 to 6 hours)
Some people say soaking enhances digestibility and the beans will cook a little quicker. If you have the time (before you leave for work or the night before), cover the beans with 3 times their volume of water, add a little salt (this helps as well), and let them soak for 6 to 8 hours. Drain the soaking water and add fresh water to cook with.

Quick soak (1 to 2 hours)
Put the beans in a pot of unsalted water, bring it to a boil, turn off the heat, then let the beans soak in the hot water for an hour or two. Drain, add fresh water, and simmer until done.

No soak
Millions of people who cook beans don't bother to soak. We like those odds so we say the same. The outcome will still be good; however, this will add at least 30 minutes to the cooking process.

✳ how to cook them ✳

Spill the beans into a large pot. Add enough water to cover by 1 inch. Bring the pot to a boil over high heat, then turn the heat down so the water is simmering. If you want beans that keep their shape in a salad or vegetable soup, cook them without a lid (you might need to add water at some point) until they're firm but not crunchy, their skins intact. For soft creamy beans, cook with a lid. Most beans are done in 1 to 1½ hours. However, it's important to use the cooking times as suggestions only. Taste a few beans long before you think they're done, and keep tasting.

Oh, and that shmutz in the cooking water is just protein from the beans coagulating on the surface. You can prevent that by adding a bit of oil to the water, or just skim off the scum with a spoon. (Don't add to your petunias!)

1 cup dried beans yields approximately 2½ cups cooked.

....

✳ how long to cook them ✳

Black beans
Soaked: 1½ to 2 hours. Unsoaked: 2 to 2½ hours.

Chickpeas (garbanzo beans)
Soaked: 2 hours. Unsoaked: 2½ hours.

Black-eyed peas, great Northern beans, kidney beans, navy beans, pinto beans, and pretty much any other small fancy bean
Soaked: 1 hour. Unsoaked: 1½ hours.

....

✳ how to flavor the cooking water ✳

There are fervent opinions as to whether you may or may not add salt to the cooking water (some say it toughens the beans), so hedge your bets and add it midway, or do whatever your mom did—she probably had it right.

Why not throw in half a head of garlic or half an onion, peels and all? Once soft, slip them out of their peels and into the beans. A bay leaf is always good; so are fresh herbs that might otherwise have been thrown out. A teaspoon of cumin seeds or half a stick of cinnamon will yield a delicious pot of beans. Adding a strip of kombu seaweed is a taste magnifier, as you are adding natural glutamates, sea salt, and minerals; it is also said to improve digestibility.

Do not, however, add acidic ingredients like vinegar or tomatoes until the very end, as they can toughen the beans.

....

✳ how to store them ✳

Store dried beans in a dark cool cupboard. Enjoy cooked beans within 4 days, or freeze them for up to 3 or 4 months.

✳ a special note on lentils ✳

Lentils are baby sisters to beans—healthy, hearty, and tasty legumes, with an extra dose of iron. You don't need to soak them before cooking, but do check to make sure they're pebble-free and well rinsed.

You cook these differently: In a pot, cover the lentils with double their volume in water. Bring the pot to a boil, then turn it down to a simmer. As with beans, the time they take to cook depends a bit on how fresh they are and whether you want them soft and creamy for a soup, or al dente for a salad, so check a few minutes before you think they are ready.

The regular flat brown (called "green") lentils you find in most supermarkets will cook in 25 to 30 minutes. The little round black beluga lentils and the French green Le Puy lentils can take a little longer, up to 40 minutes. Both of these hold their shape well, making them perfect for salads and pilafs. The tiny pink and yellow lentils you find in Indian markets cook up quickly, as little as 15 minutes. They don't hold their shape well, though, so they are best for purees and soups.

....

✳ how to use beans in many new ways! ✳

Now that the legumes have cooked, here are a few ways they fortify your food.

* Use a plate of warm beans as a bed for sturdy greens like endive or Kneaded Kale (page 122) and drizzle with a lemony dressing, making sure some hits the beans. The contrast between hot and cold, crunchy and soft, savory and tart is beautiful.

* Serve beans in a bowl topped with a little grated cheese, a drizzle of olive oil, and a sprinkle of herbs, and you'll feel happy and warm all over.

* Top them with Sautéed Greens with Garlic (page 211) and a fried egg (page 80) and you might also do a little dance.

* Grill or toast some country bread and ladle beans or lentils on top. Sprinkle with arugula, chopped tomatoes, shards of Parmesan, and a drizzle of good olive oil.

* Slide a fried (page 80) or poached (page 79) egg atop a bowl of legumes; sprinkle with salsa or tomato sauce and a shower of cheese. Serve a salad on the side . . . a perfect dinner.

* Make A Very Simple Kale Salad (page 124), divide it among bowls, add beans, maybe some quinoa, and drizzle with a little Quick-Roasted Red Pepper Sauce (page 241).

* Sauté onions, garlic, cumin, and a big tablespoon of curry powder; add cooked lentils and stir until hot. Serve with brown rice, a drizzle of yogurt, and a dollop of chutney.

* Toss cooled garbanzo beans with plenty of thinly sliced celery and/or fennel, add toasted cumin and fennel seeds, the juice of a squeezed lemon or two, some good olive oil, maybe a can of BPA-free tuna or salmon. Serve sitting under a parasol.

Grains (and Seeds!)

Want more whole grains in your diet? The easiest and perhaps most delicious way to do this is simply by throwing grains into a big pot of water and boiling them until they're tender, nutty and go pop in your mouth. You can't get any more whole than that.

Rice

We're lucky there are so many types of rice in our stores today—brown, red, and even beautiful purple/black rices that look gorgeous on your plate. Rice packaging will indicate whether the grain is long or short. The quick difference between short and long rice is that long becomes light and fluffy when cooked, and shorter rice is plumper, moister, and stickier. "Sweet rice" is not really sweet, but is the stickiest of all, so it is often used in Asian dishes like rice bowls and desserts.

White rice has had its bran removed (goodbye fiber and minerals!), then it is buffed, sometimes precooked, and finally—due to its total lack of nutrition—"re-enriched" (to put back some phony vitamins). So stick with brown rice and whole grains—they're better for you!

....

* how to cook it *

To cook rice you usually just add 2 cups of water for every 1 cup rice . . . but not all rices absorb the same amounts of water. So to avoid the guesswork, here is a simple method of cooking brown rice:

First, rinse your rice. Bring a big pot of salted water to a boil, just like you would for pasta. Pour in ¼ cup rice per serving (bearing in mind some people eat more than that, and leftovers are always useful) and boil uncovered for 35 minutes. Drain the rice. Then return it to the pot, cover the pot, and set it aside to allow the rice to relax comfortably for 10 minutes. Done.

One cup raw rice yields about 3 cups cooked.

Other grains:
spelt, wheatberries, kamut, farro (emmer wheat), einkorn, and barley

Before grains are milled, depriving them of their bran (fiber, antioxidants, B vitamins, phytochemicals, and minerals), before they are stripped of their germ (which is rich in vitamins, minerals, and unsaturated oils), before they are flattened, fluffed, and bleached to become bagels, Ring Dings, or wedding cake . . . before all that, grains are whole and good, nutty and sweet—simply perfect the way they were born.

....

* how to cook them *

If you have the time, let grains soak in water overnight—this will speed up the cooking process and give you plumper more evenly cooked grains. Bring a big pot of salted water to a boil, as you would for pasta, and for every 2½ cups cooked grains needed, throw in 1 cup raw grain. Turn the heat to low and simmer covered until the grain has reached the consistency you desire (that's the definition of "done"). The cooking times for these grains are wildly unpredictable, so start tasting after 45 minutes and figure it can take up to 90 minutes for a grumpy batch of wheatberries or spelt. Once cooked, whole grains will keep well in the fridge for 5 days, or frozen for a couple of months.

Grains can be found in "pearled" varieties, which means that some (semi-pearled) or most (pearled) of the outer bran has been polished off. This means that the grain will cook much more quickly (15 to 20 minutes instead of an hour or more for farro and barley, for example), but the trade-off is that it's not quite as nutritious.

....

* how to use them *

Boil up a big batch of any grain and whip up the following:

* Serve hot with warm milk, honey, and apples for breakfast.

* Sauté them until crunchy, along with kale, and serve them under a couple of Crispy Eggs (page 810).

* Throw grains into salads for lunch.

* Use them as you would pasta or rice for dinner.

* Simmer pearled grains while stirring madly for a faux "risotto."

* Slip a spoonful into each bowl of Tomato Red Pepper Soup (page 106).

* Place grains on top of a roasted sweet potato with a dollop of plain yogurt and a dab of chutney.

Quinoa

We love quinoa. LOVE.

It takes only 15 minutes to cook and is an easy super healthy alternative to rice or pasta. Quinoa is actually a seed from South America that has a fluffy, creamy, slightly crunchy texture, and a flavor not unlike pasta or couscous (since it's not a grain, it's gluten-free!). One of the world's true superfoods, quinoa is a complete protein, containing all 9 essential amino acids, and a great source of fiber, iron, and magnesium. It generally comes in white, red, and brown, which can be used interchangeably; just bear in mind that black and red quinoa are a little crunchier and need to be cooked a minute or two longer than white quinoa.

....

* how to cook it *

Unless your quinoa comes prerinsed (the package should tell you), rinse it well until the water runs clear (quinoa has a natural bitter coating called saponin). Bring a pot of salted water to a boil, as you would for pasta, then add ¼ cup quinoa per serving. After 10 to 12 minutes, taste a few seeds. They should be tender, but still a bit crunchy. Drain the quinoa well, fluff it with a fork, and let it sit covered in the pot for a few minutes so it has time to dry out, fluff up, and relax.

1 cup raw quinoa yields about 3 cups cooked.

Use quinoa in any way you would use rice, couscous, or pasta.

- ★ Throw it into soup and onto salads.

- ★ Stir-fry cooked quinoa with vegetables, serve with tomato sauce and meatballs, or layer instead of noodles in lasagna.

- ★ For a tasty morning porridge, toss it with nuts, seeds, and chopped fruit, maybe a drizzle of honey and warm milk.

Other seeds
millet, amaranth, and teff

Millet, amaranth, and teff are tiny but powerful. All pack protein, vitamins, minerals, amino acids, and fiber into their little bodies. An added benefit is that they are quick cooking, making them perfect for weekday meals. Cook them as you would quinoa, tasting them after 12 minutes, and draining them when they have reached the "doneness" you prefer. Millet cooks up fluffy like quinoa and can be used as a breakfast porridge or to toss into salads and as a side dish. Amaranth and teff are a bit stickier in consistency, so they are great for porridges, to thicken soups, and as dinner "polentas."

refrigerator lentils

makes about 8 cups of lentils for your fridge
PREP TIME: 15 minutes   COOKING TIME: 30 to 40 minutes

A bowl of lentils is a springboard for quick improvised dishes. They can even be served as is, simple and comforting. Or you can mix them up with a variety of different spices and preparations (see below) for international flair!

Olive oil, for the pot

2 medium onions or 3 leeks (white and light-green parts only), chopped

4 to 5 garlic cloves, chopped

2 carrots, chopped (unpeeled if organic)

1 pound green or brown lentils (about 2¼ cups), rinsed

A sprig of fresh thyme or rosemary, or a bay leaf

4½ cups water

Salt and freshly ground black pepper

1 Heat a soup pot over medium high heat and drizzle the **oil** in to cover the bottom. Add the **onions** and cook until soft and golden, about 5 minutes. Add the **garlic** and stir until fragrant, about 30 seconds.

2 Add the **carrots**, **lentils**, **herbs**, **water**, and 1 tea-spoon **salt**. Bring to a simmer over medium heat and continue to simmer until the lentils are tender but still toothsome, the skins still intact, 30 to 40 minutes.

3 Drain, if necessary. Season to taste, cool, cover, and refrigerate up to 6 days.

Indian lentils

Sauté a good amount of onions (2 to 3) in olive oil in a large skillet over medium-high heat. Add a tablespoon or so of Indian curry powder, then throw in some diced sweet potatoes and peas, a few cups of cooked lentils, and maybe a little coconut milk. Cook until the potatoes are soft, about 15 minutes, and you have an Indian flavored dal in no time. Serve with a dollop of yogurt and naan. Pass the chutney!

French-inspired lentils

Sauté cubed sausages with chopped shallots in olive oil in a large skillet over medium-high heat. Add a glugg of red wine and sprig of rosemary. Stir in a few cups of cooked lentils and simmer until heated through and the wine has evaporated. Give the dish a drizzle of olive oil. Enjoy with a simple green salad.

Spanish lentils

Sauté some garlic in olive oil in a large skillet over medium-high heat until golden and fragrant. Add a diced tomato and a chopped green or red bell pep-per or two and sauté until ten-der. Throw in some chorizo and smoked paprika, too, if you hap-pen to have some. Stir in some cooked lentils and shower with chopped parsley. Serve hot with a splash of vinegar.

DIY condiments

for dipping and drizzling

sesame sauce

makes 1¼ cups
PREP TIME: 15 minutes   COOKING TIME: 5 minutes

Sesame sauce is good drizzled on rice bowls, hot steamed vegetables, or cold leftovers. Use it for salad rolls, as a vegetable dip, or as a tasty little sauce for a plain chicken breast.

½ cup unhulled  sesame seeds

2 garlic cloves, chopped

½ cup water

2 tablespoons toasted sesame oil

2 tablespoons white or yellow miso paste, or 2 tablespoons soy sauce mixed with 1 teaspoon honey or maple syrup

1 tablespoon rice vinegar or lime juice

A pinky-size slice of fresh ginger (optional)

1 Heat a small skillet over high heat. Add the **sesame seeds** and **garlic** and toast until golden, about 4 minutes. Transfer to a blender.

2 Pour the **water, sesame oil, miso, vinegar,** and **ginger** (if using) into the blender and blend until smooth, stopping to scrape down the sides if necessary. Taste and adjust the flavors. Pour into a small bowl, garnish with any extra sesame seeds, and serve right away or store in the fridge for 4 to 5 days.

why  'cause . . .

Sesame seeds are a good source of calcium, but it's all in the hull, so leave it on!

cucumber yogurt sauce

makes 1½ cups
PREP TIME: 10 minutes

This tangy little sauce goes well with salmon cakes, wraps, or atop a bowl of lentils.

½ medium English cucumber or 3 mini (Persian) cucumbers, seeded and finely diced

1 cup Greek yogurt (whole or low-fat)

1 tablespoon fresh lemon juice

2 tablespoons finely diced red onion or shallot

1 tablespoon finely chopped fresh chives, dill, or mint

Salt and freshly ground black pepper

Wrap the **cucumber** in a clean kitchen towel or cheesecloth and squeeeeze out the moisture ❓. Combine the cucumber with the **yogurt**, **lemon juice**, **onion**, and **herbs** in a bowl. Season with **salt** and **pepper** to taste. Serve right away or store in the fridge for up to 2 days.

 why ❓ 'cause . . .

If you don't squeeze, the cucumbers will release water into your sauce, making it runny.

 play ✳ with it

Add:

✱ Grated lemon zest for sparkle

✱ 1 tablespoon each Dijon mustard, mayo, and chopped pickles or capers for "mock tartar sauce" (good for salmon cakes)

✱ 1 teaspoon toasted ground cumin for an Indian flair

✱ ¼ cup tahini paste for a Middle Eastern moment

no high-fructose corn syrup here!

homemade ketchup

makes 2 cups

PREP TIME: 15 minutes   COOKING TIME: 30 minutes

Sure, you can just buy ketchup, but sometimes it's nice to have condiments on the table whose ingredients are completely recognizable. Homemade ketchup hasn't a trace of high-fructose corn syrup—just tomatoes, whatever spices you choose, and a (big) dollop of pride.

Olive oil, for the pot

1 large onion, chopped

5 garlic cloves, chopped

2 teaspoons ground cumin

½ teaspoon ground allspice (optional)

1 can (14 ounces) crushed tomatoes

1 can (7 ounces) tomato paste

2 tablespoons maple syrup or brown sugar

2 tablespoons apple cider vinegar or red wine vinegar

Salt and cayenne pepper

1 Heat a medium heavy-bottomed pot over medium-high heat. Drizzle in the **olive oil**. Add the **onion** and **garlic** and cook until they soften, 3 to 5 minutes. Add the **cumin** and **allspice** (if using) and cook until fragrant. Transfer to a blender. Add the **crushed tomatoes**, **tomato paste**, **maple syrup**, and **vinegar** and blend until smooth.

2 Return the ketchup to the pot and simmer, uncovered, for 25 minutes, or until it reaches the desired thickness. Season with **salt** and **cayenne** to taste. If you prefer it very smooth, coax it through a strainer. Transfer to a jar with a tight-fitting lid and refrigerate up to 2 weeks. Alternatively, put in a freezer-safe container and freeze up to 6 months.

play  with it

After sautéeing the onions, add any of these:

* 1 to 2 chipotles in adobo sauce, chopped

* 1 to 2 teaspoons smoked paprika

* A pinch of ground cinnamon or cloves

* A dash of hot sauce

* A squeeze of lime juice and some chopped cilantro

* 1 tablespoon fish sauce or a chopped anchovy

a green all children seem to love

green summer pesto

makes 1 cup
PREP TIME: 20 minutes

Grab a bunch of basil and inhale deeply . . . aren't you happy now? Once you've made your own pesto from beautiful fresh-tasting basil, you will never, ever want to use the kind from a jar again. Luckily it is very simple to make and freezes well, so from now on you can pick fresh pesto over . . . that other stuff. Toss it into a bowl of hot or cold pasta, slather it on sandwiches, serve it with fish, brush it on grilled vegetables, or dollop it into soup.

¼ cup pine nuts or blanched almonds, gently toasted

1 to 2 garlic cloves, peeled

½ cup freshly grated Parmesan cheese

2 cups lightly packed fresh basil leaves

⅔ cup olive oil, plus more for storing

Salt and freshly ground black pepper

1 Combine the **pine nuts**, **garlic**, and **Parmesan** in a food processor or blender and pulse until finely chopped. Add the **basil** and pulse until minced, turning it off and scraping down the sides of the bowl every now and then. With the machine running, add the **olive oil** in a thin stream and process until smooth. Do not overprocess ❓. Taste and season with **salt** and **pepper**.

2 Transfer the pesto to a refrigerator or freezer container. Pesto gets insulted and darkens when exposed to air, so to prevent that, pour a thin layer of olive oil on its surface before storing to keep it green. Kept in an airtight container, it can be refrigerated for up to 4 days or frozen for a few months.

why ❓ 'cause . . .

Sometimes if olive oil, especially extra virgin olive oil, is blended too long it will become bitter, so treat it gently. The same goes when making dressing or mayonnaise with olive oil.

play ✳ with it

* Mix fresh parsley, spinach, or mint with the basil.
* Add a little grated lemon zest for sparkle.
* Steam a small bunch of chopped kale, squeeze out the moisture, and continue with the recipe using kale instead of basil (particularly during winter).

cook's 🥄 tip

Here's a little trick to keep your pesto bright green: Blanch your basil. Heat destroys the enzymes that cause oxidation and the resulting discoloration. Drop fresh basil into a pot of boiling water for a few seconds, just until it wilts, then shock it in a bowl of ice water. Dry it completely, then proceed with the recipe.

tangy, smoky, and brilliantly colored

quick-roasted red pepper sauce

makes 2½ cups

PREP TIME: 10 minutes

Perfect for quinoa cakes, sandwich wraps, and Crunchy Chicken Strips (page 171).

1½ cups drained fire-roasted red peppers from a jar or home-roasted*

½ cup toasted almonds (smoked almonds are perfect)

1 garlic clove, peeled

2 teaspoons red wine vinegar

Salt and freshly ground black pepper

See "How to Roast a Pepper," page 106.

Combine the **roasted peppers, almonds, garlic, vinegar,** and **salt** and **black pepper** to taste in a blender and puree until smooth. Taste and adjust the seasonings. Serve right away or store in the fridge for up to a week.

sweeties!

how do you get kids interested in cooking?

All it takes is one sentence: "Who wants to bake cookies?!" Baking with your kids is a sweet way to whip up a batch of lessons including:

Chemistry: The perfect amount of baking soda + acid makes cakes and cookies rise. Too little makes them flat and too much makes them flop.

Math: ¾ cup + ¾ cup = 1½ cups. If there are 3 teaspoons in 1 tablespoon (there are) and there are 4 tablespoons in ¼ cup, how many teaspoons are there in 1 cup?

Patience: If you read the whole recipe first, measure properly, and follow all the instructions, you will succeed.

Common sense: If you use a stick of butter and eat half the pie, then you have eaten half a stick of butter, and that is probably why you feel yucky.

Self-esteem: A homemade treat, made from scratch from real ingredients, begets lots of compliments and confidence to tackle new challenges.

Homemade desserts should be in our lives, but on special days, incorporating wisdom, respect, and delight. We believe in the ritual of dessert, which extends the time we spend together around the table. But let's redefine what dessert is: a large slice of a perfectly ripe peach, half an orange, slices of apple; a square or two of dark chocolate; one dessert, four forks; or a simple cup of tea.

berry, berry good frozen yogurt!

makes 4 to 6 servings
PREP TIME: 15 minutes

Here's the easiest way in the world to make frozen yogurt: You just throw all the ingredients into the food processor, pulse a few times, and ta-da, it's ready, no waiting at all! Serve it with toppings in little bowls to add sprinkle, crunch, and lots of smiles. (And eat it all up today—it gets rock hard if left in the freezer.)

1 pound good-quality frozen fruit, such as strawberries, raspberries, or blueberries (do not thaw!)

½ cup honey or maple syrup (more or less depending on how sweet the fruit is)

¼ teaspoon salt

1 cup plain Greek yogurt (whole or low-fat)

Combine the **fruit**, **honey**, and **salt** in a food processor and pulse until the fruit is coarsely chopped. Add the **yogurt** and process until smooth and creamy, scraping down the sides of the bowl once or twice. The frozen yogurt should be firm enough to be served directly from the food processor; if it's a little soft, cover and freeze for about 30 minutes.

why  'cause . . .

Salt in dessert? Isn't that crazy? Nope. Salt works as a flavor amplifier. It does cool stuff like make bitter ingredients (like dark chocolate) less bitter and brightens bland flavors. Next time you make plain porridge, try putting a pinch of salt in one bowl, and none in another. What do you think?

play  with it

★ Add a dash of vanilla, a sprinkle of cinnamon, or a pinch of citrus zest.

★ Serve with toppings such as chopped fresh strawberries, mangoes, and bananas; crunchy cereal; dark chocolate chips; or chopped nuts.

coconut soft serve

makes 4 or 5 servings
PREP TIME: 15 minutes   FREEZING TIME: 4 to 5 hours

This is so easy to make and dizzyingly delicious—the hardest part is waiting for it to freeze. Make it plain the first time and next time fancify it with fresh mint and chocolate chips, or make it zingy tart with lemon juice and zest, or swirl in some strawberry jam! (Eat it all up today—it doesn't last in the freezer.)

1 can (14 ounces) unsweetened coconut milk (you can choose "lite" but it will end up tasting icy)

2 to 3 tablespoons honey or maple syrup

2 teaspoons vanilla extract

1 Pour the **coconut milk**, **honey**, and **vanilla** into a 1-quart resealable plastic bag and shake. Carefully place the bag on a level shelf in the freezer and freeze until it is as firm as ice cream, 4 to 5 hours.

2 While it is still in the bag, snap the frozen coconut mixture into small chunks. Transfer them to a food processor and pulse, scraping down the bowl with a rubber spatula, until very smooth. Taste. Refreeze if you like it a little stiffer.

play with it

★ Before freezing, stir in the grated zest and juice of ½ lemon.

★ After processing, fold in some chopped fresh mint and chocolate bits.

a little fruit, a little crumble, a lotta joy

fruit crumble

makes 6 to 8 servings
PREP TIME: 15 to 20 minutes   BAKING TIME: 40 minutes

The best thing about a crisp or crumble is that you can quickly toss together dessert by using any fruit you have on hand. Small berries can just be thrown in whole, while larger ones like strawberries are better cut in half. Stone fruit, like plums and apricots, need to be pitted and sliced into bite-size pieces. Apples and pears should be cored and sliced, but no need to peel them. You can also use frozen fruit as long as you thaw it first and drain the liquid (if the liquid is tasty, add it to your water pitcher!)

FILLING

4 pounds fruit (if large, cut into bite-size pieces)

1½ tablespoons cornstarch

1 to 4 tablespoons sugar, honey, or maple syrup (optional)*

1 to 2 tablespoons fresh lemon juice (optional)*

TOPPING

¾ cup flour (whole wheat, spelt, or gluten-free all-purpose baking flour)

½ cup chopped walnuts, pecans, or almonds

¾ cup old-fashioned rolled oats

½ cup brown sugar or granulated maple sugar

Pinch of salt

1 stick (4 ounces) cold butter or ½ cup cold coconut oil

1 Preheat the oven to 375°F.

2 **For the filling:** Combine the **fruit, cornstarch, sweetener,** and **lemon juice** (if using*) in a large bowl and toss to coat. Transfer to a 9 × 13-inch baking dish. Set aside.

3 **For the topping:** Combine the **flour, nuts, oats, salt,** and **sugar** in a large bowl. Cut the cold **butter** or **coconut oil** into small pieces and add them into the bowl. Using your hands, rub the butter into the flour mixture until it resembles lumpy sand.

4 Scatter the mixture in an even layer over the fruit. Bake until the fruit is soft and bubbling and the topping is crisp, about 40 minutes.

* Start by tasting the raw fruit. If it's very tart, add 1 tablespoon sweetener. If it is a bit lackluster, add a squeeze of lemon, then taste again before you add more sweetener or lemon (remember it's going to be blanketed by a sweet topping). Next time your fruit might be so perfect it won't need any sweetener at all.

play  with it

* Add a little vanilla, ginger, or grated citrus zest to the fruit.

* Add "pie spices" like cinnamon, allspice, and cardamom to the topping.

kids  in charge

* Be the official fruit taster.

* Toss the fruit.

* Cube the butter with a table knife and count how many tablespoons in 1 stick.

* Measure all the ingredients.

* Rub the butter into the dry ingredients.

whipped coconut cream

makes 5 servings

PREP TIME: 5 minutes   CHILL OUT TIME: 2 to 3 hours

If a fluffy white peak of whipped cream on your dessert makes you happy, but cholesterol or dairy or weird chemical ingredients do not, this recipe is for you: fluffy, creamy, and delicious whipped coconut cream.

1 can (15 ounces) full-fat coconut milk

1 tablespoon honey or maple syrup (optional)

1 teaspoon vanilla extract (optional)

1 Chill the can of **coconut milk** in the refrigerator for 2 to 3 hours until it is very cold.

2 Open the can—the milk will have separated into a firm "cream" at the top and thin "milk" at the bottom. Scoop the top cream layer into a large bowl and save the milk for something else, like smoothies.

3 Whisk by hand or use a mixer on high speed to whip the cream until it is soft and fluffy, about 8 minutes by hand and 3 minutes in the mixer.

4 Add **sweetener** and **vanilla** to taste, if desired.

oatmeal chocolate chip cookies

makes 60 cookies

PREP TIME: 20 minutes   BAKING TIME: 10 to 12 minutes per batch

Some people prefer chocolate chip cookies, others prefer oatmeal cookies. Here is a cookie that will make everyone happy—it's both! This recipe makes 5 dozen: a few for today, a few for your friends, and the rest for the freezer (hidden from plain sight).

2 cups old-fashioned rolled oats

1½ cups all-purpose flour or gluten-free all-purpose baking flour

1 teaspoon baking powder

12 ounces milk, semisweet, or dark chocolate chips

2½ sticks (10 ounces) salted butter, room temperature

1 cup granulated sugar

1 cup packed light brown sugar

2 eggs, room temperature

1 Preheat the oven to 350°F with the racks in the upper and lower thirds. Line 2 baking sheets with parchment paper or grease them with the butter wrapper.

2 Combine the **oats, flour, baking powder,** and **chocolate chips** in a medium bowl.

3 Combine the **butter** and **sugars** in a medium bowl. Using a wooden spoon, beat together until it is fluffy (or close), then vigorously mix in the **eggs** and stir until it is well combined. Stir in the oat mixture.

4 If you have the patience, chill the dough in the fridge for at least 30 minutes. If not, go ahead and drop grape-size balls onto the baking sheets, spacing them about 3 inches apart. Bake for 6 minutes, then rotate the baking sheets front to back and switch racks ❓. Bake until the edges are golden brown, 4 to 6 minutes longer. Then gently transfer to a rack to cool.

why 'cause . . .

Most ovens are temperamental beasts, burning hot in some spots and cooler in others. By rotating the pans front to back and switching the racks they are on, everything gets cooked evenly . . . outwitting the oven.

play ✳ with it

* Add a cup of toasted walnuts or pecans.

* Add a handful of raisins or dried cherries.

* Add a pinch of cinnamon, a dash of vanilla, or a little coffee extract.

* Replace ¼ cup of the flour with unsweetened cocoa powder.

cook's tip

A secret trick for stellar baked goods with nuts is to toast them first . . . the same goes for oats. To toast, pour your desired amount into a dry skillet and stir over medium heat until the oats start to turn golden, then proceed with the recipe.

easy-peasy, yet elegant

almond cake

makes 10 servings

PREP TIME: 20 minutes   BAKING TIME: 55 to 60 minutes

This is a perfectly simple cake that you can serve simply too, with mint tea and sliced plums. Or for celebrations, doll it up with fresh raspberries, a drizzle of chocolate, and a sprinkle of toasted slivered almonds. You can buy almond flour, or make it by putting blanched almonds in a food processor and whizzing a couple times until it's a fluffy flour.

2 cups almond flour

1 cup all-purpose flour or gluten-free all-purpose baking flour mix

1 teaspoon baking powder

¼ teaspoon salt

10 tablespoons (1¼ sticks) butter, room temperature ❓

1 cup sugar

6 eggs, room temperature ❓

½ cup honey

2 teaspoons vanilla extract

1 Preheat the oven to 325°F with the rack in the middle. Grease an 8-inch-round cake pan with butter and line the bottom with a round of parchment paper.

2 Whisk together the **flours**, **baking powder**, and **salt** in a medium bowl.

3 Combine the **butter** and **sugar** in the bowl of a stand mixer* and beat on high speed until light and creamy. Beat in the **eggs** one at a time, then beat in the **honey** and **vanilla** until well combined. Gently fold in the flour mixture. Pour the batter into the cake pan.

4 Bake until a toothpick inserted into the center of cake comes out clean, 55 to 60 minutes. Cool in the pan on a wire rack for 15 minutes. Turn out onto a serving plate, cool, and serve.

* If you don't have a stand mixer, no worries–use a big bowl, a hand mixer or a whisk, and vigorous arm movements.

why ❓ 'cause . . .

If the butter and eggs have cold hearts, they won't marry well, leaving your cake heavy, dull, and full of holes. If you are in a rush, put the eggs in a bowl of very warm water for 10 minutes and grate cold butter with a cheese grater to speed up the softening.

play ✳ with it

Into the finished batter, fold:
★ A cup of dark chocolate chips
★ A bit of citrus zest
★ A cup of raspberries

Onto the baked cake:
★ Drizzle melted dark chocolate.
★ Top with a fine dusting of powdered sugar and toasted almond slices.

cook's 🔑 tip

Make it a coconut cake! Replace the butter with room-temperature (but not melted) coconut oil and add ½ cup unsweetened coconut flakes or shreds to the batter with the almond flour. Sprinkle with more coconut flakes before popping it into the oven.

Chia seeds!

Once we knew them only as the green hair on Chia Pets, but now we are getting reacquainted with chia as a powerful whole food in a tiny seed package. Here are a few very good reasons to add chia seeds to your diet.

They are high in brain- and heart-boosting fatty acids—each tablespoon contains 1 gram of omega-3s and 2.5 grams of omega-6s—and contain a complete chain of essential amino acids, making them a great vegetarian source of protein. They have twice the potassium of bananas and three times more antioxidants than blueberries. They even have 5 grams of fiber in each tablespoon, which helps regulate blood sugar.

When you hydrate the seeds, they absorb up to nine times their volume in water. This helps keep your body hydrated longer, and fills you up, keeping hunger at bay.

Finally, they are curiously buoyant and profoundly weird looking, so they are fun to add to any kind of clear beverage either hot or cold. Once they swell up, they swirl about like a natural bubble tea.

....

* where to find them *

They are often found in the bulk or grain aisle of natural food stores and specialty supermarkets. Sometimes they can also be found in the tea and herb section of Hispanic markets. Costco sells them, too. They are also easily ordered online. The difference between light and dark seeds is mainly an aesthetic one.

....

* how to use them *

The seeds are flavorless, if slightly nutty, so you can add their crunchy goodness to baked goods, or sprinkle them onto cereal or salads, just as you would flaxseeds.

However, they are best digested if they have been hydrated, either by adding them directly to liquids or by making them into a gel you keep in the fridge. Add a tablespoon or two to smoothies, juices, iced teas, salad dressings, puddings, and martinis (just kidding about the last one . . . maybe?).

chia gel

Combine ⅓ cup chia seeds and 2 cups water in an airtight jar, shake, and wait 15 minutes before using. Refrigerate up to 2 weeks. *Makes 2 cups.*

chia agua fresca

A lemonade with substance! Combine the juice of ½ lemon, 2 teaspoons chia seeds, 1½ cups cold water, and honey or maple syrup to taste in a 16-ounce glass and stir vigorously. Let soak for about 10 minutes, stirring a few times. Fill with ice and enjoy. *Makes 1 serving.*

coconut-mango chia pudding

makes 6 servings

PREP TIME: 5 minutes   CHILL OUT TIME: up to a few hours

All you have to do is shake, shake, shake, then wait, wait, wait! Then you'll have a very tasty soft pudding, full of omegas, protein, fiber, and antioxidants.

1 can (13.5 ounces) whole-fat or "lite" coconut milk (see Cook's Tip)

1½ cups dairy milk or unsweetened nut milk

¾ cup chia seeds

2 tablespoons maple syrup or honey, or to taste

1 mango, diced, or 1 cup chopped frozen mango or berries (save a little for garnish)

1 teaspoon vanilla extract

¼ teaspoon salt

1 Put **all the ingredients** in a large glass jar or a bowl with a lid. Stir, then shake, shake, shake at least 30 times (or stir, stir, stir). Set the jar on the counter for 15 minutes then shake again so all the seeds float free and don't clump on the bottom.

2 Put the jar in the fridge and wait, wait, wait for a few hours, or until it has thickened. When you are ready to serve it, give it a good stir and garnish with the extra mango.

 play with it

Before shaking, add:

* 1 teaspoon unsweetened cocoa powder or ¼ cup unsweetened coconut flakes

* Grated lime or orange zest and a squeeze of juice

 cook's tip

So many coconut milks . . . What's the difference?

* **Canned coconut milk** is made from mature coconut meat ground with water and then strained. This creamy milk tends to separate into cream and milk in the can; shake it well before opening.

* **Coconut milk in a carton** is often found in the refrigerated section with the milk. It is made using a similar method as the canned version, but the fat content is lower and the flavor a little more neutral so it can be used as you would use regular milk.

* **Coconut water** is thin and watery and comes from the middle of the coconut—it's the sloshing you hear when you shake a coconut. If the coconut is young and fresh, the water is very sweet.

* **Cream of coconut** is an altogether different item, with lots of added sugar and often found in dusty cans at the very back of home bars, where it probably should stay.

for the love of chocolate, with all the benefits of chia

chocolate chia pudding

makes 6 servings

PREP TIME: 10 minutes   CHILL OUT TIME: up to a few hours

Serve with chopped fruit, toasted nuts, or just a spoon.

3 cups dairy milk or unsweetened nut, soy, or rice milk

6 ounces (about 1 cup) chocolate chips

Maple syrup or sweetener of your choice

⅔ cup chia seeds (any color)

¼ teaspoon salt

1 In the microwave or on the stove, heat up 1 cup of the **milk** until simmering. Remove from the heat, add the **chocolate**, and stir until smooth. Add the remaining 2 cups **milk**, **sweetener** to taste, **chia seeds**, and **salt**. Stir, stir, stir vigorously . . . wait 10 minutes, then stir again so the seeds don't all settle on the bottom.

2 That's it! You are done! Just pour into a medium bowl and pop the pudding into the fridge for a few hours, or until it has thickened. Stir once in a while if you remember to.

play  with it

* After the chocolate has melted, stir in 1 teaspoon vanilla extract or 1 teaspoon instant coffee dissolved in 1 tablespoon hot water.

* Stir in 2 tablespoons peanut or hazelnut butter (it helps if you microwave it for a few seconds so it is soft).

* Layer the finished pudding with bananas.

it's okay to go bananas over this one

chocolate-covered bananas

makes 8 or 12 pops
PREP TIME: 20 to 30 minutes   FREEZING TIME: 4 to 5 hours

Freeze a banana and it becomes cold and creamy like ice cream. Then make it even more fabulous by dipping it in luscious chocolate and crunchy nuts. You can make these in advance, or you can bring the frozen bananas and bowls of melted chocolate and nuts to the dessert table so everyone can make their own banana pop.

4 very ripe bananas

8 to 12 thick pretzel sticks or wooden craft sticks

1 cup of your favorite nuts, toasted and chopped

8 ounces good-quality dark chocolate, chopped

1 Put a piece of parchment paper or plastic wrap on a tray small enough to fit into your freezer.

2 Peel the **bananas** and cut crosswise into halves or thirds. Carefully insert a stick into the end of each banana piece. Place on the tray, uncovered, and freeze 4 to 5 hours.

3 Kindly ask your big helper to melt the **chocolate** (see how to below) . Meanwhile, pour the **nuts** into a wide shallow bowl. Pour the melted chocolate into a tall heatproof glass. Dip each frozen banana into the chocolate, turning it to coat, and immediately roll it into the nuts. Return them to the tray. Enjoy right away or put the tray back in the freezer. Once the chocolate is completely hard, transfer the pops to a freezer container and freeze for up to 2 months.

cook's tip

why 'cause . . .

How to Melt Chocolate
The microwave way: Finely chop the chocolate and place it in a microwavable glass bowl. Microwave, uncovered, on medium (50%) power in 15-second intervals, stirring in between, until the chocolate is melted.

The stove-top way: Finely chop the chocolate and place it in a wide metal or glass bowl. Fill the bottom of a pot with a few inches of water and place over low heat. Set the bowl into the pot so that it is snug; it should not be touching the simmering water 🄿. As the chocolate begins to melt, stir, heating until smooth.

If chocolate gets too hot, it will punish you by going amuck and separating into chunky bits. If this happens, you will have to start over again (and save the chunky stuff for hot chocolate). Also, do not let a drop, wisp, or spritz of water touch your chocolate, as it will seize up into a tight-fisted wad.

an easy ooey gooey delight

swedish mud cake

makes 10 servings

PREP TIME: 10 minutes   BAKING TIME: 20 to 25 minutes

It takes five glorious ingredients and 10 lickety finger minutes of stirring to make the world's easiest pie: firm on top, muddy inside, and very, very good.

10 tablespoons (1¼ sticks) salted butter, cut into pats, wrapper reserved

3 eggs

1 cup sugar

¼ cup unsweetened cocoa powder

½ cup all-purpose flour or gluten-free all-purpose baking flour

1 Preheat the oven to 325°F with a rack in the middle. Use the butter wrapper to butter an 8-inch pie plate.

2 Gently melt the **butter** in a small saucepan over low heat (or carefully melt it in the microwave). Let it cool for a few minutes.

3 Combine the **eggs** and **sugar** in a bowl and beat with a fork until frothy, then fold in the melted butter, **cocoa powder**, and **flour** (including any extras that excite you in Play with it!, below).

4 Scrape the batter into the pie pan and pop it into the oven for 20 to 25 minutes. Carefully check the cake: The top should be baked, but the inside still should be jiggly. Don't bake it past this point, because then it becomes a clumpy clay pie.

play  with it

To the batter, add:

★ ½ cup chocolate chips or nuts

★ 1 teaspoon vanilla extract

★ A pinch of ground cinnamon

★ 1 teaspoon instant decaf coffee dissolved in 1 tablespoon hot water

Before serving:

★ Shower with powdered sugar.

★ Serve with berries and a dollop of whipped cream.

Let's Talk Trash

Dinner is over, the dishes are done, and someone still needs to take out the trash. But before we do, let's have a chat.

Of all the rooms in the house, the kitchen produces the most waste. Food scraps are the number one contributor to landfills today, making up 21 percent of all landfill trash by weight.[1] That doesn't even include food packaging. Yes, we need to recycle, but it's even more important to avoid creating waste in the first place. Here are some suggestions.

1. Purchase kitchen tools that will last many years (i.e., won't wind up on landfills) and that you really will use. Fall in love with stainless steel or cast-iron skillets that you will never have to replace. Think twice before you buy any plastic kitchen gidgetybob . . . are you really going to use it?

2. Reduce the single-use items in your kitchen, like paper plates, plastic cups, and straws. Every year, Americans throw away enough paper and plastic cups, forks, and spoons to circle the equator 300 times.[2]

3. Buy fruit that isn't perfect. A lot of good fruits and vegetables are thrown out because their size, shape, or color are a bit off. Choose produce that's unique and you'll find they're not only delicious, but you'll be reducing food waste.

4. Use your freezer. Freeze fresh produce and leftovers before they go bad for a quick, healthy meal on days when your time is limited.

5. Use durable glass, metal, or porcelain containers for storing leftovers. Challenge yourself not to use plastic wrap and bags for a week and invite your family and friends to join in. We use glass pie dishes and dinner plates to cover bowls of food. We love our glass canning jars, which we use to store leftovers and to hold our bulk pantry goods like grains and pasta. They even go to school and picnics.

In 2011, containers and packaging amounted to 75.6 million tons of total kitchen waste generated.[3]

6. Keep several reusable grocery bags in your car so they will never be forgotten (and reuse any little plastic produce bags you need). After you unload your groceries, leave the bags by your front door, ready for their trip back into your trunk!. Every piece of plastic ever produced still exists in some form. Every year, Americans use approximately 102.1 billion plastic bags, creating tons of landfill waste and pollution in our waterways.

7. Keep a pitcher of water and a few filled reusable water canteens ready to go in the fridge—it's an easy way to reduce the number of plastic water bottles in the world. Most tap water is healthy, and in fact tap water is more regulated for contaminants than bottled water. Also, many plastic bottles con-

tain the chemical BPA, which is a nasty hormone disrupter that you don't want to drink. Go to EWG. org for more information on BPA. Eighty-six percent of plastic water bottles used in the United States become garbage that ends up in landfills throughout the country. Considering that approximately 60 million plastic water bottles are used every day in the United States, we can assume that nearly 18,834,000 end up in the landfill *each year.*

8. Buy a stack of reusable dishcloths for cleaning, instead of using paper towels and napkins, and use cloth napkins at the table. Cloth looks better, it's more economical, and you'll save trees. Beware of paper towel abusers in your home. Of the 741 pounds of paper used by the average American each year, close to 55 pounds is tissue paper (which includes paper towels, napkins, facial tissue, and toilet tissue).

9. Dip into bulk bins. You will have less packaging to dispose of, it will cost you less, and you get to store the goods in those nice Ball canning jars we always talk about. Another benefit is you can buy just what you need for a particular recipe instead of an entire jar that will gather dust.

10. Compost! If you have a garden, get a compost bin—some cities give them away for free.

You will feel so much better about all those peels, tips, tops, and tails when you are tossing them into a compost bin. The amount of trash in your bin will reduce at the same speed as your garden will grow.

11. Rethink your plate size. Dinner plate sizes have increased 36 percent since the 1960s. Consider going back to a 9- or 10-inch dinner plate. Less space makes less waste . . . and smaller plates will fit more snugly in the dishwasher (bonus: more water efficiency). Less space also makes less *waist*: Research shows that most of us tend to eat what's put in front of us, so smaller cups and plates curb consumption.

12. Love your leftovers. Eat them as time-saving small meals or repurpose them into something new: Toss them with grains, fold them into eggs, or blend them into soups. Become an expert at this and you'll save time, money, and aggravation.

13. Most important, don't buy more than you will use. It is unconscionable how much food we throw away every day. (See "A Fresh Look at the Expiration Date," page 28.) Forty percent of the food purchased in the United States today goes uneaten! For more information about food waste, please visit the NRDC at nrdc.org/food/wasted-food.asp

Now that you've made a delicious dinner, it's time to sit down, dig in, and enjoy each other's company. With email and pinging iPhones changing the way we all communicate, dinnertime is more important than ever as a quality opportunity to catch up, discuss, listen, and learn. To that end, here are some conversation starters to kick off a great dinner discussion. These are excerpted from our co-venture with the *Huffington Post's* **Table Talk,** a weekly blog that offers a timely topic and great questions for the whole family to engage in. Visit the HuffingtonPost.com every Friday for a new topic.

lol & the dictionary

Every year the Oxford English Dictionary (OED) announces the addition of new words to the pages of its 150-year-old publication. Among the most recent are many modern-day expressions, or "initialisms" as the OED calls them—terms that have exploded in popular usage because of their efficiency in expressing certain sentiments over email, text messaging, Twitter, and other platforms where speed and character limits come into play. These include "LOL," "OMG," "IMHO," "TMI," "BFF," "FYI," and the heart symbol (♥).

Although, according to the OED, these words are associated with "a younger generation," their researchers uncovered some surprising earlier uses of the terms. For example, "OMG" first appeared in 1917 in personal correspondence, "LOL" appeared as early as the 1960s and referred not to "laughing out loud" but to "little old lady," and "FYI" actually originated in memoranda in 1941.

Do you think words like these belong in the dictionary? What are some other expressions you have begun using that you think should be considered for next year? What are some words and expressions that your parents grew up with that aren't heard very much anymore?

what if you found $45,000?

It sounds like a dream come true: After purchasing his family's first home, Josh Ferrin discovered about $45,000 in cash stored in metal boxes (maybe it wasn't a coincidence that the Salt Lake City suburb he moved to was called Bountiful). Although it was tempting to keep the cash, Ferrin knew that the money must have belonged to the recently deceased owner, who had left the house to his children, and that he should give the money back.

Ferrin explained, "I don't believe you get a chance very often to do something radically honest, to do something ridiculously awesome for someone else, and that is a lesson I hope to teach to my children." Kay Bangerter, the oldest of the six children of the previous homeowner, called the money's return "a story that will outlast our generation and probably yours as well."

What would you have done if you were Josh Ferrin? Do you think that honesty is always the best policy? If you really needed money, would it have been okay to keep some of it? Is it stealing if you find something on your property, even though it's not yours? If $45,000 dropped into your lap, how would you spend it? How do you save money? Have you ever kept something that wasn't yours?

cheating

Students from one of the top high schools in the country were caught cheating on a test, but they didn't just get detention. Everyone involved was arrested because they cheated on what is arguably one of the most important tests given—the SAT.

Out of the seven students involved, six were high school seniors, minors under 18 years of age, who paid between $1,500 and $2,500 for someone to take their test for them. Since the test taker was 19—no longer a minor—he was arrested on felony fraud charges, and could go to prison for up to 4 years. The attorney representing the test taker said, "Cheating on tests is something that should be handled in schools, not in criminal courts."

Do you think that the students should be treated as criminals? What do you think the right punishment for this kind of cheating is? Do you ever feel the kind of pressure at school that these teenagers must have felt? Is there someone you can talk to about feeling pressured?

giving back

New York Times columnist Nicholas Kristof writes about Rachel, a 9-year-old girl who, from a young age, always had the desire to give back and donate to charity. Charity has no age boundaries, and children are often able to contribute, whether it is by donating long hair to children who have lost their own due to cancer, becoming friends with a child with developmental disabilities, or running a lemonade stand that raises money for cancer patients.

A nonprofit is a charity organization that uses the money it raises to help it pursue certain goals. Nonprofits can exist in many forms, from helping the environment to helping the homeless, from finding cures for diseases to pushing for better human rights.

If you could start a charity or a nonprofit, what would you start? Who would it help? What causes are you passionate about? Are there organizations at school that you would like to join? How do you help people? How can kids get more involved with nonprofits?

luscious lips

Heavy metals might not be something you'd generally associate with makeup—but a recent study from the University of California at Berkeley's School of Public Health found the presence of metals including aluminum, chromium, cadmium, and manganese in eight lipsticks and 24 lip glosses available in stores. According to preliminary research, the cosmetics involved could be harmful to your health due to exposure to these ingredients over time. Many teens and tweens reapply lip gloss several times a day (according to the study, the average number of times is two to three), and may not realize they could be ingesting these metals every time they lick their lips. Tonight, let's talk about the importance of paying attention to the ingredients in products we use every day.

Are you surprised by this research? Why do you

think cosmetics companies make products with ingredients that are potentially dangerous? What other products do you regularly use that may have chemicals in them?

saving water

Water—it's in us, around us, good for us . . . but sometimes we take it for granted. Recently, the *New York Times* reported that Levi Strauss & Co. discovered that on average a single pair of their blue jeans goes through enough water to fill 15 spa-size bathtubs. *Fifteen.* How does that happen? Because Levi's needs water to grow the cotton in jeans. Then, when we buy those jeans, it takes more water to wash them over and over again.

Some of us may think the answer is not to wash our jeans. But, Levi's has an idea to save water before we even see new jeans in stores. They've created a program called "WaterLess," which starts by teaching farmers in India, Pakistan, and other countries where jeans are made to use more sustainable techniques. For example, they can stonewash jeans with rocks instead of water. Which seems like how it should be done anyway since it's called *stone*washing, right?

Levi's is a big name doing big things to help save our planet, but we can pitch in, too. Currently an American taking a 5-minute shower uses more water than a typical person in a developing country slum uses in a whole day. Since water is something we need, not just to wash ourselves and our clothes, but to survive and stay healthy, figuring out better ways to conserve it is an important conversation.

What else do we wash TOO much? Why are people worried about running out of water in the world? How would it affect your family if you didn't have enough water? What are simple ways we can save water? Would you prefer to wear clothes from a company that's doing things like Levi's?

getting real about what's fake

Open a copy of almost any fashion magazine and you'll come face-to-face with beautiful men and women (or girls and boys) in trendy clothes. Chances are they don't look a lot like you and your friends. Many people see these photos and feel bad about themselves, wondering: How can anybody look this perfect?

Maine teenager Julia Bluhm felt bad when she saw these pictures, too, so she decided to take a stand by writing a petition addressed to the editor of *Seventeen*.

In the petition, she said: "Here's what lots of girls don't know. Those 'pretty women' that we see in magazines are fake. They're often Photoshopped, airbrushed, edited to look thinner, and to appear like they have perfect skin. A girl you see in a magazine probably looks a lot different in real life." According to Bluhm's petition on Change.org, more than 65,000 people agree with her.

In her petition, Bluhm also made a specific request: "I'm asking *Seventeen* magazine to commit to printing one unaltered—real—photo spread per month. I want to see regular girls that look like me in a magazine that's supposed to be for me." Whether or not *Seventeen* ever agrees to the terms of Bluhm's petition, it's clear that this teenager has raised an issue many people feel strongly about.

Do you think the photographs you see in magazines are "too perfect"? Does this bother you? What makes a person beautiful? Do you need makeup and a "perfect" body shape to be attractive? What's one thing you see in the world around you that you want to change? What are the first steps you can take toward making that change happen?

the crush of school work

School brings a ton of pressure for kids—the burden of homework, barrage of midterms, state standardized tests, college applications, etc. Harvard family therapist Carleton Kendrick describes how, over the years, he has seen growing numbers of "frightened, pressured high achievers" who have "trouble finding their own voices." They "had been advised, persuaded, and professionally coached," he explained, "into believing that school's only purpose is to get the grades that will gain them admission into an elite college."

In short, kids of all ages are getting mightily stressed out. And the data backs this up: the *New York Times* recently reported that the emotional health of college freshmen is at its lowest level on record. Campus counselors across the country are seeing more and more students arriving at college stressed and depressed.

Are you stressed about schoolwork? What stresses you out the most? What do you think homework accomplishes and do you think you get too much of it? Is there a case to be made for no homework at all? Do you feel that there's a distinct path toward college that you're unable to deviate from if you want to succeed? Can learning be fun?

win at all costs?

Good Sportsmanship is an expected part of all athletic endeavors, so it was particularly surprising when an adult coach for the New York Jets tripped a player for the Miami Dolphins in the middle of a play during a football game. The Jets strength and conditioning coach, Sal Alosi, deliberately stuck out his knee as Miami's Nolan Carroll was running up the field, causing him to tumble to the ground. There was nearly universal outcry at the coach's unsportsmanlike behavior and, given that it was caught on film, the coach had no choice but to offer an apology for his action, saying, "I made a mistake that showed a total lapse in judgment. My conduct

was inexcusable and unsportsmanlike and does not reflect what this organization stands for." As punishment, the NFL suspended the coach for the rest of the season without pay, and fined him $25,000.

Does this story shock you? Have you witnessed unsportsmanlike behavior at your sports games or practices? A common sports expression is, "Winning isn't everything, it's the only thing"—does that philosophy justify any action taken to win a competition? What are some things that people do in other areas of life that you think are similar to the coach's behavior in this incident?

the "anti-ice cream truck"

What's better than an ice cream store on wheels? In many neighborhoods, the ice cream truck is a beloved summer tradition, bringing cold sweetness to kids (and their parents) on the hottest of days. But would you still visit the truck if it brought healthy snacks instead of a sugar rush? That's exactly what's happening in New York City right now, as the Food Bank for New York City's "Change One Thing" truck visits different parts of the city, giving teens nutritious snacks and recipes to try at home.

No, this is not a prank. (Someone else started driving an anti-ice cream truck to be funny, too.)

The point is not to make people feel bad about enjoying a treat every once in a while; as "Change One Thing" explains on its Web site, "Eating healthy doesn't have to mean overhauling your diet or buying expensive 'health food.' It can start with just one healthy choice per day." Tonight, let's talk about this idea—and how to build a healthy lifestyle, one choice at a time.

What is your reaction to the "anti-ice cream truck"? What kind of healthy foods do you like to eat? What's one healthy choice you can make to improve your diet every day?

Acknowledgments

We would like to send out a huge and heartfelt thank-you to the fantastic Rodale team, headed up by our guardian angel Alex Postman. We wish every author had an editor as smart, thoughtful, and caring as Alex. One of her most loving acts was to assign this book to Kara Plikaitis, our super talented art director. Who in turn connected us with Quentin Bacon, a phenomenal photographer who is as much fun to work with as his pictures portray. He spread his kindness by finding us prop stylist extraordinaire Maya Rossi, who lives by the rule that you can never have too many wooden spoons to choose from. We agree! Madeline Miller assisted Quentin and enchanted us all with her fancy computer work.

Paula Bolas provided steadiness, calm, and foresightedness as our kitchen assistant. Thank you, Paula!!

We all had a ball together shooting this cookbook, eating all the leftovers, constantly running down to the garden to grab herbs and more kale, and enjoying the superb New England fall weather.

In the "we couldn't do it without you" category, a gigantic thank-you to Dawn Woollen, our associate extraordinaire, who researched, fact-checked, read and reread, recipe tested, and kept us organized and on time. Dawn is the master keeper of "the book" and once again gets our MVP award.

A hearty thank-you to the following people for providing us with the most up-to-date and accurate information on childhood obesity and the food systems that are wrecking havoc on our diets. They include: Dr. Harvey Karp, Dr. Mark Hyman, Dr. Robert Lustig, Dr. Kelly Brownell, Dr. Yoni Freedhoff, Kristin Wartman, Dr. Urvashi Rangan, Dr Wendy Sue Swanson, Margo Wooten, Robyn O'Brien, Harold Goldstein, and everyone at CSPI.

Thank you to the rest of team at Rodale, including Maria Rodale, Mary Ann Naples, Nancy N. Bailey, Yelena Nesbit, Aly Mostel, Brent Gallenberger, and Kate Slate, for helping to make our dream for this book a reality.

Thanks to the great staff at the NRDC, including Dana Gunders, Jonathan Kaplan, and Francesca Koe, and for all the great work at the Environmental Working Group, headed up by Ken Cook.

A special thank-you shoutout to our friend Marina Gilboa, who has always been an inspiration to us in the kitchen and the garden.

To all of our models: Matthew Dix, Joshua Dix, Isabella Thorpe, Sieun Ahn, Adam, William, and Peter Miller, and the inimitable Jessica Harris, who won the award for best volunteer by showing up at the shoot with her very own homemade bloody Marys!

Of course, food tastes a lot better when it's homegrown and for that a big thank-you to Camilla Westby, who oversees the veggie garden growing at Wise Owl Farm and teaches us new things every day. On that front, we have to recognize North Tabor Farm and our dear friend Rebecca Miller, who mentors us, starts our seeds in her greenhouse, and is our partner in our new and budding sweet potato enterprise.

Thank you to all the HuffPost writers who helped write the Table Talk column throughout the years, including Roy Sekoff, Sarah Hoyoon Lee, Farah Miller, Emma Mustich, Carey Polis, Jessica Samakow, Colin Sterling, and Nina Zipkin. A heartfelt thank you to my mentor, Arianna Huffington, for the years of support, trust, and wisdom.

Thank you to John Pierce for his generous and patient lending of Kirstin. (At least I have never heard him complain.)

Thanks to Romy and Cazzie for recipe testing, tasting, and talking all these years around the kitchen table. And to Bella for being such a good sport posing for photos and for learning to love kale and quinoa!

Thank you to the inimitable Katie Couric for caring so deeply about all the issues that cross the dinner plate. Thank you Meredith Kennedy for all you do. A profound thank-you to the director of *Fed Up*, Stephanie Soechtig, who tackled a film about our health problems with so much grace, brains, and fortitude.

Thank you to all of our recipe testers: From 3 years little to 83 years wise, we are very grateful for every single one of you. Thank you for licking spoons, chopping, simmering, and tasting. Thank you for every thoughtful question you asked, for photos and videos, for stories of flops and words of praise. Every single one of your comments made this an even better book: Anne Ward, Ian Roberts, Emily and Claire Sures; Aase Schoen, Josh, and Zach; Andrew, Ragnhild, Daniel, and Jonas Green; Anna, Julia, Joe, and Lone Thwaites; Barbara and Nicole Pierce; Cami and Cap Gordon; Chef Sylvie Staboli; Claudia Calderon, Sofia and Gabriella Galvez; Emma Kofman; Heidi, Henry, and Clara Earle; Jane Tran; Jennifer, Mike, Alexander, Benjamin, and Rebecca Schiff; Jessie Nelson; Jill Hansen; Julie Jampolis; Kim, Symmie, and Cailey Bitto; Liana Schwarz, Mike Montgomery, and Ella Montgomery; Mavis, Chris, and Hudson Hillin; Merete von Eyben; Michelle and Aki Kaneko; Michelle Topolsky; Monina Von Opel, and Edward Miller; Nancy Rosenberg, Jacob, Jordan, and Joshua; Olwen and Mark Turtle; Pamela Van Summern; Rebecca Miller; Risa, David, Noah, and Jordyn; Rosie Highgate; Rosita Godycki, Sasha, and Shaya; Susan and Jack Woollen; Madia and Holly Bellebuono, Tracey Hohman, Nat and Gus Silverman. And the whole fantastic Uhrenholdt family (tusind tak!!).

Thank you to our contributors Chef Asata, Daniel Klein, Alex and Ben Schiff, and Monina Van Opel.

Lastly, but most heartedly, thank you to my husband, Robert Thorpe, for creating the beautiful organic farm where we grassfeed our animals, grow our own veggies, and shot these gorgeous cookbook photographs.

. . . And, from Kirstin, to the finest (organic, pasture raised) ingredient one could wish for when cooking up a book: Laurie. My gratitude cannot be measured. Your boundless enthusiasm, kind support, chutzpah, humor, and wisdom makes for a recipe everyone should know by heart. (P.S. I did sneak the teaspoon of honey back in.)

Home-Cooked Sundays

Here is our parting gift for you: Home-Cooked Sundays!

Inaugurating this ritual will radically simplify your cooking routine during the busy work or school week and guarantee you healthier, calmer, and happier meals. A Home-Cooked Sunday is your family's day to shop, prep, cook, and enjoy a great sit-down dinner together—all the while getting your fridge ready for the week.

To get started, sit down in a comfortable chair with an inspirational cookbook (!) or a box of recipes and write out a plan for three dinners: one for tonight—maybe it's just a Sunday soup (page 112) made from all the leftover veggies in the fridge—and two easy dinners for midweek. Then write a shopping list for the recipes and the staples you will need for the whole week (see page 24). Take the kids along!

Once you get home from shopping, put on comfortable shoes and your favorite music. Have your kids pitch in by giving them a task they can learn by heart (for the little ones, something like pulling broccoli apart and mixing the salad dressing—or, for the older ones, making a batch of tomato sauce). Invite good friends to take part. Pour yourself a glass of wine or a cup of tea and cook up a delicious start to your week.

Every Sunday...

Prep a few of these recipe staples so you'll always have them on hand when needed:

* Peel three or four onions and one or two heads of garlic (don't chop them yet–they'll get funky) and store in airtight containers.

* Wash, peel, and slice plenty of carrots, celery, and peppers. Chop up a head or two of cabbage, cauliflower, or broccoli. Store them in separate glass jars or containers (adding water to the carrots) and place in the fridge–they'll be easy to grab for snacks or to chop up for soups and salads.

* Wash and prep a large container of salad greens (page 129). Refrigerate in an airtight container.

* If you are a kale-loving family, wash, chop, and knead a couple of bunches (page 122) so they are ready for salads, as toppings for soups, eggs, and beans, or as fillings for sandwiches and wraps. Refrigerate in an airtight container.

* Mix a jar of your house salad dressing (page 137).

On the Sundays when you have a little more time...

* Simmer a pot of grains or beans (pages 230 to 233).

* Make a big pot of soup or white bean chili (page 201).

* Toss a quinoa or chopped salad to last a few days (pages 126, 132).

* Simmer a batch of tomato sauce (page 210) for the fridge and freezer.

* Roast up a bunch of vegetables—such as cauliflower, Brussels sprouts, and sweet potatoes—so you have a week's head start on side dishes, fillings for sandwiches, salads, and soups.

Join *The Family Cooks* challenge and make every Sunday a Home-Cooked Sunday! Visit **TheFamilyCooksBook.com**, **FedUpMovie.com**, and **Huffingtonpost.com** for more inspiration.

FED UP

Notes

1. Liquid Candy Report, CSPI http://www.cspinet.org/new/pdf/liquid1/4candy1/4final1/4w1/4new1/4supplement.pdf

2. A Review of Food Marketing to Children and Adolescents, FTC http://www.ftc.gov/os/2012/12/121221foodmarketingreport.pdf

3. http://pediatrics.aappublications.org/content/118/6/2563.full

4. www.matthewkarpinski.com/burn-fast-food-calories/

5. http://www.usnews.com/news/articles/2013/01/09/nih-study-links-soda-with-depression

6. http://cspinet.org/fooddyes/index.html

7. http://www.huffingtonpost.com/dr-mark-hyman/diet-soda-health1/4b1/42698494.html

8. http://www.ftc.gov/os/2003/11/slottingallowancerpt031114.pdf

9. http://www.vendingmarketwatch.com/magazine/autm/issue/2013/jun

10. http://www.ers.usda.gov/topics/food-choices-health/food-consumption-demand/food-away-from-home.aspx#.UmgjgpRgZjG

11. http://www.mayoclinic.org/mrsa/

Let's Talk Trash

1. http://www.epa.gov/foodrecovery/

2. http://www.cleanair.org/Waste/wasteFacts.html

3. http://www.epa.gov/osw/nonhaz/municipal/pubs/MSWcharacterization1/4fnl1/40607131/421/4rpt.pdf

Index

Underscored page references indicate sidebars. **Boldface** references indicate photographs.

EAT ANYTHING YOU
WANT, JUST COOK IT
YOURSELF!

MICHAEL
POLLAN